Rural Sociology, Human Migration and Social Work

Rural Sociology, Human Migration and Social Work

Dr. Shweta

KUNAL BOOKS

New Delhi-110002 , India

KUNAL BOOKS
4596/1A, First Floor,
11, Daryaganj, New Delhi-110002
Phones: 9811043697, 011-30125412
E-mail: *Kunalbooks@gmail.com*

Rural Sociology, Human Migration and Social Work

First Published 2010

ISBN - 978-93-80752-05-1

Published in India by Prem Singh Bisht for Kunal Books, and printed at **Deepak Offset Press**, Delhi.

PREFACE

Rural sociology is a field of sociology associated with the study of social life in non-metropolitan areas. It is the scientific study of social arrangements and behaviour amongst people distanced from points of concentrated population or economic activity. Like any sociological discipline, rural sociology involves the examination of statistical data, interviews, social theory, observation, survey research, and many other techniques. In contrast to rural sociology, urban sociology is the study of urban social life.

The movement of people from one place to the other to stay on for a considerable period of time for various reasons is known as migration. It is one of the three components of the population change the other two being mortality and fertility. Migration is associated with the socio-economic development of the country. In India one of the side-effects of unprecedented population growth is industrialization and economic development which helped in a rapid increase in internal migratory movements. Internal migration is the movement of people from one region to another within the country. In internal migration there are different forms of migration such as "Rural-to-rural" Urban-to-urban migration "Rural to urban migration "Urban to rural migration and International migration is the migration from one country to another country.

Rural flight (or rural exodus) is a term used to describe the migratory patterns of peoples from rural areas into urban areas. In modern times, it often occurs in a region following the industrialization of agriculture when fewer people are needed to bring the same amount of agricultural output to market and related agricultural services and industries are consolidated. Rural flight is exacerbated when the population decline leads to the loss of rural services such as stores and schools, which then leads to greater loss of population.

The loss of population in rural areas leads to the abandonment of small towns, turning their once thriving downtowns into empty or underutilized storefronts. The rise of corporate agricultural structures directly affects small rural communities, resulting in decreased populations, decreased incomes for some segments, increased income inequality, decreased community participation, fewer retailed outlets and less retail trade, and increased environmental pollution.

Post-World War II rural flight is caused by the growing industrialization of agriculture, in which small, labor-intensive family farms grow into, or are replaced by, heavily mechanized and specialized industrial farms. While a small family farm typically produced a wide range of crop, garden, and animal products, all requiring substantial labor, large industrial farms typically specialize in just a few crop or livestock varieties, using large machinery and high-density livestock containment systems that require a fraction of the labor per unit produced.

Contents

1

Introduction

County agricultural agents, foresters, social workers, soil conservationists, civil engineers, and other professionals inevitably come into contact with such social systems as cooperatives, unions, families, churches, and schools. For those who use organisational structures as channels of communication to reach people with programs, or for others who must establish communication between members, the concrete social system is more meaningful in most cases than abstractions of a different order. Considering the present stage of development in sociology and anthropology, and considering the limited knowledge of social processes possessed by many technically trained professionals who work with people, we believe the contribution of these disciplines may be accepted more readily if we deal with concrete social systems familiar to potential users. Cast in the framework of social systems, it is hoped that the student of rural sociology may gain a better understanding of rural group life, its interaction, functioning, and change.

One may think of social systems on two different levels, which, for our purposes, do not often require differentiation. In the first place, a social system may be considered as concrete, or a cooperative social structure such as a football team, a Farm Bureau local, a family, a church congregation, a school, or even a silo-filling ring. It can be shown that these organisations are composed of persons who interact more with members than with non-members when operating to attain their objectives. When considerable action is involved, as in a football game, it is not difficult to distinguish the players from the non-players.

Even in such relatively simple situations, however, there may be a central system and various sub-systems. The usual starting line-up, for example, represents the central core, and the substitutes organized into various groups represent the sub-systems. In the second place, a social system may be viewed as abstract, or one in which patterns of relationships prevail from generation to generation and from region to region. Viewed in this way, social Systems consisting of elements or patterns that persist do not require that specific persons be considered as parts of the system. A Catholic church official of a given order and status, for example, can quite easily fit into or adjust to the sub-systems in different parts of the world or even into the same sub-systems of earlier generations.

According to our conceptual scheme, the subject matter for sociology and cultural anthropology is human culture and interaction. Although such subject matter may be viewed in many ways, we choose to make the various types of social systems our chief concern. As the significant unit of social systems, we accept Sorokin's "meaningful interaction of two or more human individuals" and his requirement that interaction be an event "by which one party tangibly influences the overt actions or the state of mind of the other." Social systems are made up of social interactions and the cultural factors which structure these interactions.

What do seemingly diverse social systems such as the Michigan State College, a combat fighter squadron, or the X families of Middletown have in common? What instructions can be given a stranger so that he may identify these or others as social systems? What are the significant differences in social systems? Volumes can be written in answer to these questions, but key elements of concern to those interested in understanding personality formation, social interaction, and culture can be outlined.

ELEMENTS OF SOCIAL SYSTEMS

That interaction between persons within a functioning social system is greater than interaction between those within and those outside has already been mentioned as characteristic of social systems. Although a large number of elements might be suggested, the authors feel that certain components related to the structure, value orientation, and locus of social systems are most important. These include the following:

1. Roles or that which is expected of individuals in given situations.
2. Status or the ranking given individuals, based upon the consensus of members as to what traits and qualities are to be rated high and low.
3. Authority or the right and power of individuals to influence others (a concept that also implies certain duties).
4. Rights or the immunity from authority, and duties, or the required obedience to authority and the requirements associated with the individual's role.
5. Ends and objectives or those changes (or perhaps the maintenance of the *status quo*) which members of the system expect to accomplish through the operation of the system.
6. Norms or those rules which govern the application of means in the accomplishment of the ends or objectives.
7. Territoriality or the locus and space requirements of a social system.

If other elements of social systems remain, the authors believe they are so inextricably interrelated that any classification which separates them is not realistic. For our purposes, however, we shall consider roles, status, and authority as primarily parts of the structure of social systems. The ends or objectives and norms we consider as primarily aspects of the value orientation. Thus, although some overlapping may occur, the social structure and value orientation are the two basic type-parts of social systems.

As applied to a specific social system-a football team-the elements just outlined may become clearer and more realistic. At a very early age, a child in American culture learns that different players on a football team do different things and are designated by the positions they play. Such positions we call roles, or what is expected of one in a given situation. The child also learns that some players are considered better than others. The basis for rating players, rooted in a general consensus as to what qualities are to be rated high and low, gives the players different status. It will also be perceived, particularly if the signals are called aloud, that the one player who calls signals influences the actions of others more than any single individual influences the action of the signal caller.

The child may properly ask why this player or the coach has the right to influence others. This right and power to influence others is authority. A person with great authority holds permission-granting rights and gets those over whom he exercises authority to do his bidding much more than they get him to do their bidding. Great authority is usually coupled with much one-way action, an extreme case of which is hypnosis, a relationship in which the subject has little apparent influence. Two-way action implies less authority, as in the case of the committee chairman who has members of the committee do only those things the committee has previously determined should be done.

Studies have shown that the element of authority is not restricted to human groups. For example, among chickens there is a well-defined "pecking order." That is, chicken A may peck any other member of the flock; chicken B may peck any member except A; and so on to chicken Z, a very frustrated chicken that can peck no other chicken. Although pecking orders are seldom as regular as this, similar behaviour has been observed among baboons and goats studied in captivity. In football, the coach has the right to influence the players. He is an authority. When he sends the team onto the field to play, the authority is temporarily and partially transferred to a player who calls the signals.

The coach further designates which players will play certain positions, or certain roles. With the authority and role go both rights and immunity from influence, and duties, or required obedience to authority and conformity to requirements associated with the roles being played. A child who sees a football squad running signals soon notes the interaction pattern sufficiently to distinguish between team members, spectators, and others who may be near. Furthermore, he will be able to readily differentiate football teams from other teams and groups. In more generally applicable phraseology, he will detect changes in the situation which the organisation or its leaders hope to bring about by the action. The child learns the team's ends or objectives-what the team is trying to do.

As football teams play in competition, officials are empowered to declare penalties for violations, thereby rewarding the other side. These penalties are determined by the rules of the game. We call this aspect of social systems norms, which govern the application of means to achieve the end or objective. Whether they are written or not, all systems rely upon norms. Territoriality or location in space is also a very important element which should not be omitted in the description of social systems. In football the rules of the game not only specify the dimensions of the playing field but also the spatial relationships of the various players. In offensive play the football center, for example, cannot trade places with the end. The roles are assigned to physical locations as related to the other players.

In considering systems as a whole, territoriality is also important. In warfare, control of areas is basic to strategy. When countries are occupied following a war, boundaries become very important because they indicate the extent of the occupying army's authority. In systems such as concentration camps and prisons, territoriality is of extreme importance. In kinship groups, the authority pattern and other factors are related to the manner in which marriage settles the spatial relationships of the two families of orientation. Furthermore, territoriality is of importance to discussions of locality groups such as neighbourhoods, trade centers, and cities, as well as of governmental units such as townships, counties, municipalities, states, and nations.

VALUE ORIENTATION AND MORALE

Many groups are not organized for specific objectives. Associations in MacIver's sense, or special-interest groups in Toennies' sense usually have rather specific objectives; but in the case of friendship and kinship groups, the value orientation includes the objective which, if it can be expressed at all, may be as broad as "preserving our way of life" or "keeping our gang together." Any group will have some of this type of motivation, which may be characterized as "persistence of aggregates"; but non-purposive behaviour of intimate face to-face groups makes the interpersonal relationships ends in and of themselves.

A typical family will not disown a son because there is an opportunity to adopt another child who will make the family more efficient in this or that respect. On the other hand, the football team that does not use the most efficient players will probably win few games. These differences are due to differences in value orientation. Even though all systems have patterns of authority, roles, rights and duties, and status, they may vary greatly in their value orientations.

Many elements, of course, are related to the morale of a social system. Roethlisberger has stressed the importance of open and effective communication between authorities and the various levels of subordinates. Of importance also is the relative emphasis placed upon objectives and the possibility of attaining them. Thus the integration of all the elements of a system is important for the greatest personal satisfaction and security of its members. Zeleny has developed socio-metric methods for measuring what he calls morale. His measurements in reality deal with congeniality.

Likert and the Morale Division of the United States Strategic Bombing Survey measured morale in terms of the absence of willingness to accept unconditional surrender, absenteeism in industry, loss of faith in leaders, belief that one's own group or class was getting the worst of it, and such general conditions as defeatism, fear, hopelessness, fatalism, and war-weariness. It should be obvious that regardless of whether morale is high or low in a given system, it is dependent upon the functioning of the communication system and the integration of the elements outlined.

High morale exists when all members of the system are in accord with its ends, agree upon its bases of attaining status, have confidence in its leaders, conform to its norms, and are willing and ready to make great sacrifices to defend the system. A system that places excessive emphasis on "success goals," or on norms, protocol, and customs, and frustrates achievement, will probably have lower morale than a system in which such elements are balanced.

APPLICATION OF CONCEPTS

Variations in both social structure and value orientation make for a general over-all variation in the nature of social systems. Many writers have attempted to describe these variations by what may be called "sponge" types. Many types are in use.

However, their practical utility has been questioned. It is not difficult to understand why many sociologists and anthropologists who are required to assist in directing human affairs can see little or no value in such "sponge" concepts as *Gemeinschaft* and *Gesellschaft*, mechanical solidarity and organic solidarity, sacred and secular society, Apollonian and Dionysian societies, folk and civilisation, primary and secondary groups, or familistic, mixed (contractual), and compulsory interaction.

Useful as such concepts, configurations, and themes of social systems may be in analyzing human behaviour and culture, few administrators and executives would be enough interested to listen to a sufficiently complete explanation of these concepts to make them useful. Nevertheless, such concepts may be very important in major social movements. The Nazi movement would never have been what it was without the *Volks Gemeinschaft* or "community of fate" idea, nor would the socialist and communist movements be what they are without the Marxian concept of the *buergerliche Gesellschaft* or middleclass capitalistic society. These and similar concepts have played and will play major roles in wars, race riots, and revolutions.

Consciously or unconsciously, everyone whether a scientist or a director of human affairs is continuously using similar concepts. When they are of such a nature that they may be defined, their elements specified, and their over-all or Gestalt qualities described in objective terms, they may be instruments of science. When not, they may be useless, or they may be used to accentuate prejudice, thus augmenting race hatred, religious strife, and class conflict.

The authors devised an instrument whereby students in rural sociology classes could compare aspects of the value orientation and social structure of various systems with which they had had experience. In the winter and spring terms of 1949 there were 90 students who had had experience in the armed forces during World War II. They were requested to compare the military unit with which they had had most experience with their own families, most of which were farm families. In making this comparison they were requested to recall how they were related to their fathers and other family members when they were from 10 to 15 years of age.

In comparing the family and army units, the following instructions were given: "In each case please assume the following conditions: A sudden emergency about which no member of the group had any warning requires that the permanent location (residence of the family, and offices or quarters of the other group or groups) be moved within twelve hours. All possessions and equipment used by the group and its individuals must be moved by the group itself to a new location several miles away." The stability of the averages and the similarities in the profiles of the many rural sociology and other classes whose members have compared the military units they know best with their own families during their youth demonstrate the workability of the instruments and illustrate the importance of the elements which were chosen for the continua used. The findings for the 90 veterans will be described below, but we must now turn to the three concrete social systems which are also to be analyzed through the use of the continua.

CONCRETE SOCIAL SYSTEMS TO BE COMPARED

To illustrate the use and components of the type of concepts employed, in addition to comparing the rural sociology students' appraisal of their own families and military units, it is proposed to compare an Amish family, a Latin-American ditch association, and a federal government bureau in the United States Department of Agriculture. Because the authors know these social systems very well and because the systems differ from one another fundamentally they will be described and compared to illustrate the nature of and variations in social structure and value orientation.

THE AMISH FARM FAMILY

The family to be described is a typical Amish farm family living on the outskirts of the Older Order Amish settlement in Lancaster County, Pennsylvania, which numbers about 3,500 persons. The culture of these people has been described in detail elsewhere. Unfortunately, it is not possible in the space available to describe the history and many other facts of importance concerning these people.

The family considered here lives in the mother settlement from which colonies have gone out into various states. The land was rented and the income was somewhat below average-elements that prevented location in a more central part of the settlement, where land values are almost ten times higher.

The more central location insures families more isolation from the "gay" people or non-Amish outsiders. Among Amish families the chief elements from which status is gained are: (1) conformity to the sacred mores of the Amish; (2) success in farm operation; and (3) hard work and thrift. Within the family, status is determined according to many of the same principles. Wholehearted obedience and willingness to participate in the cooperative activities of the family are very important.

The Amish think of themselves as a people apart-God's plain people-who have always been persecuted by outsiders. Their norms, which taboo the use or possession of many conveniences, considered as part of the profane, ungodly world outside, are the most significant characteristics making the Amish people different. Thus, tractors cannot be used for draft power in farming. Neither can the Amish own automobiles, trucks, electric lights, lightning rods, radios, telephones, bicycles, electric refrigerators, indoor toilets, or elaborate house decorations. Plain clothes, without buttons, are prescribed for work, church, and visiting. Standardized "plain" grooming in hair styles is characteristic.

Few groups have restricted the occupational roles of their members more than the Amish. Only farming and a few related non-urban occupations are open to children. School beyond the eighth grade or beyond the age of 14, musical instruments, non-biblical books, membership in non-church organisations, and many other activities and objects are tabooed. Dress and grooming mark the Amish as a people apart, and great value is placed upon being in "full fellowship." Violations of 'taboos' or failures to abide by prescribed customs may deprive one of the rights to communion or may even lead to shunning. In the latter case, even the nearest relatives refuse to interact with the violator until he repents and makes amends.

The alternative is to "go gay"-that is to say, give up the privilege of "full fellowship." Limitations on the possession of such American symbols of status as automobiles, education, house furnishings, clothing, and the like are accompanied by great emphasis upon success in farming and upon hard work. Many dairy farmers arise at 4:00 A.M. and retire regularly at eight at night. According to the investigator's notes, the family under consideration included the mother and father, a 19-year-old son, and seven daughters, ranging from an infant to one 17-year-old girl. With the exception of the baby, of course, the entire family worked as a team.

Each had certain functions and duties to perform. At nine o'clock one morning in April, the family was engaged in the following activities: the father, Christopher, was plowing with the three-horse sulky; the son, David, and the investigator were loading and spreading manure; the mother and three older girls were currying the twenty cows; a younger daughter was feeding the chickens; and the baby was cooing in a basket in the barn. The family had all arisen at 4:30 A.M. The mother had quickly started a fire in the range and had left one of the youngest girls to cook the cereal and boil the coffee. She had then followed her husband, son, and daughters to the barn to help feed and milk the twenty cows. Milking was done by hand, and each person had specific cows to milk and other specific duties to perform.

However, if one member of the family was sick or if another, such as the investigator, was added to this work team, the father had no difficulty in readjusting the work in such a way that a new equilibrium was formed with little frustration or friction. Other Amishmen sympathized with Christopher for having only one boy left at home, because, in general, the heavier field work falls to the men. On this farm, however, the girls and mother all participated in field work. The roles and functions were assigned in accordance with required strength and abilities. A general consideration, however, specifies that the women's first duty is that of caring for the house, poultry, and pigs, while that of the men is almost exclusively outside household affairs. Accounts and buying are the man's business, although in this family the woman's superior education resulted in her participation in these affairs.

The family had two buggies, which could not, however, be used interchangeably by the father and the son. Since David was in the courting stage, he had an open buggy, harness, and several blankets. If David followed the recommended practice of the Older Amish, he would attend barn singings, court a girl, and marry her at about twenty years of age. After the wedding he would sell the open buggy and buy an enclose d, grey-topped one similar to his father's. He would then grow a beard, and his wife would bring her hope chest and dowry to the newly formed household. After the wedding, the bride no longer wears her white cap and white apron, and neither she nor the bridegroom attends the singings. All these developments designate important changes in both roles and status of the two young people. Marriage constitutes an important transition in the life cycle and is associated with impressive rites of passage.

The Amish family has often been described as patriarchal. To this the authors would most certainly agree. Some superficial observers, however, have described the Amish father as a dictator. It is true that the Amish wife and children are supposed to be submissive to the father and the children to the mother when the father is absent. Chapple's and Arensberg's interaction measurements would show a high origin-response ratio for the Amish father. This would indicate that he ordered, suggested, and directed, and that the wife and children conformed and obliged. Such quantitative measures, however, may misrepresent the authoritarian pattern.

If one heard the Amish father order his son to fix the fence in the pasture, he might sound dictatorial. However, his order would assume a different meaning if the son himself had previously said that the fence needed repairing, lest the cows attempt to crawl through. Many of the directives that Christopher gave resulted from similar discussions. Nevertheless, wives and children are expected to obey fathers, and children are expected to obey both parents. As will be shown later, the Amish father's interaction with other members may superficially resemble that of an authoritarian system such as an army unit. Their basic characters, however, are quite different. This will become evident as the conceptual scheme we plan to employ is developed.

The function of the ditch association in New Mexico is to clean, maintain, repair, and control the irrigation system of El Cerrito, a village of twenty-five families. Since few cultivated crops grow in the village without irrigation, the ditch association, next to the family and the church, is probably the most important organisation. All families owning land in the valley are eligible for membership. Although there is no formal constitution, the association is almost as old as the village itself. No dues are paid. Instead, each family contributes labor in accordance with the area of irrigated land operated. One day's labor is usually required for each acre of irrigated land. If the dam is washed out or if any other catastrophe occurs, the labor involved is allocated in accordance with the number of acres to be watered.

Authority or control of operation is placed with the ditch boss or *mayordomo*, who, with the ditch committee of three members, is elected by a popular vote of all members of the village. The role or function of the boss as an official is to plan the cleaning of the ditch, an event which assumes the character of a community fiesta. Other functions are to inspect the ditch at regular intervals and to call out the men to work when the ditch is to be repaired. In many New Mexican villages the ditch boss has great status in the community. At El Cerrito the duties are equal to or exceed the rights attached to the role, and the office is passed around to all who will function in it. No pay is received. The only reward, other than the prestige attached to the position, comes by virtue of the fact that the boss is not expected to do any labor, since he is a supervisor.

Except for the priest, ditch bosses and all other authorities are called by their first names by those of the same age group. Only first names are used among the members. If enmity develops between members, they may address one another by last names. However, this is not common in this association. In the roles as members of the ditch association, committeemen are expected to make new rules for the regulation of the association and to see that the old ones are enforced. They must regulate water according to supply and need. The authority of the officials is not questioned, but they usually follow tradition or consult with other leaders.

Another aspect of the value orientation is reflected in the fact that a violation of the code of the association may bring about a suspension of water rights or heavy penalties in the form of labor. Such sanctions are seldom necessary. However, people are expected to be, and usually are, cooperative. One's status in the community depends in no small measure upon willingness to submerge self-interest. If a member fails to do his share for good reason, he is pardoned. The people say, "It's the spirit that counts." In general, there is a definite status system for cooperators. Those who fail to do their share in the cooperative undertaking find help less readily in other events in which assistance is needed. Although one's contributions in this rather timeless society are certainly not accurate to the minute, the value placed on doing one's share is very great.

THE DIVISION OF EXTENSION AND TRAINING

The Division of Extension and Training, like the Technical Collaboration Branch of which it is a part, came into being as a result of the war, but nevertheless it is a typical division of a governmental bureau. It became an arm of a cooperative agricultural program concerned with returning the growing of rubber, cinchona for quinine, and cubı for rotenone and other sprays to the Western Hemisphere. These crops had originated in South America but in large part had been transplanted to the East, where they, along with certain fibers and other important crops, were appropriated by the Japanese after Pearl Harbor. To re-establish the production of these crops in areas accessible to the United States, cooperative experiment stations were established in various Latin-American countries.

As a part of this program, trainees were brought to the United States to learn American agricultural techniques. Specialists were sent to Latin America to make rural sociological and cultural anthropological studies preparatory to beginning adult education and extension work. The division is expected to handle foreign trainees, to make cultural anthropological studies, and to establish extension or adult education work at the experiment stations. As in other government bureaus, directors, chiefs, and leaders directed activities or gave the permission necessary to carry through a line of work. The rights and responsibilities of functionaries at both professional and clerical levels are specific. The authority of director, chief, head, and leader is limited to the individual employee and does not extend to members of the employee's family. The personal lives of employees and their families are sharply separated from their professional lives.

The roles and functions of the bureau have evolved as time passed. Functions could not be as specific as in many bureaus because an employee, although traveling in a foreign country, was expected to look after the affairs of the various other sections, including those of crop production and station management. Upon returning, he was expected to help assign foreign trainees to various government bureaus or land-grant colleges. All were expected to watch for capable technicians who might study agriculture in the United States and carry improved methods to agriculturalists in their own countries. Division of function was less than in many bureaus.

In general, status was represented by one's professional rank, i.e., by P-1, P-2, and other ratings. In this system, status is not accorded in exact relation to rank and salary. Lower ranked and salaried persons receiving the basic P-3 salary but having considerable foreign experience and mastery of foreign languages, for example, may be accorded more respect than a Senior Scientist with higher salary, or even a Principal Scientist (P-5) with a much higher salary but with little foreign experience and mastery of foreign languages. Since the organisation was made up of research workers, the standing in the scientific professional groups was also important. Because the men were away from central controls a great deal of the time and were continually travelling, much more freedom was enjoyed than in most government bureaus. While in travel status, to be sure, certain duties had to be performed outside one's regular work. A formal call, for instance, had to be made at the American Embassy, which led to other duties of protocol.

As the division grew, procedures grew. One could not do this but must do that. Letters had to be written in five copies of different colors. Letters for the director's signature were written one way, those for the secretary's signature another, and if in either case they went to the Department of State, a more impersonal form had to be used. Even so, anyone accustomed to European bureaucracy, particularly of the prewar type, would class this division as relatively informal and personal. It was not uncommon for those below section heads to call division heads by their first names. Chiefs would be called by their first names only by section leaders, unless those below had been former friends. Nonprofessionals such as clerks, secretaries, and stenographers seldom call their bosses by their first names, but bosses frequently call them by first names or nicknames.

FUNDAMENTAL ATTRIBUTES OF SOCIAL SYSTEMS

As social systems, the Amish family and the government bureau are, of course, essentially different. The outstanding difference resides in their value systems, or that which Sorokin calls law-norms. The Amish family is more of the familistic *Gemeinschaft* type; the government bureau more of the contractual *Gesellschaft* type.

These two concepts, the latter word of each pair developed by Toennies and the former by Sorokin, are not found in actual life but represent types which are "extremes" or "ideal types." Like the components of atoms in nuclear physics, they are fictions of the mind, invented to assist in understanding the data. The peasant family and the intimate, solidary, face-to-face relationships of the clique or friendship group are relatively familistic *Gemeinschaft* in nature. Toennies thought the attitude and behaviour of people in the stock market characterized contractual *Gesellschaft* relationships. Sorokin and Maine have thought of people associated with one another by contract as forming the prototype of what they call the contractual and what we call contractual *Gesellschaft* relationships.

In general, it may be concluded that the members of a familistic *Gemeinschaft*-type system place relatively more emphasis than do members of a contractual *Gesellschaft*-type system upon the norms rather than the specific ends of the systems. The inclusion of the word contractual emphasizes a particular type of norm and suggests a characteristic feature of *Gesellschaft* systems. As suggested previously, types such as familistic *Gemeinschaft* and contractual *Gesellschaft* are "sponge" designations. They are broad, comprehensive terms which often fail to define explicitly their elements or components. The authors have attempted to abstract some key aspects of these broad types not only in order to illustrate fundamental components of the types but also to further describe differences between the Amish family, the El Cerrito ditch association, and the division of the government bureau.

That the familistic *Gemeinschaft* and contractual *Gesellschaft* types are to be considered as extreme, polar types is familiar to the reader. For purposes of precision, we have chosen to visualize the two types at the extremes of a ten-point scale. A neutral point is arbitrarily chosen to be 0, and five points in either direction indicate the relative degrees of familistic *Gemeinschaft* and contractual *Gesellschaft* traits. Thus, on one hand, point 5 on the continuum represents the extreme or ideal type, familistic *Gemeinschaft*; on the other hand, point 5 at the opposite end of the continuum represents the ideal type, contractual Gesellchaft.

The components of the two major types under consideration are each constructed into a scale or continuum. Ratings of the Amish family, the ditch association, and the government bureau are made for each of the continua. Also, as stated above, each of ninety students in Michigan State College rural sociology classes with military experience compared their own military units and their families when they were 10 to 15 years of age, by placing them on the continua. Those components of the types considered most important to illustrate the nature of social systems include the following: non-rational versus rational action; functional specificity versus functional diffuseness;

complete or blanket responsibility versus limited responsibility; and integration of roles within the system versus irrelevance of roles outside the system.

NON-RATIONAL VERSUS RATIONAL ACTION

One of the fundamental characteristics of the contractual *Gesellschaft* as viewed by the authors is its rationality. Three non-rational types of behaviour are traditional, emotional, and sacred. The characterisation used in placing the three systems on a continuum of Non-rational versus Rational is the following: The completely rational act is considered as one in which the interpersonal relationships of the members of the system are in no sense considered as ends in and of themselves. In fact, in rational action interpersonal relations are only valuable insofar as they further some action aimed at the attainment of ends or objectives.

The non-rational act, for our purposes, is considered one in which all interpersonal ties and relationships are the only important ends. All other values are subsidiary. Obviously neither of these extreme conditions exists in reality. In large part it is the high evaluation which farm people place upon home and community ties that makes for "lack of flexibility" in the family farm, a fact which prevents it from casting off its members merely because they may not pay for their upkeep. Those economists who deplore the "inflexibility" of the family farm enterprise, which results in what they call over-population in rural areas, have failed in many cases to understand the difference in value orientation of the family on the one hand, and a bureaucracy on the other.

The 90 students with military experience ranked their military units with scores which averaged far to the contractual *Gesellschaft* side. They did not place their families so far to the familistic *Gemeinschaft* side as the rankers placed the Amish family. Similarly, the norms governing the means used in attaining objectives and the objectives themselves may be either diffuse or specific. The action pattern of the Amish family is much more blanket and much less functionally specific than that of the government bureau, considered from the point of view of the roles, authority pattern, norms, and ends.

The ditch association falls into an intermediate position. Along with the Amish family, however, it falls on the familistic *Gemeinschaft* side of the continuum. The government division falls on the contractual *Gesellsehaft* side. The average scores rural sociology students with military experience gave their military units and families fall between the Amish family and the government bureau. Interestingly enough, students without military experience tend to rate military units farther toward the contractual *Gesellschaft* side than students with military experience, who have experienced the familistic *Gemeinschaft* nature of buddy groups and so forth.

COMMUNITY OF FATE VERSUS LIMITED RESPONSIBILITY

The Amish family represents a relatively complete "community of fate," in that the hardships and sorrows are borne by all and the pleasures and satisfactions are the pleasures of all. In the case of the government bureau, financial loss on the part of a member is borne only partially, if at all, by other members of the system.

INTEGRATION OF ROLES WITHIN AND OUTSIDE THE SYSTEMS

Some systems require that members play no role outside the system which conflicts with their roles within. Usually a church will not permit its minister, for instance, to make money as a barkeeper; in fact, the freedom of ministers' children outside the church is often more restricted than is that of other children. The Amish family is close to the extreme type of the familistic *Gemeinschaft*, while the ditch association is again intermediate.

The intermediate position of the students' military units and families may be due to the fact that the systems were rated as two contrasting units independently. If each person had rated all five systems at the same time, the general pattern would have been the same, but the order of the systems on the scale might have been different.

THE SIGNIFICANCE OF THE TYPES DESCRIBED

That bureaucracy as a large-scale cooperative structure is efficient is attested by its prevalence, particularly in the modern Western world. The last two world wars were struggles between huge bureaucracies, and the outcome of future wars will unquestionably depend largely upon the efficiency of bureaucracy. Among the most important features of the dynamic and powerful nations today is the prevalence of bureaucracy. All nations of any military or industrial importance are characterized by bureaucracy or the contractual *Gesellschaft*-like organisation.

Even though *Gesellschaft*-like organisations such as the army, business, and industry are more efficient than familistic *Gemeinschaft*-like organisations, experience has demonstrated that morale in the bureaucracies can be increased if some of the characteristics of the familistic *Gemeinschaft* organisations can be introduced. The more frequent the two-way interaction between authorities and subordinates is, for instance, the higher will be the morale, in all probability. Likewise, the greater the face-to-face relationships and the greater the solidarity of the relationships, the higher will be morale.

The depersonalized, secondary, rationalized, and secular relationships in formal bureaucracy, when coupled with the high mobility resulting from assigning status, roles, and rewards on the basis of attainment rather than upon family or other criteria can be demonstrated to be related to, if not a cause of, great personal frustration and insecurity. The very groups that attain positions of authority in the organisations and professions characterized by these traits have the highest suicide and functional insanity rates.

Such movements as Nazism and present-day emotional religion are not unrelated to the frustration and insecurity which characterize modern middle- and lower-class life. Toennies and others have called attention to the satisfaction that comes to workers in large impersonal industries through participation in the social life of unions where some *Gemeinschaft*-like features are emphasized. Much of the insecurity and consequent frustration of present-day society is related to the growth of large-scale organisations which have the characteristics of the contractual *Gesellsehaft*.

This influence extends to the rural areas and has caught up the farmer in the price and market regime; as a result, the farmer has lost much of his former independence and security. The German peasant residing in a family sized farming area often supported the Nazi movement, whereas many urban labor groups sought security through labor, socialistic, and communistic groups in the cities. Roetblisberger and Dixon, in their study of the Western Electric Company's plant, and Likert, in his study of life insurance salesmen, have demonstrated that industry and business could improve morale by introducing certain aspects of the familistic *Gemeinschaft* into their organisations to offset frustration precipitated by the impersonal aspects of bureaucracy.

Attempts to restrict output are very often related to the insecurity of workers. It is obvious, of course, that great frustration would be brought about by the mixing of some familistic *Gemeinschaft* traits with some *Gesellschaft* traits. If agencies resorted to particularistic and personal criteria for awarding promotions and status in large-scale organisations, morale would most certainly suffer. Nevertheless, much of the insecurity in large-scale organisations is inherent in the strangeness, impersonality, and secularisation of the organisation. The Likert study cited above, for instance, indicates that salesmen are concerned most about the attention their supervisors give them.

The German army attempted to overcome some of the insecurity of bureaucracy induced by the rational, functionally specific, and secondary nature of the Prussian army by having unit officers learn the birthdays of their men so that they could be congratulated. Although such innovations represent a change in techniques rather than a change in value orientation, the fact that they are used proves that such bureaucracies lack features which are felt to be necessary for high morale. Mayo and Lombard demonstrated that in those departments of the aircraft industry in which the interaction pattern and the type of authority was *Gemeinschaft*-like, labor turnover and absenteeism were lower.

If society develops a means of introducing elements of security into modern industry and government, whether based upon features of security characteristic of the familistic *Gemeinschaft*, the contractual *Gesellschaft*, or both, a tremendous force will be released for productive use. This is not to say that an automobile plant can be modeled after an Amish family. Neither would the desired results necessarily be accomplished by turning private bureaucracy into government bureaucracy. The point is that those who direct bureaucracies of either type should realize that workers who are not secure in their families, communities, and occupations are not likely to have high morale in the bureaucracies in which they work.

Social science has demonstrated means of improving the morale of social systems. In this connection, the development of that branch of sociology called sociometry should be mentioned. Through special socio-metric techniques, devised to get people together who want to be together for various purposes, both group and individual efficiency has been increased. Thus work groups of children in school and camp, county agricultural agents in work shops, bomber crews on missions, and other groups may perform more efficiently when members are grouped by socio-metric techniques permitting those to function together who want to be together.

Cleavages within social systems such as those between different races or rural and urban people may be measured and special procedures such as role playing, social drama and other forms of group dynamics may be used to increase integration. It is the authors' belief that important in the explanation for back to the land movements during depressions and for the current phenomenon of small-farm purchase by workers, is the feeling of futility and insecurity in the organisations characterized by contractual *Gesellsehaft*. We also believe that underlying rural-urban conflict and the mushrooming fringe areas around the cities are the fundamentally different attitudes of people with basically familistic *Gemeinschaft* orientations and those with basically contractual *Gesellschaft* orientations. Underlying much of the unrest and disequilibrium among both rural and urban groups today is the loss of elements which have here been described as being of the nature of the familistic *Gemeinschaft*.

RURAL AND URBAN WORLDS AS RELATED TO FAMILISTIC GEMEINSCHAFT

Toennies maintained that the urbanite was more influenced in his actions by the elements of the *Gesellschaft* than by the elements of the *Gemeinschaft*. On the other hand, according to Toennies, the peasant was more influenced by the elements of the *Gemeinschaft* than by those of the *Gesellschaft*. Tomars writes: "Certainly there is a vast body of sociological analysis to attest to the reality of the rural as a type of society set off from the urban type, whether this be expressed in terms of primary group versus secondary group organisation, sentimental versus rational attitudes, isolated-sacred versus accessible-secular structures, communal versus associational groupings, or in terms of a host of other distinctions." For Sorokin the rural society is characterized by familism, the urban society by contractualism, but throughout the world he two is merging.

Rural life in general should not be spoken of as "a world" or a type. The relative significance of those elements characterized by the familistic *Gemeinschaft*, or by its counterpart the contractual *Gesellschaft*, varies in rural society from social class to social class, from type of farming area to type of farming area, from generation to generation, and in many other ways. Consider the variations represented in the huge "factory farms" on the West Coast, the Amishman's family-sized operation in Pennsylvania, the southern lower-class sharecropper's and the upper-upper-class plantation owners' operations, the slave plantations of the Roman Empire, the free peasant operations, and those of the feudal barons of the Middle Ages.

If the social systems representing all these and other operations were placed on the various continua in the preceding analysis, the oversimplification which the use of the more concrete types such as rural and urban, or even of the more abstract types such as the familistic *Gemeinschaft* and contractual *Gesellschaft*, would become evident. Cities also have their familistic *Gemeinschaft*-like elements. There are the familistic *Gemeinschaft*-like settlements of Japanese in cities like Seattle, and lower-class Italian and other groups in cities like Boston. Nevertheless, by and large, the rural groups and elements of life which are important to rural people have relatively more of the characteristics of the familistic *Gemeinsehaft*, and less of the characteristics of the contractual *Gesellsehaft*, than do comparable organisations in the cities. Future studies should attempt to be more specific in making comparisons than is possible when such "sponge types" are used.

THE VALUE ORIENTATION OF RURAL PEOPLE

The value orientation, or attitudinal characteristics, of rural people as compared with urban, when considered in relation to the components of the types we have used, are different even in the United States, where rural and urban life patterns are merging more rapidly than elsewhere. These differences will hold for comparable classes, regions, or epochs. Only a few of the most important distinctions will be treated here. On most measures of behaviour which may be used to compare the sacred as versus the secular attitudes, the farm families, class by class and area by area, spend relatively more money in church activities than do comparable city families." Studies of radio listening patterns stress the greater interest on the part of rural people for church and religious programs than that of comparable urban groups.

Taylor, in his attempt to ascertain whether farmers were more "isolationist" than others, concluded that on the whole they are more provincial in their thinking and relatively more concerned with what goes on in the family, neighbourhood, and local community than are others. Many other studies have indicated that farm people are in their basic attitudes more traditional than they are rational or nontraditional, as this continuum is used in the previous discussion. Rural people are able to preserve national culture for a longer time than are urban people, who are more subjected to the invasion of rational thinking, techniques, and high mobility.

In general, the farm family as a production and consumption unit retains its members in a unified team-work arrangement much more than does the comparable urban family. Although great variations by class and by type of farming area exist, farmers' wives and children help the farmer more with the farm enterprise than the wives and children of city families help the husbands. The fact that the life and occupation of an members of a family are inextricably intermingled so that all members consider themselves a part of a going concern affects the thinking and attitudes of rural people as much as or more than any other feature.

This assistance is not only a routine chore type of activity. Tasks and roles of all members are varied from season to season. All members must make decisions which, with the variability of the work, make for certain flexibility not present in all factory work in cities. In interpersonal relationships, responsibilities are less specific and defined than in comparable urban situations. In those areas in which the family-sized farm, owned and managed by the operator, is the ideal (and this includes most of the farming areas of the United States and the world), the farmer and peasant is both management and labor.

Physical work is respected and a high premium is placed upon initiative, cooperation, physical strength, vitality, energy, endurance, and effort. Also, property ownership and control, whatever the systems of tenure, are considered virtues. As Tomars has indicated, because "the selfrespecting farmer of the past was the owner-farmer, living in someone else's house carried the lower status of tenancy or lower still, dependency." Rural migrants have carried this attitude to the city and it is all-pervasive. Schuler and Taylor, in summarizing the results of a survey conducted by *Successful Farming* in 1945, state that about two-thirds of the farmers interviewed said that they did not believe the government should own banks, coal mines, and railroads. However, the farmers have organized to prevent what they thought to be exploitation and have fostered the cause of state ownership of distribution facilities and public utilities.

In general, the public opinion polls and surveys have shown that the farm population sides with management in their attitudes towards strikes, organized labor, wages, and the socialisation of industry. However, the farmers of the nation have several times aligned themselves with the laboring interests in national and state elections. We may thus conclude that the farm family as an operating unit, particularly in the United States, includes both the roles of manager and laborer, and, looking out to the broader society, accepts the value orientation of the middle classes, but that physical labor as an activity is respected and the role of management is appreciated.

As indicated above, this integration of roles within the family, and the accompanying attitudes, are more in keeping with the familistic *Gemeinschaft* than with the contractual *Gesellsehaft*. In American rural society we have therefore a significant paradox. In terms of material levels of living, the rural people are more like the laboring classes, but in terms of attitudes, they are orientated toward the middle classes, who, as it will be indicated, operate the contractual *Gesellschaft*-like and bureaucratic structures of society. The farm people are a repository of what is sacred and traditional in the culture, but the impact of the contractual *Gesellschaft* upon them is now tremendous.

Throughout this book the relative position of various rural social systems as related to the types, familistic *Gemeinschaft* and contractual *Geselischaft*, will be discussed. The relative sacredness, traditionalism, functional diffuseness, and importance of the integration of the various different and important roles within the farm family are extremely important and are, therefore, stressed here.

Social systems are organisations composed of persons who interact more with members than with non-members when operating to attain the systems' objectives. All social systems, whether small silo-filling rings or large farmers' organisations such as the Farm Bureau, have elements in common which the social scientist, educator, and administrator must consider if he is to understand them. The elements of both social structure and value orientation, of course, are so inextricably interrelated that any classification that separates them will be somewhat unrealistic.

For purposes of empirical procedure, we consider value orientation as including the ends or objectives and norms. The ends or objectives may be regarded as changes which the members of a system, especially its leaders or officers, expect to accomplish through the functioning of the system.

The norms may be considered the "rules of the game" which govern the application of means, especially the use made of persons and interpersonal relations in attaining the ends and objectives. Norms also include such attitudes as those which furnish the basis for social structure, particularly rights, duties, and the evaluation of persons.

The social structure, on the other hand, is composed of roles, authority patterns, and stratification. The roles or positions, based upon expectancy patterns, are those things which persons in the system are compelled by habit, custom, or duty to do under given conditions. Authority may be regarded as the right to influence others, and is obviously related to a counterbalancing element, rights, or the immunity from the influence of others. Stratification is the hierarchical or the status pattern of a system. It is based upon consensus among the members of the system as to what qualities in the individual are to be rated high and what qualities low. Stratification, roles, and authority are all dependent for their effective operation upon a common basis of evaluating human action. Hence, we may say that social structure has its basis in the value orientation, or the attitudes and sentiments concerning right and wrong, justice and injustice, good and evil.

Territoriality, or the manner in which interpersonal relationships of the members of a social system are influenced by social space, is an additional important element of social systems. Rural libraries desiring to increase circulation for people in sparsely populated areas, for example, are confronted with problems different from those confronted in populous areas. Hospitals situated in small towns with trade centers extending more than 30 miles in all directions have problems which hospitals in larger, more populous centers do not have. The nature of social systems is determined by the interrelation of all the elements enumerated.

A professional football team that does not determine who shall play on the basis of competence and performance does not succeed. A family, on the other hand, will not discharge members merely because of lack of technical competence. We take such differences for granted, but if we are to understand social systems, the elements making for such variations must be conceptualized and analyzed. To point up the differences in the value orientation of social systems, we have introduced the concepts of familistic *Gemeinschaft* and contractual *Gesellschaft.* Stated in oversimplified terms, the former embraces those relationships and associations arising from an emotionally based desire or inclination to associate; the latter grows out of rational and calculated consideration of the ends to be served by the associations.

Both concepts are regarded as "pure" or "ideal" types. To illustrate the characteristics of these types, we have compared the military units and families of 90 GI students taking rural sociology, a Pennsylvania Amish family, a Spanish-American ditch association, and a division of a government bureau in the United States Department of Agriculture, on a series of continua. Compared with the Amish family, the government bureau is much more limited in its range of authority and responsibility for members. It is more rational, more functionally specific, more secular, and less concerned about the outside roles of members than is the Amish family.

From these and other differences, the fundamental familistic Gemeinschaft-like nature of the Amish family is contrasted with the fundamental contractual *Gesellschaft*-like nature of the government bureau. The 90 GI students described their families as of the nature of the familistic *Gemeinschaft* and their military units as of the nature of the contractual *Gesellschaft*. The Spanish-American ditch association is intermediate on the continua. Problems of building morale always involve developing an effective balance in the elements described as being of the nature of the familistic *Gemeinschaft* and the contractual *Gesellsehaft*.

In both rural and urban areas, the personal security and social solidarity which were once produced by the familistic *Gemeinschaft* elements have largely disappeared. A condition results in which fanaticism of various sorts can easily take root. Emotional religion, Nazism, communism, and various extremist movements thrive in a transitional period in which the elements of the familistic *Gemeinschaft* are being replaced by the elements of the contractual *Gesellschaft*. Although rural life throughout the world and particularly in the United States is acquiring many of the elements of the contractual *Gesellschaft*, on the various continua described it remains more sacred and less secular, more traditional and less rational, more functionally diffuse and less functionally specific than urban life.

Viewed from the structural point of view, the fact that the farm family integrates within itself many roles, especially those played elsewhere by management and labor, and the fact that it uses property as both a symbol of status and a means of production are of great importance to the total of society. Although the majority of farmers have material levels of living comparable to lower- or lower-middle-class families in the cities, their attitudes toward property and most other issues resemble those of the classes above them. Nevertheless, the farmer is both a planner and a doer; he represents both labor and management.

2

Social Systems and Social Change

An Effective Understanding Of Group Life And of groups experiencing change would be difficult, if not impossible, without consideration of relevant social systems, the elements comprising them, and the important processes involved in change. This chapter is devoted to an attempt to isolate and explain those elements and processes believed to be essential to the understanding of rural groups. It is possible to conceive of social systems as existing on two different levels which, for our purposes, will not often requite differentiation. In the first place, a social system may be considered a concrete interactive social structure, such as a Farm Bureau local, a family, a church congregation, or a dairy herd improvement association.

The members of such organisations interact more with members than with non-members when participating in the organisation as an on-going concern. In concrete social systems, the greater the interaction between members, the easier it is to ascertain who is part and who is not part of the system; that is to ascertain the boundaries of the system. For some systems, such as communities in family sized farming areas, the interaction and loyalties of members are so often diffused throughout other systems that only a crisis will reveal some aspects of the community system. Even in the case of a simpler system, such as a family or a school, there is usually a central system and various sub-systems.

For the typical family of the Western world there may be the conjugal core composed of father, mother, and children, and others related to the core-for example, grandparents, uncles, aunts, and cousins. For a farmers' organisation, the local may be the unit of observation and may be considered a system, or the whole organisation with its central organisational core may be considered a system and the various state, county and local units' sub-systems. Obviously, even when we are studying organisations as on-going concerns, we must focus upon relevant sociological aspects of social interaction.

In the second place, a social system may be viewed as a more abstract unit, or one in which patterns of relationships prevail from generation to generation and from region to region. Social systems consisting of persistent patterns do not require that specific persons be considered as parts of the system. A Catholic Church official of a given order and position, for example, could easily fit into or adjust to Catholic sub-systems in different parts of the world. Furthermore, he could imagine himself as fitting into the same sub-system of earlier generations.

Social systems, whether studied as going concerns in the present or from a historical point of view, are composed of social interactions and the cultural factors which structure these interactions. As the significant unit of social systems, we accept Sorokin's "meaningful interaction of two or more human individuals" and his requirement that interaction be an event "by which one party tangibly influences the overt actions or state of mind of the other." We also accept Parson's observation that Participation of an actor in a patterned interactive relationship... is for many purposes the most significant unit of the social system."

What do such apparently diverse social systems as a local church, a Cooperative Extension Service, a rural school, the X family of Middletown, or the old fellows clique in rural Ireland have in common? What instructions should a stranger is given so that he can identify such systems? What instructions should be given organisation experts who specialize in introducing innovations through such systems? What are the significant differences in such systems? Volumes have been written in attempts to answer these questions, and key elements of concern to those interested in understanding social change and social interaction may be outlined.

ELEMENTS OF SOCIAL SYSTEMS

ENDS OR OBJECTIVES

Those changes which members of the social system expect to accomplish through the operation of the system are considered ends or objectives. In some instances systems have as ends or objectives retaining the *status quo*. The prevailing objectives of a family may be broad and diffuse-those of a bank more specific. A family may strive to provide all its members with a level of living compatible with its standards, and this may be the family's end or objective. A bank may direct its activities toward the end of increasing its earnings which may usually be measured in dollars and cents.

Norms

The rules or guiding standards which prescribe what is socially accepted or unaccepted are the norms of a system. Hence norms govern the application of means in the attainment of ends or objectives. In everyday terminology, they are "rules of the game" and, as such, play a major part in establishing expectancy patterns for action in a given system. Norms as we use the term are more inclusive than written rules, regulations, or laws. They constitute the standards determining what is right and wrong or good and bad in given situations with respect to relationships with team mates and fellows as well as with non-members and opponents. In athletics involving team play, the norms not only include what is specified in the rule book, but also what is included in such concepts as "fair play" and "good sportsmanship."

Status-roles

That which is expected in a given status or position we regard as status-role. It is the active aspect of such positions as father, son, teacher, or pupil. We use the double term "status-role" in preference to "role" in order to eliminate from consideration psychological concepts of role, such as the Milquetoast role, Don Juan role, and glamour girl role, which do. not require membership or participation in a specific group. The emphasis on status-role, rather than status or position, enables us to stress the active aspects of function or process rather than the static aspects of structure.

For purposes of illustration, we may take the status-roles of father and mother. In the farm families in which the authors grew up, it was expected that the father as a part of his role would do the heavy labor in the fields and that the mother as a part of her role would prepare the meals. Surprise would be expressed if these activities were regularly reversed.

Power

Power, as we use the term, is control over others. Power has many components, which we classify under two major headings: authority and influence. Authority may be defined as the right, as determined by the system, to control the actions of others. Implied in this concept of authority is the uncritical acceptance of this right on the part of subordinates and certain immunities from influence on the part of superiors. Sanctions, as outlined later, also are implied.

Influence may be regarded as control over others which is of a non-authoritative nature. Such influence may be based upon skills in human relations, social capital based upon such things as past favors, superior knowledge of interrelations of members, certain types of wealth, or even outright blackmail. Some aspects of influence in a given social system may be derived from relationships outside of the system.

Generally the status-role, the active aspects of a position held by a member, articulates his authority. Influence may be related to role performance and many other factors. For example, when salesmen visit farm families seeking to sell farm implements, the father is usually sought. It is the father who has the authority and the right of decision-making concerning such matters. This is not to say, however, that the mother and the children may not exercise considerable influence in such decisions.

Social Rank

Social rank of members of systems is based upon consensus as to what is to be rated high and what low insofar as this is relevant to the system under consideration. In conformity with our meaning, the term "standing" could be used instead of rank. As we use the term, it must refer to a system, i.e., rank in the Methodist Church, rank in Wagon Mound community, or rank in Family X. A member's rank in a given social system may be derived from more than one status-role in the system, from status-roles outside the system (insofar as these influence his value to the system), and from power and wealth both inside and outside the system. Various personal factors not directly related to the elements just mentioned, such as personal appearance and morals, may also be important.

As we use the term, social rank results from an over-all appraisal. When applied to an individual farmer in a relevant system (let us say, a neighbourhood), it may involve evaluations related to and based upon the following: (1) The non-active aspects of positions (often called status) which he has in the neighbourhood. These may be the status of adult, male, father, husband, farmer, church member, and farm organisation officer. From these non-active aspects of positions he derives his prestige. (2) Status-role performance in the neighbourhood. From his performance he derives esteem. (3) Prestige and esteem from status roles outside the neighbourhood (insofar as these influence his evaluation in the neighbourhood). (4) Power.

It will be noted that social rank in our terms is the social value placed by members on these four items relating to the specific reference group. The sociological concept of rank, as we use it, is comparable to the economic concept, price is a summary term which expresses money value of an object due to utility and scarcity. In fact, the money value or price of a professional baseball player to his club is not unlike our concept of rank evaluations. Used in this manner, social rank is a summary term which is quite different from the other elements of social systems we are employing. Social systems evaluate their various sub-systems so that groups as well as individuals have social rank. Individuals derive their rank in the community from various reference groups by which they place themselves and are placed, using a society, nation, or large system as the most pertinent reference groups. Individuals of the same rank make up the strata of systems. Such strata may be in the nature of castes determined by birth or achievement. As we shall see, the family and clique to whom a person belongs are very important in the status evaluation of individuals and larger systems.

SANCTIONS

Those potential satisfaction-giving or - depriving mechanisms at the disposal of the system, which induce compliance with ends and norms, are considered sanctions. Sanctions may be positive or negative. Positive sanctions are the rewards, available to members from the system, including prestige resulting from authority, rights, privileges or immunity from authority, esteem, and other social or economic returns. Negative sanctions are the penalties or the deprivation of those items just mentioned as rewards at the disposal of the system. All familiar with farm families will be able to recall instances of both punishments and rewards applied by parents in order to make the family function as a unit.

FACILITIES

Facilities may be defined as the means used by the system to attain its ends. Facilities as used here are a residual category and not intended to include phenomena more correctly associated with the elements outlined previously. For a farm or ranch family, facilities involve property, such as equipment, livestock and real estate used in the farming operation; for schools, facilities include the plant, books, and equipment. Human relations skills, credit, knowledge, technology, and other resources available to a system and not included in the elements outlined may be considered as facilities.

TERRITORIALITY

The spatial arrangements and requirements of a social system are considered territoriality. It is obvious that all social systems are influenced by spatial considerations. The mere fact that a number of related families live in one house, for example, pose different problems than where each related family lives in its own house, separated by space.

Since social action and human life constitute a totality, all conceivable segments of which are inextricably interrelated, categories such as those mentioned are not mutually exclusive. The value of the concepts can only be determined by their usefulness. Since we are concerned with directed social change in addition to considering the above elements, we must be aware of the nature of social change in general.

SOCIAL CHANCE

What is conceived as social change depends upon the observation point (more correctly called the point of reference), and the scope of one's vision. This may be illustrated by the differences in conception of what is going on when a fire fighting crew deploys to get a large and fast moving forest fire under control. The view of the superintendent directing the fight from a helicopter is different from that of the individual fire fighter working on the ground near the fire.

The wild life specialist may be expected to view the situation in a different way than the mineralogist or the specialist in wood utilisation. The view of the sociologist or anthropologist would be different from that of other specialists. In our analysis of change, we hope we may have under consideration the more important sociological aspects of both systems and sub-systems. However, our frame of reference is limited, since we are focusing primarily upon guided change in the most common social systems.

SOCIAL CHANGE AS RELATED TO SOCIAL EQUILIBRIUM

Essential to our conception of social change are the concepts of equilibrium and the related concepts of boundary maintenance, integration, and solidarity. Equilibrium, as employed by some biologists and used here in an analogous way, is a useful point from which to begin this discussion. Equilibrium is considered a state in which, if a force is impressed upon a system, resultant modifications are produced within the system; when the force is removed the system will tend to return to its original state. To this concept one may add the idea of a biological system undergoing normal growth, constituting a moving equilibrium.

Equilibrium in a social system implies interrelatedness of the elements mentioned previously. It implies an ordering (in contrast to randomness) of interaction of the elements within the system. It also implies in interaction with other systems in such a manner that the core patterns of interrelatedness tend to maintain themselves. Our conception implies, as in the case of growth in biological systems, a moving rather than a static equilibrium. For example, the interaction of a family may remain in equilibrium as its members age, the interaction in a society may remain in equilibrium as its leaders are replaced by others, or a plantation may remain in equilibrium through the various crop seasons.

However, the concept of social equilibrium implies integration. In addition to implying cooperation of members in attaining objectives, integration also implies that any attempt on the part of outside agencies to change the manner in which interrelationships are patterned will be resisted; further, that pressure will be exerted to enforce conformity to the norms of the system, since there is a vested interest in the maintenance of the system itself. Hence, we may say that internal or external forces which change the equilibrium will impose strain on the system.

Although somewhat over-simplified, the following example may serve to illustrate the functioning of equilibrium. An attempt was made in Costa Rica to change the status-role of village school teachers to include tasks other than the mere teaching of reading, writing and arithmetic in the classroom. The change in the teacher's status-role, designed to improve village life, involved the added responsibility of teachers to give instruction in improved sanitation, simple health and agricultural practices through activities inside and outside the classroom.

The inspectors who supervised the teachers had no standards by which to appraise the new activities and resisted this change, or using our analogy, attempted to re-establish the equilibrium. The villagers also resisted. Many villagers said that the privies, installed by some through the teachers' efforts, were not the proper concern of the teacher. In this attempt to change a status-role, the norms of the villagers were involved. Forces within the school system and related external forces exerted pressure to re-establish earlier arrangements, or previous equilibrium.

Boundary maintenance signifies activity to retain the identity value orientation, and interaction pattern of a social system. The process of boundary maintenance requires that the system actively resist forces which tend to destroy the identity and interaction pattern. If integration is resent, we say the system is functioning as a team. That is, individual effort contributes to the ole effort which moves the system toward its goal. Solidarity refers to the extent to which members are agreed as to the ends and norms of the system, and the extent to which members identify with the system as a value in and of itself.

IMPLICATION OF ASSUMPTIONS RELATED TO EQUILIBRIUM

Our conception of social systems as boundary maintaining units implies that changes may be expected to set up strains in the existing systems. Strain sets up re-equilibrating processes, but resistance must be expected, especially if the change interferes with the basic values guiding action. In our considerations of social change, we are not focusing attention upon whole cultures, civilisations, or societies as have Sorokin, Toynbee, and Spengler. Perhaps the most interesting aspect of change as described by these writers is the reaction or counteraction of large units to major changes. Sorokin describes the weakening of what he calls the sensate culture, in which the primary objective is that of satisfying the senses.

According to Sorokin, the sensate culture in the West which grew out of its counterpart, the ideational culture of the middle Ages must pass through a crisis before the ideational type is re-established. In describing the reaction of the East to the invasion of western culture, Toynbee writes:

The Russians have taken up a Western secular social philosophy, Marxism; you might equally well call Marxism a Christian heresy, a leaf torn out of the book of Christianity and treated as if it were the whole gospel. The Russians have taken up this Western heretical religion, transformed it into something of their own, and are now shooting it back at us. This is the first shot in the anti-Western counter-offensive; but this Russian counter-discharge in the form of Communism may come to seem a small affair when the probably far more potent civilisations of India and China respond in their turn to our Western challenge. In the long run India and China seem likely to produce much deeper effects on our Western life than Russia can ever hope to produce with her Communism. But even the comparatively feeble native civilisation of Mexico is beginning to react... and what is happening today in Mexico may happen tomorrow in the seats of the native civilisation of South America: in Peru, Bolivia, Ecuador, and Colombia.

Although we recognize the importance of the broad kinds of change just described, our attention will not be directed to social and cultural changes involving systems of such great magnitude as those considered by Sorokin, Toynbee and Spengler. We shall focus our attention on social systems such as the rural family, friendship group, school, and church-systems which were also considered by the great theorists. Changes in these smaller units are related to changes involving whole cultures and societies, but we shall not attempt to specify in detail the nature of these relationships.

RATE OF CHANGE

It is possible to compare rates of change as reflected in vital statistics when such data are available. One may say, for example, that the birth rate is falling more rapidly in Japan than in Puerto Rico, or that the suicide rate is increasing more rapidly among rural than urban residents. What the causes and consequences of these rates in terms of social and cultural systems may be, however, are very difficult to determine. To compare rates of social and cultural change under the best conditions is not easy. Perhaps the most difficult comparisons to make are between systems of entirely different types.

The theory of "cultural lag" maintains that one segment "lags" behind another. It is maintained that forms of material culture-houses, factories, machines, raw materials, and foodstuffs-change more rapidly than non-material things-beliefs, philosophies, laws. Davis argues that such comparisons are of dubious validity and that "it may seem absurd to speak of relative rates of change in such non comparable matters-like asking if a giraffe moves faster than a cell divides-but it is sometimes done." It is more meaningful to compare rates of change of similar traits or items in varied settings, than to compare the rates of change of entirely different traits or items, even in the same setting.

IDEAL TYPES OF SOCIAL ACTION-GEMEINSCHAFT AND GESELLSCHAFT

Types of social systems and relationships which are *Gemeinschaft*-like are those in which the relationship is an end in itself, as contrasted to those which are *Gesellschaft*-like in which the relationships are means to ends. That part of life which is rationally or instrumentally oriented is *Gesellschaft*-like in the sense that people and facilities are considered means to ends rather than ends in them. In general under given conditions, a process is rational when specified action results in a system producing the most for the least effort or cost. Thus, a factory which is *Gesellschaft*-like will adopt a process which turns out a more valuable product at minimal cost.

If the use of an iron corn grinder, to turn from human relationships to material things, requires less effort than the *metate* or stone corn grinder, the former will be substituted for the latter, provided only rational or instrumental considerations are involved. However, if the activities organized about the use of the *metate* are ends in and of themselves (or *Gemeinschaft*-like) in that they may be recreational or expressive, or if they serve moral or integrative functions (such as religious symbols), they are less likely to be discontinued merely because they are less efficient. Experience indicates that group acceptance of more efficient means is not inevitable if the activities being changed or displaced are expressive, because it is more difficult to demonstrate the efficacy or result of the proposed change.

Changes which involve activities related to the basic values threaten group solidarity and may be resisted, even if their efficiency can be easily demonstrated. This is true because such change is thought to threaten the security of both individuals and groups. Thus we say that *Gesellschaft*-like activity or systems are more instrumental than those which are *Gemeinschaft*-like. Activities and systems, the functions of which are integrative or moral are sacred, or *Gemeinschaft*-like. In summary, for a given system instrumental or rational action is primarily *Gesellschaft*- like, whereas integrative or moral action is primarily *Gemeinschaft*-like.

GEMEINSCHAFT-LIKE RELATIONSHIPS

As indicated in *Rural Social Systems*, *Gemeinschaft*-like relationships and systems are characterized by functional diffuseness. This means that one actor (for instance, a mother) reacts to another (for instance, her child) in such a way that *all* concerns and desires of the child are pertinent to the actor who is held responsible for them. *Gemeinschaft*-like relationships and systems are determined by norms which are personal or particularistic. The relationship itself, not duty or responsibility to larger reference systems, determines what is done. Relationships within systems which are considered *Gemeinschaft*-like are characterized as emotional or affective behaviour. Relationships within systems which are described as *Gemeinschaft*-like are characterized as solidary, all members constituting a kind of "community of fate."

GEMEINSCHAFT-LIKE COMPARED WITH GESELLSCHAFT-LIKE RELATIONSHIPS

The *Gemeinschaft*-like system has been described as one in which the norms are in many ways opposed to the *Gesellschaft*-like system. The peasant family has been characterized as being *Gemeinschaft*-like in nature; a military unit as being *Gesellschaft*-like in nature. In the peasant family, the scope of interest of an actor for his object is diffuse, while in the military unit it is specific. The norms which determine the relationships are personal and particularistic in the instance of the peasant family; they are impersonal, universalistic and not bound to specific persons or relationships in the military unit.

Furthermore, relationships are conditioned by emotion or affectivity in the family, while they lack emotion and are governed by affective neutrality in the military unit. Treatment of the actor as object is based upon ascription in the first instance; upon achievement or performance in the second case. In the first there are few relationships which are private or individual. Each individual is bound to fellow members of his system by personal relations of a diffuse nature, many of which are established at birth by ascription in the peasant family.

DIRECTION OF CHANGE

As underdeveloped societies adopt Western culture, the tendency is for various social systems involved in rational or instrumental activities to become *Gesellschaft*-like. In general, the rational or instrumental action (such as that found in bureaucracies), the traits of specificity, achievement universalism, and affective neutrality are linked. Therefore, the blanket term *Gesellschaft* has meaning in considering the direction of social change. Also, as in the case of the family, diffuseness, ascription, particularism, and affectivity are linked, and therefore, the blanket term *Gemeinschaft* has meaning. There may be variations in the extent of linkage, as for example when the relations between father and son approach affective neutrality, but these exceptions can be described as they are encountered.

The specific directed changes we discuss will involve primarily rational or instrumental action. Such action is characteristic of *Gesellschaft*-like systems, and is action which is neither recreational nor religious. Insofar as we treat the direction of change in general, it will be on the continuum of activities which are *Gemeinschaft*-like at one extreme and *Gesellschaft*-like at the other extreme. We consider modern, Western, urban, technological society more *Gesellschaft*-like than that of the underdeveloped societies.

It is possible to appraise the relative emphasis a society or system places upon various types of activity at one time as compared with a later period. Assuming that the ends of a system are expressed in the amount of time used by the members in various types of activities, we may note how these change in time. One could study the time devoted by different segments of the population to recreation or other expressive pursuits which are ends in and of themselves. Redfield, for example, found that people in Tepoztlan, Mexico, spend one third of their time in fiestas and holidays.

The time devoted to religious activities which the social scientist would say serve the function of reinforcing the values of the group, could be measured. The time devoted to the production of goods and services as distinct from expressive or religious activities may also be measured. If one had a measure of the time spent by sample groups at different epochs in history one could rank them in primacy of orientation. Using Parsons' terminology, one could classify the sample groups in relation to action which was: (1) instrumentally, (2) expressively, and (3) morally oriented.

TYPES OF SOCIAL CHANGE

Social change may be classified according to various principles. We are more concerned here with directed change, or that which a change agent is consciously attempting to introduce. The social changes transpiring at any moment in a rural community are usually directed in part and non directed in part. In either case changes may result from any one or combination of the following: (1) Changing the relative importance of the different social systems in society. The school, for example, may take over functions previously performed by the church or by a craft. Factories may take over the functions performed by families. (2) Creating new social systems. An agricultural extension service, for example, may be organized in a country which formerly did not have one. (3) Changing the elements of the systems and their relation to one another as well as creating new elements. Thus, the role of the school teacher may be changed to include community responsibilities such as those mentioned in the discussion of equilibrium.

An informal friendship group may become formal, as when a group of friends organize a cooperative. A series of hypotheses concerning the importance of social factors in social change as related to these possibilities may be developed. To cite only one: "Individuals of lower prestige accept culture traits from those of high prestige more readily than the reverse."

TYPES OF CULTURAL CHANGE

Cultural change is a category of change broader than social change, including changes in technology, philosophy, belief systems, systems of expressive symbols or art, and systems of values. Although few societal changes do not involve both social and cultural changes, one may think of them as being separated.

The introduction of the germ theory of disease to a people, who had no previous knowledge of this cultural trait, would normally bring changes in the social systems dealing with sickness and disease prevention. Clinics and hospitals may be used as examples of both cultural and social change. Changes in systems of mathematics or scientific procedures are cultural changes, and may be studied *per se* in the same way that changes in armies, churches, clinics, and governments as social systems may be studied.

In discussing change, Ralph Beals writes: "If I were to rate the acculturative forces I have seen at work in various communities, I think I would suggest that one road is worth about three schools and about fifty administrators." This statement, as well as our knowledge of change, suggests several hypotheses. The greater the felt need for a cultural item, for example, the easier it is to relate a proposed change to the ends of the system involved. Further, the better a cultural trait is understood, the easier it will be to introduce the change. If two cultural items are available, according to Parsons, the one which costs the least in effort and yields the greatest satisfaction will be accepted. According to others, "Traits compatible to the culture of one group will probably show greater compatibility to a neighboring culture than to a distant one."

The greater the functional need of a system for a trait, the easier and more rapid will be its acceptance. It is the felt, not "real" need in terms of various scientific standards that is set against the apparent or latent incompatibility that determines acceptance or non-acceptance. Five gallon oil cans, for example, have displaced pottery containers for liquids among preliterate peoples, generally because users believe them superior. Machetes, sewing machines, and corn grinders spread more generally among indigenous Latin American peoples than bed springs or water sterilisation. In considering agencies and influence of change, we usually do not separate the social from the cultural. Thus, the germ theory of disease, a cultural item, is not separated from hospital organisations, medical organisations, and schools which are considered by some to be social.

IMPORTANT PROCESSES INVOLVED IN SOCIAL CHANGE

As the elements of social systems previously discussed are articulated in social action, the processes of communication, decision-making, boundary maintenance, and social-cultural linkage are of special importance. It is convenient in discussing change to differentiate what is called the "target system" from the "change agent system." The latter is the person or system attempting to introduce or effect a change; the former is the group which the agent and his system is attempting to change. If, for example, the agricultural extension service in a given community is attempting to organize the cotton growers into a one-variety cotton community, the extension service is the change agent system and the community involved the target system.

COMMUNICATION

By communication we mean the process by which information, decisions, and directives pass through a social system, and the ways in which knowledge, opinions, and attitudes are formed or modified. Communication may be carried out through mass media, such as radio, television, and motion pictures, in which the agency receiving the communication cannot, interact directly with the agency imparting the information. Mass media provide one-way communication from imparter to receiver.

Communication may be carried on through formal and informal social channels which usually provide the opportunity for two-way interaction in which individuals are both imparters and receivers of information. A vivid illustration of how the communication process operates in rural areas is the Telephone

Company or community signal and message. The coming of a blizzard, a flood, or other events may be communicated by telephone, radio, or television to large groups. Usually not all people are listening to such communications but they are further spread by word of mouth.

DECISION-MAKING

This is the process whereby alternate courses of action available are reduced. If a rural family in a flood area is notified that flood conditions approach, decisions must be made concerning evacuation. In many farm and ranch families much decision-making occurs at mealtime. In patriarchal families much family decision-making rests with the father, who has greater power than other members.

The strategy of change involves decision-making on the part of the change agent in terms of the allocation of effort, facilities, and personnel, in relation to those status-roles, patterns of power, and social rank of the target system. Decisions concerning such allocations must be made with a view to maximizing the possibility of cooperation on the part of the target system and minimizing "costs" to the change system. The decision-making of the change agent must result in effective timing of events which requires intimate knowledge of the functioning of the change target in terms of social structure, value orientation, and the important processes related to change.

BOUNDARY MAINTENANCE

This is the process whereby the system retains its identity and interaction pattern; that is, retains its equilibrium involving both integration and solidarity. Boundary maintenance may be illustrated by the various folk admonitions concerning an outsider taking the part of one member in a family quarrel. These proverbs usually imply that the quarreling family members will unite and turn on the outsider no matter how just his cause for supporting one side of the dispute. Folk beliefs and scientific findings show that systems which are challenged from outside defend their values.

SOCIAL-CULTURAL LINKAGE

This is the process whereby the elements of at least two systems come to be articulated so that in some ways they function as a unit. Thus, social-cultural linkage usually requires that the value orientation and the social structure of the change agent system and the target system are brought together in at least temporary closure. In order to be effective, a teacher must have his role accepted by students, and the teacher in turn, must accept the students in their roles as students. When a family borrows money from a bank, social-cultural linkage is accomplished between the two systems and the roles of debtor and creditor express this linkage.

Social-cultural linkage involves the following three processes: initiation, legitimation, and execution. Initiation is the process whereby the change system brings the proposed or advocated change to the attention of target system. Legitimation is the process whereby the proposed change is made "rightful" to the target system. Prestigeful sponsors, rituals, prayers, and other legitimizing procedures are used in the strategy of change. Execution is the process whereby the social-cultural linkage is put into effect.

AN ILLUSTRATION OF A SOCIAL SYSTEM AND SOCIAL CHANGE

A FOOTBALL TEAM

The concepts we have discussed as elements of systems may be effectively illustrated by a football team. Change and social-cultural linkage may be illustrated by the description of the attempts of coaches and schools to accept a new trait, such as the split-T formation. Directed change may be illustrated by the processes whereby the coaching staff as a system brings the team into its participation orbit.

In a football team, as with other athletic teams, each separate position clearly represents a different status-role, as we have defined the term. Fullbacks perform different functions than guards because their status-roles are different. Authority may be illustrated by the general control coaches' exercise over the players, particularly the quarterbacks to whom coaches delegate considerable authority during games. Non-authoritative power, or influence, may be illustrated by human relations and leadership skills on the part of exceptional coaches and players. Sanctions, in the form of rewards, may be illustrated by letters, plaques, and citations received by the team or individual players. Rewards may also take the form of prestige and esteem, and bids to play professional football.

Negative sanctions for violating norms may result in team penalties or individual penalties. Social rank may be illustrated when the team members select the "most valuable" player. Immediate ends such as those of winning games are rather obvious in the case of athletic teams. Norms or the rules of the game as prescribed in the rule book are also obvious, but other norms such as those falling under the heading of sportsmanship are less obvious. Norms concerning rewards a player may or may not receive and how players may or may not be recruited are also important. Territoriality, or spatial relationships, may be illustrated by the requirements of the various positions in relation to one another and the boundaries of the field. Facilities, including field house, practice fields and equipment, are also obvious.

The social processes whereby athletic teams develop superiority and high morale are not well understood by sociologists, but the same processes involved in effective operation of other social systems may well be applicable. Communications involving the means whereby teams are prepared for high level performance are not well understood by social scientists, and should constitute a profitable area of study for those who wish to understand human organisation. No doubt high morale or the willingness to sacrifice for a social system, as well as the confidence in its capacity to achieve its goals, are related to the decision-making process on and off the field. The degree to which members believe allocation of rewards, roles, authority, and status square with existing norms is probably very important.

The process of boundary maintenance would be revealed, for example, if a high school coach at midseason attempted to turn his football team into a basketball team. The status-roles in football would not be given up without resistance any more than a successful team would permit a member to be misused.

3

Geographical Social Philosophers

All the so-called geographical determinists have felt compelled to modify geographical determinism by the recognition of other factors. The pure geographical determinists should, of course, say that "man is a child of the earth," and that therefore everything that he achieves is "earthy," in the sense that it is determined by geographical conditions. Perhaps no one would deny that all human societies show some conditioning by geographical factors. But hardly anyone any longer seeks for adequate interpretation of human social life through geographical conditions. We are forced, therefore, to select an author who is only in part a geographical determinist. Perhaps we cannot do better than take Henry Thomas Buckle, because he first brought this way of looking at human affairs into prominence in the nineteenth century.

Buckle's purpose was to produce an inductive science of human history. Nevertheless, it is fair to say that he had no very clear or carefully thought-out method. As we have seen, he was essentially a self-educated man. Through his reading in the physical sciences, he had gained a strong materialistic bias, and attempted what we should now call a materialistic interpretation of history. He was particularly opposed to the doctrine of human free will, and sought to bring all human actions under the determinism of laws as fixed as those of the physical world. It is doubtful whether he clearly understood what was meant by free will or by fixed laws.

But he made use of statistics to show that all human behaviour is governed by fixed laws. He used also the arguments of the classical economists to support his materialistic interpretation. But strangely enough, he appealed to human intelligence to explain what could not be explained by geographical forces or by economic laws. Thus more than one historian of social thought has classified Buckle among the ideological theorists. This inconsistency is one reason why we can say that he had no very clear method. It is perhaps not unfair to add that, while he professed scientific impartiality, he showed most of the prejudices of the average Englishman of mid-Victorian times, especially in regard to political and economic matters. He was decidedly a child of his age.

BUCKLE'S SOCIAL PHILOSOPHY

Buckle attempts primarily an interpretation of human society in terms of its physical environment. He lays it down at the very beginning that there must be an intimate connection between civilisation and physical laws; for all that man has done has been a result of the interaction of his mind and physical conditions, especially geographic conditions. "Civilisation," he tells us, "begins only where conditions make it possible to produce a surplus, where supplies of food are regular and reliable, and a leisure class is made possible."

Only in lands where man can live and accumulate surplus wealth does civilisation develop. Buckle discounts the possibility of race or heredity being much of a factor. In general, he holds that we have no right to believe that race and heredity have any influence upon mentality or culture. So far as we know, all races have about the same endowment, and their social differences must therefore be due to the differences of their geographic environment.

DOCTRINE OF SOCIAL DEVELOPMENT

Rejecting all other factors, Buckle divides the factors of social development into geographical and intellectual. He classifies the geographical factors that produce social differences among peoples under four heads: climate, food, soil, and the general aspects of nature. Climate, soil, and food influence the social life of peoples, Buckle says, mainly through the accumulation of wealth, because some accumulation of wealth is necessary for leisure, and there can be no high development of knowledge without leisure.

It is the surplus resulting from an excess of production over consumption that makes the accumulation of wealth and the existence of intellectual classes possible. Therefore the fertility of the soil and the conditions of climate are "the great physical causes by which the creation of wealth is governed." As all civilisation is based upon the economic factor, it follows that ultimately it is based upon these geographic factors. Especially in the early stages will the development of civilisation be found to depend entirely upon soil and climate?

After the accumulation of wealth, comes the matter of its distribution. As soon as any degree of wealth is accumulated, the population divides into two classes, the employers and the employed. Accepting Ricardo's iron law of wages, namely, that wages paid will, in the long run, amount to only that which is sufficient to maintain the laborer and his family and allow him to reproduce, Buckle says that the price paid for labor will depend largely upon the cheapness or dearness of food. Agreeing with Malthus that food is the most important factor affecting the growth of population, Buckle says that where food is most abundant the increase in population will be greater than where food is scarce and difficult to secure.

Now it is obvious that in warm and fertile countries food is more abundant than in cold and barren countries and is more easily secured. In such countries, therefore, there is a greater tendency toward an increase in population, and as labor may be regarded as a commodity, it cheapens the price of labor and lowers wages.

Therefore, Buckle said, "There is a strong and constant tendency in hot countries for wages to be low and in cold countries for them to be high." The increase of population decreases wages and the average wealth of the laborers; that is to say, it is the main factor responsible for the poverty of the masses. This poverty weakens the laboring classes and gives greater power into the hands of the wealthy.

The result is the subjection of the lower classes, politically as well as economically. Hence, both in hot countries and on fertile plains democracy and free government do not easily flourish. Only under conditions of life where food is scarce, wages high, and the great accumulation of wealth practically impossible, do we find the natural conditions under which free governments and free societies can flourish. Other conditions give rise to classes and the poverty and degradation of the masses. Another geographical factor that greatly affects the social development of peoples is the general aspects of nature. If natural phenomena are such as to inspire feelings of terror or of great wonder, or powerfully inflame the imagination, then man, contrasting himself with the forces and majesty of nature, becomes painfully conscious of his own insignificance. His sense of inferiority inhibits his will to achieve.

On the other hand, where the works of nature are small and feeble, man regains confidence, comes to understand, and finally to harness natural forces, and so his mind has a chance to act. Cool intelligence and reason have no chance to develop when the aspects of nature are overpowering. To illustrate, Buckle contrasts the civilisation of India, where the works of nature are of startling magnitude, with that of Greece, where they are smaller, feebler, and less threatening to man. Practically all of the countries outside of Europe discourage all attempts on the part of man to subdue nature. Consequently, "Looking at the history of the world as a whole, the tendency has been, in Europe, to subordinate nature to man; out of Europe to subordinate man to nature."

Hence, Buckle says, the fundamental division of human history, to be made if it is written scientifically, is the division between the civilisation of Europe and the civilisation that is non-European. In European civilisations, geographical conditions have favored the development of that critical scientific spirit upon which all social progress must depend. Hence, European civilisation is what it is fundamentally because in Europe man is stronger than nature. Europe is the only continent where this is true. In other continents, nature is stronger than man. In Europe the human mind is not overawed by nature.

The mind can work and can overcome nature. Moreover, climate and soil, as we have seen, are favorable to a balanced economic development. Consequently, if we are to understand the history of European countries, we must make the growth of knowledge and of intelligence our principal study. "The advance of European civilisation is characterized by diminishing influence of physical laws and an increasing influence of mental laws." Consequently, "These mental laws, when ascertained, will be the ultimate basis of the history of Europe"; that is, if the history is written scientifically.

Only in Europe then, Buckle thinks, have the human intellect a fair chance to function, and four laws of the functioning of the intellect in social development and progress become evident: (1) The first of these laws is the law of the exclusion of other factors than the intellect, such as race or moral qualities. The progress of mankind, Buckle says, depends upon the success with which the laws of phenomena are investigated and the knowledge of these laws diffused. Moral qualities are relatively static and have no bearing upon progress. It is knowledge alone which counts. (2) The native faculties of men do not improve, Buckle tells us, but civilisation rests solely upon intellectual progress, upon the increase of knowledge. There is no evidence, he tells us, that the hereditary qualities of mankind, either physical or mental, have improved. These qualities are static. The accumulation and diffusion of knowledge is therefore the only dynamic factor. (3) It follows from the first two laws that scepticism in every department of thought has been invariably a preliminary to social progress, because it has led to the examination of old beliefs and to the search for new knowledge. To get a basis for social progress we must have the critical attitude of mind. Even destructive criticism is necessary for the progress of truth. (4) Again it follows that the great enemy of civilisation-the great enemy of human progress- is "the protective spirit," by which Buckle means the church teaching men what to believe and the state teaching them what to do. If church and state would leave men to determine their own beliefs and actions, social progress would be more rapid. Thus Buckle, like Nietzsche, takes his stand for a *laissez-faire* individualism.

CRITICISM

The two parts of Buckle's social philosophy, the geographical and the intellectual, hardly harmonize. The geographical part of his social philosophy is the logical basis of all materialistic conceptions of human history. There is, however, not much evidence to sustain even as much geographical determinism as Buckle seeks to establish. Indeed, he himself was forced to admit that the evidence was better for primitive society than for present civilisation. Buckle's division of human history into European and non-European upon the basis of the determinism of geographical factors seems to us now almost ludicrous. Naturally, this idea of Buckle's was not well received in America. The idea itself was a manifestation of European ethnocentrism.

Not much more can be said to support Buckle's four so-called "mental laws." Hardly any trained social thinker today would make the progress of mankind depend upon the accumulation and diffusion of scientific knowledge. We now know too much about human nature and the mind of man. It is evident that knowledge as knowledge cannot function alone. After all, the question of progress, no matter what sense we may attach to the term, depends upon the human will. And the human will depends upon impulses and emotions quite as much as upon knowledge. Social progress, therefore, depends upon the diffusion of altruism and good will not less than upon the diffusion of knowledge and intelligence. It is not correct to say, as Buckle said, that social progress has not been affected by moral qualities.

Buckle's law of the function of scepticism in social progress is almost taken for granted today and seems harmless enough, though at the time it was put forth by Buckle, it caused a great storm of protest. It is true that we must have the critical attitude of mind in order to improve or progress. But it is also true that destructive criticism may be carried so far that it results in confusion and in a loss of ability to take constructive attitudes. Destructive criticism may become a mere intellectual bad habit productive of nothing except the destruction of old values. Again, Buckle's *laissez-faire* individualism, if carried to an extreme, could hardly result in social progress.

Buckle fails to see the church and the state as great cultural agencies, maintaining civilized traditions and standards. If Buckle's *laissez-faire* individualism were to be carried out, the state could scarcely carry on education for good citizenship. His attitude, and this seemed to be his personal belief, was that the schools and education should be private concerns. We have given up that attitude for very good reasons. Moreover, we know that all human beings need guidance in the development of their ideals and standards. It is the business of the church to teach men ideals and standards that will function in the direction of social progress.

It is equally the business of the state to enforce minimum standards of conduct that will enable human communities to live at peace within them and to build for future progress. There are, of course, dangers in what Buckle calls "the protective spirit," but no human community has been able to build a high civilisation without some use of this protective spirit; and there is no reason to think that the protective spirit necessarily makes men either moral weaklings or intellectual slaves. We are forced to conclude, therefore, that the crude naturalism of the nineteenth century led Buckle into error, both in the direction of geographical determinism and in the direction of *laissez-faire* individualism.

It is only fair to add that geographical influences in human society have been treated more sanely and hence more adequately by a great number of other writers. For example, Friedrich Ratzel, the great German geographer of the nineteenth century, did this in his work on *Anthropo-geographie.* His pupil, Miss Ellen C. Semple, did so in her work on Influences of Geographic Environment. These authors are not altogether free from criticism, but in general they did not make the crude errors of Buckle. The most modern school of geographers, which recognizes to the full the influences of culture in determining the social behaviour of man, has made available many studies of the influence of geographical factors that are unobjectionable.

THE INDIVIDUALISTIC SOCIAL PHILOSOPHERS

Fichte said, that the self alone is real. This is extreme philosophical individualism, the doctrine that the human individual is a self-determined and self-determining whole. In a broader sense, individualism is the doctrine that the human individual is an independent, self-determining entity, both in the universe and in human society. It assumes not only that the individual self is the center of experience, a view to which all would agree, but also that there are no values outside of the individual. There have been many such individualists in the history of social thought.

Epicurus in ancient times, for example, with his doctrine that there is no such thing as human society, but only an aggregate of individuals, was an individualist. Hobbes, with his doctrine of the social contract between independent individuals, was an individualist. Rousseau, with his exaggerated emphasis upon the rights of the individual, was an individualist. Indeed, it has often been said by historians that the crest of individualism reached its height with Rousseau. But many more extreme individualists than Rousseau lived in the nineteenth century. It is impossible for us to give more than a single example. Leaving aside the whole school of philosophical anarchists, we shall take Friedrich Wilhelm Nietzsche as our example of extreme nineteenth-century individualism. If in him individualism seems pushed to an absurd extreme, it is only because he carried out with relentless logic the implications of this one- sided social thinking.

F. W. NIETZSCHE

Nietzsche was born in 1844. His father, of remote Polish descent, was a cultured Lutheran clergyman. Nietzsche's mother, however, was German, and as his whole culture was so thoroughly German, nothing should be attributed to his Polish blood. He was a very precocious child, learning to read the Greek and Latin classics at the early age of five or six years. Thus he became very early steeped in the lore of Greece and Rome, and, as in the case of Machiavelli, these countries awakened his admiration; but his admiration was rather for early Greece than for Rome. Nevertheless, young Nietzsche was destined for the ministry, and went to study at the University of Bonn with this intention. Soon, however, he gave up theology for classical philology, following his professor in the latter subject to the University of Leipzig.

At the same time he became a great admirer of the German pessimistic philosopher, Schopenhauer. Upon the recommendation of his teachers, Nietzsche became at the early age of twenty-five a professor of classical philology in the University of Basle, Switzerland. There he formed a close friendship with Richard Wagner, the great German composer, who was living at Triebschen, near Lucerne. Nietzsche had long admired Wagner, and now found in him an exponent of Teutonic paganism, which again became one of his ideals. On account of ill-health, Nietzsche gave up teaching in 1876, and was finally put on the pension list of his university in 1879. In the meantime he had discovered that his idol, Wagner, had feet of clay. This produced in Nietzsche a very intense emotional reaction, and may have had something to do with the unbalancing of his mind.

From 1872, when Nietzsche produced his first considerable book on *The Birth of Tragedy,* until 1889, when he was declared hopelessly insane, Nietzsche was continually busy producing, one after another, a series of volumes in revolt against modern ideals of life. Here a word must be said about the nature of Nietzsche's illness. According to reliable medical authorities, during all this period, Nietzsche was suffering from the gradual onset of paresis, a form of neurosyphilis. On this account, it has often been said that no attention should be paid to Nietzsche's thought. However, thought stands upon its own basis, whether uttered by sane or insane, sick or well. We cannot dismiss a man's thinking, for example, because we know he has tuberculosis.

All arguments against Nietzsche's philosophy on account of his physical condition fall short of their mark. Morbid geniuses are comparatively common in the history of thought, especially in modern times. Perhaps we may rightly say that it requires a certain degree of mental unbalance to carry out with relentless logic the implications of certain mental and social attitudes. Moreover, we are bound to take Nietzsche into account because his followers in western civilisation have been so numerous, whether directly acquainted with his writings or not.

The chief reason, however, for calling attention to Nietzsche's illness is the undoubted fact that it affected very greatly his thinking. His glorification of health, brute strength, and power was undoubtedly in part a reaction from his physical condition. Thus his chronic invalidism had much to do not only with the form, but with the content of his thinking. It is carrying the matter much too far, however, to attribute the quality of his thought wholly or even chiefly to his invalidism. Nietzsche himself said that he was but carrying out the social implications of the doctrines of Charles Darwin. He claimed that he merely took over from Darwin the idea that the individual struggle for existence and supremacy was the whole content of the human social process.

Nietzsche was probably mistaken in this, but we cannot deny that a crude sort of social Darwinism was in the air at the time that Nietzsche wrote. But beyond Darwinism was the individualism of the nineteenth century, and its general emphasis upon a crude naturalism in its social thinking. If, as Dr. Durant says, Nietzsche was not "the last great scion of the lineage of Rousseau," he was certainly at least a direct descendant. Both Rousseau's naturalism and individualism stand out in Nietzsche in an exaggerated degree.

Nietzsche chief works are *Human, All Too Human* (1876), *The Dawn of Day* (1881), *Thus Spake Zarathustra* (1883), *Beyond Good and Evil* (1886), *The Genealogy of Morals* (1887), *Antichrist* (1889), and *The Will to Power* (1896). Of these, probably *The Will to Power* is the best introduction to Nietzsche essential ideas, though it is a fragmentary work, written in periods of lucidity after he was declared hopelessly insane in 1889.

NIETZSCHE'S METHOD

Nietzsche had no scientific method. One is inclined to say that he had no scientific mind at all; for he threw logic out of the window. One of his mottoes was, "Let the truth perish, let there be life." As Durant says, he does not prove, he announces and reveals. Yet Nietzsche had certain points of view from which he proceeded. One was his exaltation of instinct against thought; another, of the individual against society. Like Rousseau, he held that "instinct is the most intelligent of all kinds of intelligence." Like Rousseau, too, he emphasized that all values must be found in the feelings and emotions of individuals; but of all instincts and emotions, "the will to power" is the strongest and most fundamental. It is not simply the will to live, but the will to power and to overpower that explains all life and therefore all human society.

It must be remembered that, above all, Nietzsche was a literary man, a poet and an artist. As a literary artist he was, moreover, an impressionist, and so fitted in with a strong tendency of his time. Perhaps, however, all this is inadequate to explain the vogue of his writings in the early years of the twentieth century. Two additional explanations of his vogue should be given. First of all, Nietzsche's writings became popular because they were in harmony with a certain spirit of the times that depreciated Christianity and humanitarianism.

They harmonized with the *Zeitgeist,* particularly in Germany. But another reason for the vogue of Nietzsche's writings was his style. Nietzsche knew something about the psychology of the human mind. He knew that it took short, catchy sentences to appeal to th e popular mind. He disregarded, even shattered, the traditional periodic style in which German, previous to his time, had been written. To this extent he was perhaps right in saying that in the future the history of the world would be divided into the time previous to his writing and the time after his writing.

NIETZSCHE'S DOCTRINE OF SOCIAL ORIGINS AND DEVELOPMENT

According to Nietzsche, man is simply an animal among animals, stronger, more energetic, more cunning, and with a greater will to power than other animals. The origin of human society was accordingly in the act of a horde of strong individuals who established themselves as masters over weaker individuals and reduced them to slavery. Society is merely a means for the enhancement of the power and personality of individuals; the group is neither a reality nor an end in itself. All this is particularly illustrated, Nietzsche says, by the overrunning of Europe by Teutonic tribesmen. These men were not burdened with morals. They "were free from every social restraint; in the innocence of their wild beast conscience they returned as exultant monsters from a horrible train of murder, incendiarism, rapine, torture, with arrogance and compromise as if nothing but a student's freak had been perpetrated."

These men, "a herd of blond beasts of prey, a race of conquerors and masters, with military organisation, with a power to organize," supplied the ruling classes for Germany, Scandinavia, France, England, Italy, and Russia. Very similarly, in pre-Socratic Greece, the barbarous Hellenes, coming down from the north, established ruling classes in the Greek city-states and set up the worship of Dionysus, the pagan god of life, enjoyment, music, dancing, and all that goes with the revelry of power.

It was especially the pre-Socratic Greeks, with their childlike love of life and enjoyment, whom Nietzsche seemed to regard as the social ideal. From pre-Socratic Greece down to the present, Nietzsche seemed to hold, there had been progressive degeneration. This degeneration began with the teaching of Socrates, Plato, and Aristotle, whom Nietzsche regarded not as true Greeks, but as aberrations from the pagan ideal. This movement was continued by the Epicureans and the

Stoics. It made its conquest of western civilisation, however, through the Jews and the Christian movement. The Jews, as a conquered race, had developed what Nietzsche called "a slave's morality."

Through the Christian church, they were able to foist this slave's morality upon the world. While the Romans at their best had a master morality, this was undermined through the influence of the Christian movement, and Rome fell because it was emasculated and feminized by Jewish-Christian ethics. Gradually the Christian church, which Nietzsche called "the greatest of all imaginable corruptions," gained power and set up in the medieval world this slave morality as its ideal. The Renaissance, if it had been allowed to pursue its course, would have restored the master morality of the early Greeks and Romans and of the early Teutonic tribesmen. But just when the modern world was pursuing its course back to Greece and Rome through the influence of the Renaissance, Luther and the other Protestant reformers pulled it back again to the ridiculous slave morality of the Jews.

The triumph of the Jewish-Christian ethics resulted in the rise of the modern democratic movement. The democratic movement gave birth to humanitarianism, and then to socialism and feminism, all of which represent progressive degeneration from master morality. Nietzsche thinks, however, that there is still some hope of the revival of paganism.

The will to power still manifests itself beneath all of these attempts to smother it by the Christian and democratic movements. In Napoleon, Nietzsche sees a true manifestation of his ideal of the superman. Moreover, Christianity as a theology is dead. It is only Christian ethics that survives, an ethics that is responsible for all of our evils, and is cowardly and weak. We need only return to the pre-Socratic Greeks, with their joy in life and power and beauty, to restore health to the modern world.

DOCTRINE OF SOCIAL ORGANISATION

Nietzsche's doctrine of social organisation is vague and inconsistent. It may, perhaps, be characterized as aristocratic anarchism. First of all he insists, however, that there must be gradations of rank. The common people must not be allowed to drag down the exceptional, superior individual. The whole process of civilisation should be such as to produce these superior individuals.

The masses, the common people, Nietzsche says in a vigorous metaphor, are nothing but the manure to fertilize the genius of the transcendent great. Society should be organized so as to make possible the exploitation of the inferior by the superior. It should be a true aristocracy with just enough organisation not to hinder or hamper the development of the strong man.

Moreover, life for all is to be an adventure. Its motto should be, "Live dangerously." Instead of war being discredited, all war should be regarded as good. "A good war," Nietzsche tells us, "halloweth any cause." Revolution is good if it does not lead to the supremacy of the masses. "Live in a state of war," Nietzsche says. However, the ideal society will be divided into rulers, officials, and producers.

The last two are to be the servants of the first class. The rulers will be men of refinement, as well as of courage and strength. They will be united by courtesy and *esprit de corps,* rather than by formal government; for Nietzsche regards the state in its present form as another manifestation of social degeneration. These aristocratic supermen will constitute a caste that will not contaminate and weaken its blood by marrying rich vulgarians. No equality will be permitted between classes or between men and women. The whole organisation of society is to be such as to exploit the masses for the benefit of the superior few. Aristocracy is the key to ideal social organisation.

NIETZSCHE'S ETHICS

It is hardly worth while to discuss Nietzsche's conception of social progress. So far as he had one, it seems to have been a return to the paganism that we have already sketched, plus the eugenic breeding of "supermen." It is the ethics of strength, of power, however, rather than eugenics, politics, industrial organisation, or anything else, which Nietzsche regards as the foundation for the establishment of an ideal human society. He tells us that there are two kinds of morality in nature-the morality of the lamb and the morality of the eagle. The morality of the eagle produced the master morality of the pagan world, the egoism that did not hesitate to take what it wanted, keep it, and take all that it could get.

The morality of the lamb was developed into Jewish-Christian ethics, and has resulted in such manifestations of degeneracy as democracy, socialism, and feminism. Hence, Nietzsche sets up a program to restore human society to a normal, natural condition in which the biological forces of struggle and selection that have produced man can again function: (1) All obstacles to the individual's development are to be removed, so that the superman may be produced. (2) The only obligations that are to be recognized as binding on the individual are those of enlightened egoism. (3) All institutions and ideals connected with the doctrine of altruism are to be done away with.

The vigorous application of these rules, Nietzsche believes, will restore human society to a natural condition and will result in the further evolution of man, in the production of the superman. Finally, it should be noted that Nietzsche's superman is to be "a blond beast." But why "blond"? This seems to show that Nietzsche was also infected by the "Nordicism" which was rising in the later half of the nineteenth century, and which held that the north-European blond is alone capable of the highest civilisation.

CRITICISM

It seems idle to use space to criticize such ideas. Yet millions of people in western civilisation, most of whom have never heard of Nietzsche, have acted in whole or in part upon these principles. After all, they are simply the principles of a crude naturalism and of an extreme individualism. Nietzsche pretended that his doctrines were the logical outcome of Darwin's teachings, and a whole school of social Darwinians endorsed, in part, such principles. But it is hardly necessary to say that there is no support given these ideas in modern biology. Although Darwin may have made the mistake of considering the struggle for existence a purely individual one, his successors have long since corrected that idea.

The paganism that Nietzsche preached, instead of bringing forth a new and superior race of men, would probably result in human degeneration, if not in human extinction. There is every reason to believe that the movement to interpret human social life in crude biological terms would result in something like Nietzsche's social philosophy. But it must be pointed out those other influences than the biological tradition had to do with the shaping of Nietzsche's philosophy. After Machiavelli had declared that moral principles had no application in political life, and after Rousseau had exalted savage man above civilized man, it was quite easy for Nietzsche's diseased mind to come to the conclusions that he did. Moreover, the worship of pagan antiquity, the approach to its ideals on hands and knees, again led Nietzsche easily to the conclusions he reached.

Finally, we must remember that the undermining of the philosophical foundations of the Christian movement almost inevitably led, considering the circumstances which we have just mentioned, to an attack upon Christian or humanitarian ethics. It was Nietzsche's distinction that he did not deign to discuss Christian theology, but openly attacked Christian ethics, the last stronghold, so to speak, of the Christian movement.

Whether Nietzsche is only an aberrant social thinker or whether he is the herald of a new civilisation based upon pagan ideals of life, only time can decide.

RACIAL SOCIAL PHILOSOPHERS

We have already seen that Nietzsche's biological view of human society and human history tended to a glorification of the blond race. If one takes the biological view of human society as an individualistic view, it issues logically into something like Nietzsche's philosophy. But if one takes the biological view from the standpoint of race, it issues in a racial view of human society and human history. It is the latter view that is ordinarily thought of as the biological theory of society. It is the theory that blood, race, and heredity account for all social and cultural differences among human groups. The theory is very old, having roots again in classic antiquity, but the development of biological science in the nineteenth century, and especially the scientific theories of heredity of that century, gave the racial view new vitality.

To some extent, the eugenics movement also worked in the same direction. But the fact that racial problems and interracial struggles came to the front in the nineteenth century probably had even more to do with the recrudescence of racial theories. Racial sociological theories, at any rate, gave birth to an enormous sociological literature in the latter half of the nineteenth century and in the early decades of the twentieth. The foremost advocate of these theories, or, at any rate, the first modern thinker to put them into definite form, was a Frenchman, Count Arthur de Gobineau.

ARTHUR DE GOBINEAU

Count Arthur de Gobineau was born in 1816 and died in 1882. He came from a French family of some standing, which claimed descent on one side from the old Norsemen who had founded Normandy. He entered political life, and soon after was transferred to the French diplomatic service. He served on French embassies in South America, in Greece, in Persia, and in several other countries. It was through this experience in diplomatic service that he came to the idea that racial problems were fundamental in human history and human society. His interests, however, were largely literary and historical, rather than scientific.

While this work received at first but little attention in France, it was published at a strategic time when racial questions were uppermost in a number of countries. It immediately attracted attention in our South, where the slavery question was rapidly approaching a culmination and where the defenders of slavery as an institution were eagerly searching for confirmation of their belief that the Negro race was essentially inferior and incapable of civilisation.

Chiefly through the influence of Richard Wagner, the work also attracted attention in Germany, where the so-called "Aryan question" was beginning to come to public consciousness. Strangely enough, this work remained untranslated into English until 1915, when the first volume only was translated by Adrian Collins, with an introduction by Oscar Levy, the editor of the English version of Nietzsche's works. The book cannot be considered in any sense scientific, but it was written in a literary style that, though paradoxical, made it understandable and popular.

GOBINEAU'S METHOD

Again we must say, as we said of Nietzsche, that Gobineau seems quite innocent of any scientific method in the strict sense of that phrase. He was, as we have seen, essentially a diplomat and a literary man. He had, however, considerable knowledge of the history of various peoples, and his extensive travels gave him a basis for making social and cultural comparisons. On the whole, what he did was to generalize his impressions and, possibly we should add, his own prejudices.

GOBINEAU'S SOCIAL PHILOSOPHY

Gobineau's attempt was essentially to present a philosophy of history in terms of race that would explain the rise and fall of nations and civilisations. He finds the explanation in what he calls "a kind of historical chemistry," the chemistry of races. He tells us in the dedication of his book that, as he pursued his studies, he was "gradually penetrated by the conviction that the racial question overshadows all other problems of history, that it holds the key to them all, and that the inequality of the races from whose fusion a people is formed is enough to explain the whole course of its destiny."

But Gobineau is not content to recognize race as merely one factor in human society. He finds it to be the one and only adequate explaining factor. He says: "I convinced myself at last that everything great, noble, and fruitful in the works of man on this earth, in science, art, and civilisation derives from a single starting point." In other words, Gobineau goes the full length of racial determinism.

He divides mankind into three great races: the white or European; the yellow or Asiatic; and the black or African. These he further divides into secondary and tertiary types. Among the types of the white race he finds the north-European blond, or, as we would now say, the Nordic type, to show the greatest capacity for creative civilisation.

He identifies the blond north-European with the Aryans and says: "There is no true civilisation among the European peoples where the Aryan branch is not predominant." As regards the Negro, he tells us, "No Negro race is seen as the initiator of a civilisation. Only when it is mixed with some other can it even be initiated into one." Furthermore, "No spontaneous civilisation is to be found among the yellow races." Whatever civilisation they have developed is due to Aryan intermixture, and stagnation supervenes as soon as Aryan blood is exhausted.

Thus it is clear, according to Gobineau, that culture or civilisation is wholly a product of race. His argument seems to be somewhat as follows: The way people think depends upon their nervous structure, which in turn is dependent upon heredity, or upon the purity of breed. Purity of breed results in unity of thought and action. It follows, first, that so long as a race is pure, the way of thinking of all of its members will remain essentially the same; second, people will think differently where there is mixture of blood, and antagonisms will develop; for manifoldness of blood produces manifoldness of ideas; third, the white race alone in human history has shown itself capable of high civilisation, and where the white race is purest, as in northern Europe, you will have the highest and best civilisation.

At this point, Gobineau develops a new definition of social degeneracy. He says: "Societies perish because they are degenerate and for no other reason." But the word "degenerate" means that the race has deteriorated. This deterioration comes essentially through intermixture of blood. When a nation no longer has the same blood in its veins, because of continual adulteration through intermixture, it can no longer maintain its original qualities, and its civilisation decays. Unity of action and ideas is now no longer possible. Conflicts break out and finally revolutions occur. Thus revolutions are an indirect result from mixture of blood, as South American countries already show. "Peoples degenerate only in consequence of the various admixtures of blood which they undergo," and "their degeneration corresponds exactly to the quantity and the quality of the new blood."

Gobineau then argues that human institutions are simply an expression of racial qualities, and that institutions are powerless, therefore, to stop or prevent the decay of a people.

The institutions of law, government, religion, and morality, he says, have no influence upon civilisation. Even physical environment has no direct influence. Only the purity or mixture of its blood has any significance for the history of a people.

As regards the qualities of the three races, Gobineau finds the black race represents passion, the yellow, mediocrity in everything, and the white, god- like reason. He finds that the white is endowed not only with reason, but with energy, generosity, and physical beauty. The supreme sub race in the white is the Aryan, of which the Germans are the purest modern representatives. Gobineau sets forth the theory that all the other civilisations of the world have sprung from the conquest of weaker peoples by Aryans.

Thus the civilisation of Egypt was produced by Aryans, but when they mingled with the natives, Egyptian civilisation declined. In both China and India, a similar process took place. As for the future, Gobineau thought that for America there is little hope, for there all nations are intermingling. In southern Europe and western Asia, the white race is rapidly losing its purity. He thought that for northern and Western Europe, civilisation might be secure yet for a few centuries. Thus his conclusion regarding western civilisation was pessimistic, because the purity of its blood was rapidly being lost.

CRITICISM

There is, of course, no scientific evidence that civilisation is dependent upon racial heredity. Civilisation, or culture, seems to be wholly an acquired trait. It consists of the accumulation of inventions that have been diffused through a process of teaching and learning. The most that racial heredity can do is to give a bias in certain directions. All of the evidence from history and experience fails to justify Gobineau's theories.

On the contrary, all the races of mankind seem to be capable of taking up the essentials of both material and spiritual civilisation. Differences of racial temperament and endowment may result in different peoples developing their civilisation in different directions. To acknowledge this, however,. is very different from acknowledging Gobineau's strictly biological, racial theory. We are not justified in taking Buckle's position that race counts for nothing. But, on the other hand, we cannot agree with Gobineau that race accounts for everything. Modern biology no longer upholds Gobineau's position of the all-might of racial heredity.

The political dangers of such one-sided social philosophy as Gobineau's are well shown in present-day Germany. Here the racialism of Gobineau was popularized by Houston Stewart Chamberlain, who, though the son of a British admiral, became a German citizen, and in his *Foundations of the Nineteenth Century* preached the superiority of the Nordic type. Chamberlain's book became, in Germany, a sort of Nordic bible, and in spite of the boasted culture and scientific achievements of the German people, their whole national policy under Hitler has been based upon this one-sided social philosophy, resulting not only in the persecution of the Jews and other non-Nordic elements in Germany, but also in arousing throughout the world racial antagonism to an extent scarcely known in previous generations. The inadequacies and dangers of one-sided social philosophies, when converted into practical political policies, were never better illustrated.

4

Transnational Migration, Crime, and Popular Justice

An effort to bring into a single field of vision transnational migration, crime, and popular justice may appear strange. However, these categorically different activities can, in fact, be related to one another as distinct responses to economic and political fields of power reconfigured through Mexico's deepening incorporation into international capitalism. None involves organized resistance or presents a viable alternative around which progressive political movements might coalesce.

Yet these responses problematize rule - even as they (temporarily) prop it up - because they appear in many circumstances to be the products of subject identities that reject the state's claims to rest its authority on a purported social contract. Delinquency involves a rejection of law, lynching reflects a breakdown in the institutionalized justice system, and transnational migration challenges the state's sovereign control of territory, especially when economic and political decisions affecting relations in rural Mexican communities are made by transmigrants in New York City or California.

SOCIAL FIELDS OF POWER

Pierre Bourdieu's idea of social fields provides a useful point of departure. For Bourdieu, social fields are relatively bounded social domains, composed of "positions" endowed with differing amounts of "capital" (economic, cultural, and symbolic). The positions' occupants struggle to augment their capital or to change the field's rules or boundaries in their favor. According to Bourdieu, the strategies that actors employ are produced by "generative schemes" or "durable dispositions," which he calls 'habitus,' representing the mental form of the structured fields in which the actors themselves were shaped.

He notes that habitus is "a model for the production of practices and a system of models for the perception and appreciation of practices. And in both cases its operations express the social position in which it was constructed". By definition, social fields are complex and positions multiple, meaning that the habitus of social actors occupying those positions vary, even if the overall domination of one group gives it more latitude in structuring the field to its advantage and thus shaping the durable dispositions of the field's other occupants.

In a somewhat different context, William Roseberry referenced this when he defined hegemony as the manner in which "the words, images, symbols, forms, organisations, institutions, and movements used by subordinate populations to talk about, understand, confront, accommodate themselves to, or resist their domination are shaped by the process of domination itself." Roseberry opined that, "What hegemony constructs...is not a shared ideology but a common meaningful and material framework for living through, talking about, and acting upon social orders characterized by domination."

In his empirical work Bourdieu explores in great detail the positions, dispositions, and rules affecting struggles in specific French intellectual, religious, and educational social fields. As Bourdieu is well aware, though, social fields are not isolated but intertwined in local, regional, national, and international complexes. Neither are they of equal salience in shaping the contours of a society or the globe. To take one example,

Bourdieu maintains that writers and artists who are dominant in the field of cultural production "are dominated in their relations with those who hold political and economic power"

To analyze fields dynamically and in interaction with one another, we can incorporate Bourdieu's perspective within the global vision of Eric Wolf and Sidney Mintz. Wolf and Mintz treat social fields as multiple, overlapping, mutually affecting, and, at particular historical moments, hierarchically ordered. Their perspective is particularly important now that most local and national economies and cultures have become more open and vulnerable to outside influences because of quick, massive movements of commodities, capital, and; to a lesser degree, people.

SOCIAL FIELDS AND NEO-LIBERALISM

The end of Mexico's 30-year experiment with import substitution industrial policy brought profound economic, social, and political changes. The economic crisis that followed the collapse of oil prices in early 1982 facilitated the increased influence of international financial institutions over the Mexican economy and contributed to the rise of political technocrats who, beginning with the presidency of Miguel de la Madrid, pursued structural adjustment and adopted Neo-liberalism as their guiding philosophy. De la Madrid and the presidents who followed him privatized state enterprises, opened markets, eliminated most price controls, and sold off and deregulated financial institutions. For U.S. and European capitalists, the policies represented a "good fit" with their turn toward "flexible accumulation," put in place from the 1960s to overcome Fordist rigidities and stem the growing accumulation crisis.

Investors from advanced capitalist countries took advantage of cheap wages in Mexico to relocate Fordist-style assembly plants (maquiladoras) there, invested in privatized sectors of formerly national industry (airlines, sugar mills, chemical factories, etc.), and flooded the country with imported goods, often marketed through local outlets of multinational chain stores. By the early 1990s, thousands of Mexican firms, deprived of tariff protection, had been driven out of business; many that survived the crisis shifted from producing goods to marketing imports or entered as junior partners into joint ventures with foreign capitalists.

Structural adjustment and Neo-liberalism have been accompanied by (and contributed to) a double and mutually enforcing process of political crisis and social class differentiation. The Mexican state no longer controls the resources to maintain the corporatist relations that historically underpinned PRI-government control. The Mexican Workers Confederation divided in 1998, and the land reform sector, historically the most reliable PRI ally, has been alienated by the reform of Article 27 of the Mexican Constitution, which in 1992 legalized the break-up and sale of ejido lands.

The reversal of land reform, reduction or elimination of price supports on basic grains, and the massive importation of cheap food from the United States signal the state's abandonment of more than three million small farming families (13 million people) to an impossible competition with industrialized (and heavily subsidized) farmers in the United States. Such policies contributed to the 1994 indigenous rebellion in Chiapas. Indeed, the Zapatista (EZLN) rebellion on January 1, 1994, was in no small part a reaction to the implementation of NAFTA, which for the insurgents represented a death warrant for indigenous Mexicans.

Yet the end of the politico-economic pact between unionized workers, land reform recipients, and the state has not been accompanied by social movements of national breadth that offer viable alternatives to the neo-liberal economic agenda. As elsewhere in the world, social struggles in Mexico split into a plethora of single-issue groups (environment, urban women, debtors, indigenous people) or local/regional organisations that resist commitment to larger collectivities, partly as a means of avoiding the co-optation that spelled the demise (or state incorporation) of so many of their predecessors. Even the EZLN, which began with a broad agenda for uniting multiple collectivities, has come to focus principally on indigenous issues.

The social cleavages parallel economic ones: a massive growth in black and informal sectors of the economy, decline in unionisation, and arising dependence on the United States for capital, food and other commodities, and markets. Currently, the United States accounts for 85% of Mexico' s foreign trade, purchases eight of every 10 barrels of Mexican petroleum exports, and supplies at least 25% of the nation's intermediate demand products. John Ross refers, albeit somewhat metaphorically, to Mexico's incorporation into GATT in 1986 and NAFTA in 1994 as the latest phase of the U.S. annexation of Mexico.

Both the wealthiest 10% of the Mexican population and international investors benefited from an economic transformation that has impoverished the majority. Applied to household income, the Gini coefficient, a generally accepted measure of income dispersion, declined from about.54 in 1963 to.44 in 1984 - reflecting a reduction of income inequality - at which point it reversed course, rising to.47 in 1989 and.49 in 1992. The current income of the bottom 80% of Mexican households declined over the 1984 to 1992 period from 50.5 to 45.6% of total income (a fall of 9.7%), while that of the top docile increased by 17.5%, from 32.4 to 38.1%. Government statistics indicate that in 1994 the wealthiest 10% of households controlled 41% of the national income. Participation in current national income of the poorest 10% of the population declined by more than eight per cent between 1984 and 1992, from 1.72 to 1.58%. Between 1982 and 1995, the real value of wages fell by 70%.

The number of Mexicans living in extreme poverty has increased 53% since Ernesto Zedillo assumed office in 1994, passing from 17 million to the currently estimated 27 million (up from 22 million in 1995), even as the economy grew. By 1998, the situation of the majority of Mexicans had deteriorated to such a degree that the government withheld the results of the National Household Economic Survey carried out in the third quarter of 1996 by the National Statistical and Geographical Institute. Among 18 countries studied by the Economic Commission for Latin America (ECLA), only Mexico experienced an increase in the percentage of households living in poverty between 1989 and 1996.

Urban and rural households employ a variety of "family survival strategies" to compensate for the peso's declining purchasing power, the decline in formal sector employment, and wage stagnation. Common strategies entail reducing or eliminating the consumption of expensive foods (meat, cheese, milk) and seeking additional income by working overtime, taking an additional job, or sending additional family members into the labor force. In urban Puebla, for instance, most women in working-class families labor while the children are cared for by their elderly parents.

Some parents pull children out of school and put them to work as rural wage workers, servants to middle-class households, petty vendors, or beggars. The International Labor Organisation (ILO) estimates that at least 250,000 Mexico City children work to help out their households. Almost half labor as petty vendors; another third beg. Though child labor may help families sustain a minimal level of in come today, it "has a clear social cost in human capital terms and is a factor that will tend to perpetuate poverty and inequality in the future".

The government's own statistics indicate that the number of street children in Mexico City doubled between 1992 and 1995 from 6,875 to 13,373. Apart from their immediate and long-term costs, the strategies are of limited effectiveness, as the growing percentage of people living in poverty demonstrates. In the context of social and economic fragmentation that accompanies structural adjustment and Neo-liberalism, international migration and crime become rational (and among the few) alternatives for many people.

CRIME AND DELINQUENCY

The "crime problem" must be defined with care, lest the poor, who are the principal victims of crime, be represented in mass as its perpetrators. No less an authority than Carlos Monsivais stated recently that although "this desperation serves as a seedbed for delinquency and gratuitous violence," he did not believe, as did former president Cabs Salinas, that "in poverty there is no democracy." To the contrary, Monsivais argues that: In poverty there is and can be cultural life....The scarcity of money does not eliminate spiritual and moral resources...for which reason it is very classist to maintain that there exists a strict causal relationship between poverty and transgression of the law.

The point is fundamental. A great deal of crime is fomented by poverty. For instance, a portion of the increase in bank robberies - which rose from an average of 233 annually between 1981 and 1994 to 413 in 1995 and 485 in 1996 - is the work of unarmed and inexperienced assailants driven by desperation and operating alone. Yet exclusive focus on crimes of opportunity and desperation committed by the poor distracts attention from the hard-core criminal organisations that possess enormous wealth and have thoroughly infiltrated local, state, and national government, as well as the criminal corruption that exists in every level of government.

Organized crime is no longer restricted primarily to drug trafficking rings, but is involved in car theft, bank assaults, kidnapping, traffic in arms and persons, the violation of intellectual and industrial property rights, assaults on transporters, and house robberies, among others. A spokesperson from the Mexican Institute for the Study of Organized Crime recently stated the experience of organized crime in Mexico is unique: organized crime is joined with and protected by the state. Moreover, the most extensive and powerful criminal mafias inhabit the heart of the state, to the extent that most police forces become transformed into criminal organisations.

Organized crime, strengthened by the political disorganisation that is part and parcel of the crisis (and to which official crime contributes), is along-term problem that is unlikely to diminish with improvement in global economic performance. It threatens the integrity of any future government, whether of the long-ruling Party of the Institutional Revolution-(PRI), the conservative Party of National Action (PAN), or the center-left Party of the Democratic Revolution (PRD).

To take but one prominent example, gangs operating in the small, though historically important, state of Morelos kidnapped as many as 1,200 people (350 cases documented) between 1995 and 1997, obtaining ransoms estimated conservatively at 30 million dollars. When the kidnappings began to mount up in the mid-1990s, dozens of businesspeople sold their homes and fled the state with their families, often to San Antonio, Texas. Responding to public complaints, the state government formed the Anti-Kidnapping Unit of the Morelos Judicial Police, whose recruits, drawn from the State Judicial Police, were trained by Colombian specialists. This new organ of public order functioned under the authority of Morelos Attorney General Carlos Peredo Merlo.

On January 27, 1998, federal highway police working a stretch of the Mexico-Iguala highway in Guerrero detained Armando Martinez Salgado, the chief of this "highly trained" anti-kidnapping police, as he, along with the unit's commander and one of its agents, attempted to dispose of the body of kidnap victim Jorge Nava Aviles. Within a few weeks, both Jesus Miyazawa, chief of the Morelos Judicial Police, and Attorney General Peredo Merlo had been dismissed from their posts and placed under house arrest.

The government disbanded the Anti-Kidnapping Police and the federal Attorney General's Office, which was brought into the case by the Zedillo administration, placed its agents under investigation. With the prosecution of Martinez Salgado, Peredo Merlo, and Miyazawa, the improbable assumed the order of a fact: the state anti-kidnapping police worked closely with one of Morelos's principal kidnapping organisations.

These revelations led to the formation of a broad multiparty and multi-organisational Front for the Security of Morelos that eventually secured Governor Jorge Carillo Olea's resignation. Several years earlier, in October 1995, state human rights and civic organisations had presented evidence that implicated the Judicial Police in kidnapping, and they had pleaded, without success, for Secretary of State Emilio Chuayffet and President Ernesto Zedillo to order an independent investigation of the Carillo government.

Events like those in Morelos, which are becoming increasingly common in Mexico, undermine the government's already reduced legitimacy. The print and broadcast media inundate the public with stories of documented links between narco-traffickers, politicians, and military officers, corruption and brutality in the Judicial Police, profiteering on the sale of state enterprises, and murderous intrigues within the ruling party. U.S. President Bill Clinton's "Whitewater" and sex-related problems seem tame by comparison.

The impunity enjoyed by notorious mafiosos and corrupt public officials, engaged in what often appears to be an internecine struggle to divide the public treasury, can serve as a justification for (if not an incentive to) other forms of criminal activity. "Paco," a 27-year-old narco-trafficker and bank robber, and "Roberto," a 29-year-old assailant, compared their criminal activity to that of the "authorities" during a 1996 interview with journalist Ramon Marques in the Reclusorio Oriente (East Penitentiary). Paco began by blaming criminal activity on the government:

Look: the government is guilty of everything that happens to us, for various reasons. They've not only permitted the brutal enrichment of a group of privileged bastards, with the consequent impoverishment, to the point of misery, of the screwed ones [jodidos] - that piled resentment upon resentment - but they've also placed themselves at the forefront of violence with their famous public crimes. And the children of the screwed ones, those who have nothing, went out on the street and formed their own government: the gangs. They have to obtain by means of violence that which society has denied them. And among the things that have been denied them are education, access to work, but above all, they have been denied food.

To this Roberto added a commentary about his experiences with the police:

It doesn't suit any policeman to detain a delinquent because that would represent a reduction in his income. They are constantly on the prowl for people who violate the law, not to apprehend them and to attempt their rehabilitation, but to exploit them, to demand more and more from them every day. I wouldn't want to, or perhaps couldn't, calculate what the underworld represents monthly for the private economy of the police. And that's without taking into account their own shady businesses.

If Roberto is correct, then the already notoriously unreliable statistics on crime in Mexico - grossly underreported because a majority of victims avoid going to the authorities - would require additional revision. Given public distrust in the authorities, who regularly request payment to investigate crimes, and, even so, solve few of them, increases in reported crimes in places like

Mexico City - up 66% in 1995, 13.7% in 1996, and 2.7% in 1997 - are unlikely to be statistical artifacts caused by a higher incidence of reporting. Official figures indicate that crimes against property, such as burglary, robbery, and auto theft, have skyrocketed, while rape and homicide have risen only moderately by comparison.

Minors commit a growing number of infractions. Over the last three years the number of minors (by law those less than 18 years of age) apprehended by Mexico City police forces and accused of criminal activity rose from 2,973 in 1995 to 5,351 in 1996 and 5,420 in 1997-a three-year increase of 82%. Almost one in five violators was less than 15 years old. Youthful offenders, many of whom are members of one of Mexico City's estimated 1,300 gangs, were implicated in an average of 50 murders, 83 sexual offenses, and 2,668 robberies annually between 1995 and 1997.

Pedro Penaloza, the coordinator of Citizens Participation for Crime Prevention of the Capital Government, counts these young people among the "children of the crisis. Children precisely of disintegrated families or families with no possibilities of development". In 1997, rising juvenile crime led to a heated discussion about lowering the legal age of adulthood so as to consign older youth infract ors to adult prisons. In 1994, in response to Mexico City's crime wave, then Mexico City regent Oscar Espinosa Villarreal appointed an active-duty army officer, General Enrique Salgado Cordero, to head the police force.

General Salgado filled the top posts with 40 army officers, created several special police forces, among them the "Zorros" and the "Jaguars" (trained by the Colombian police), to deal with organized youth gangs and even placed a battalion of soldiers in the high-crime district of Ixtapalapa to substitute for the police. When these measures proved ineffective, Salgado ordered a series of controversial large-scale sweeps in high-crime areas. The first operations produced few arrests but numerous complaints to human rights groups of police harassment. Then, on the afternoon of September 8, 1997, elements of the Zorros and Jaguars carried out an operation in Colonia Buenos Aires during which they took into custody and later murdered six young men.

Testimony in this case revealed that the police picked up the youth following an armed confrontation that left one policeman and one bystander dead. They placed three of their prisoners in an ex-Route 100 bus (used to transport police to the site) and conveyed them to the Balbuena headquarters. Shortly thereafter, at 6:30 in the evening, policemen drove the prisoners to a dirt road in Colonia Zapotitlan and shot them to death. The bodies of the three, aged 17 to 21, were found the next day at the bottom of a sand mine with a dozen bullet wounds among them. Several weeks later the decomposing remains of the other three men seized in the operation were discovered in a forested area of Ajusco.

The "Buenos Aires" case, as it is known, galvanized public opinion against the false promise of having military personnel involved in internal policing functions and led to the disbanding of the 135-member Jaguar and Zorro forces, the incarceration of 52 former agents and three army officers, and the resignation on Decemb er 4, 1997, of General Salgado following the discovery of evidence that he falsified statements in which he exonerated army officers implicated in the killings. Many people expected that when he took office in December 1997, mayor Cuauhtemoc Cardenas would introduce a "Zero Tolerance" policy modeled on that used by Republican Mayor Ralph Giuliani in New York City.

Giuliani's policy has reduced crime, but at the cost of a significant increase in accusations of police brutality. Yet as Sicilia pointed out and as the Cardenas administration soon recognized when it decided not to pursue Zero Tolerance,

Mexico City's problems are quite different from those of New York, where "criminality is not the child of the disintegration of a corrupt power". Instead, Cardenas dismissed all military personnel from the police force and called upon his extensive support base to form 55,000 "crime prevention committees" throughout the city.

The "crime problem" is not restricted to Mexico City. In Puebla, Guerrero, Oaxaca, Morelos, and throughout the country, armed bands haunt rural areas, robbing passersby, cars, and trucks of merchandise and personal possessions, and kidnapping merchants and industrialists or their family members and holding them for ransom in remote hideaways. In Puebla's southern Mixteca, one of the poorest areas of Mexico and a major departure point for U.S.-bound migrant workers, the state attorney general identified 17 armed gangs in 1995, among them The Cats, The Bald Ones (who wear wigs because they have no hair), and The Baptisms, feared because "in every assault or robbery they display arms used exclusively by the Army". Ten additional armed groups have been detected along the coast and in the highlands of Chiapas.

The timing of the most recent national crime wave leaves little doubt but that it is associated with the crisis that exploded in December 1994, when the peso suffered 40% devaluation. The 1994 crisis, which resulted partly from the neo-liberal economic opening, placed severe stress on a social fabric rent by the "lost decade" of the 1980s. Financial crisis and fiscal austerity dictated by the International Monetary Fund reduced the health, educational, and recreational sectors, social spaces that are key to the production of obedient subjects. Children forced to live in the streets or to abandon school so as to contribute to household income by begging, washing car windows, selling gum, and dozens of other informal sector occupations are formed in the absence of disciplinary training in the management of time, space, and their bodies.

Historically, the training provided by schools, religious institutions, and other official and semi-official institutions helped to limit resistance or guide it, when it was unavoidable, into acceptable channels.

Where these mechanisms are absent or unavailable, many children (and to a lesser degree adults) acquire or develop practices, values, and social relations that replicate in many ways those of the larger society, but without the respect for authority that accompanies successful socialisation. They are formed in social fields that lie on the margins of state control, fields bereft of the disciplinary norms that contribute to the production of docile subjects. As such, they become potential recruits for organized crime.

Government officials seem unaware of the impact of transformed social fields on social subjects. In Mexico, as in the United States, officials either delink social subjectivity from the practices that give rise to it or they decontextualize practices from the social fields of which they are a part. This leads them to place exaggerated emphasis on "moral values" and "family," as though by force of will "family" could survive as an island of serenity unaffected by the economic and social turmoil that surrounds it.

Poverty should be unrelated to the raising of the young; parents should be able to impart moral values to their children even though they are unable to provide basic material needs, without violating the very principles that they would have their progeny uphold; but neither parents nor children should be affected by the inside deals, thefts of public funds, and the corrupt practices (the kickbacks dealt Raul Salinas, the government bailout of the banks and its current effort to saddle the public with the bill, the Maseca cornmeal scam, or complicity between government officials and narcotraffickers) that abound even as structural adjustment policies demand that the poor cinch their belts tighter.

The ruling party never mentions income redistribution due to the neo-liberal axiom that the economic pie must grow larger before workers and peasants receive a bigger piece. Statistics cited earlier demonstrate that this simply does not occur in practice. Of course, as crime increases, especially in the major cities, and the authorities prove unable to curtail violations, it, too, takes its place as a dimension of social fields to which people react. One such reaction takes the form of lynching and other kinds of citizen "justice."

POPULAR JUSTICE

As confidence in public authorities' declines, more Mexicans take the law into their own hands. Responses vary, but all are evidence of the state's weakening control over social space. Though difficult to document with confidence, an apparent escalation in the number of lynching provides one example. According to Huggins, lynching "involves citizens' actions against another citizen presumed to have committed a crime or violated some social norm." De Souza refers to it as a form of "secondary violence," in the sense that it involves "violence against some other act that is defined as criminal or violent." Lynchings have been best documented in Brazil, where de Souza accumulated data on 268 lynching and attempted lynching from selected national newspapers between 1979 and 1988 (an average of 27 annually).

However, lynching or a form of comparable vigilante justice also existed in Northern Ireland, where the IRA was pressed to provide police protection in areas under its nominal control and in revolutionary South Africa where irate citizens in shantytowns and squatters' camps frequently "necklaced" accused delinquents. Neither should we forget the United States, which "has a long history of (largely racist) vigilantism". Of the 4,730 lynching reported there between 1882 and 1952, 90% of the victims were African Americans. The decline of lynching in the United States to about one annually since the 1950s is a relatively recent phenomenon.

Lynchings in Latin America occur in many different contexts and exhibit significant variations in levels of participation, degrees of spontaneity, and other aspects. For instance, recent lynchings in Mexico have followed accusations of rape, theft, or murder; accusations of witchcraft; and attributions of child theft. The U.S. "Mexico Country Report on Human Rights Practices for 1996" stated that lynching were rising, "primarily in rural communities with limited access to the criminal justice system," and that the national press documented 21 victims between September 1995 and August 1996.

More recently, the Mahatma Gandhi Regional Human Rights Commission reported to La Jornada that nine lynching resulting in 17 deaths had occurred in Oaxaca alone over the last five years. In Morelos, civilians lynched 15 people in seven incidents during the governorship of Jorge Carillo, indicating a lack of civilian trust in police and judicial authorities during his term. Different from Brazil, where lynching is a predominantly urban phenomenon, most Mexican lynchings occur in rural areas of southern states such as Puebla, Oaxaca, and Chiapas, where justice officials are notoriously corrupt and ineffective, repressing peasants and popular movements in the service of local and regional bosses rather than fighting crime.

As crime rises in the marginalized south, driven in no small part by an economic policy that continues to drain labor and surplus from the countryside to the cities and then onward to the United States, some citizens respond with direct action. It is tempting to read in these responses the seeds of a progressive politics. Direct action challenges the authority of the state by substituting local popular authority. Are we, then, in the presence of a rural Mexican version of the "popular justice" that Foucault defended against the criticisms of his Maoist opponents?

The debate between Foucault and the Maoists centered on a hypothetical transition to socialism and the advisability of preserving the forms of the bourgeois justice system and the courts, but refunctionalizing them to serve the interests of the popular classes. Mexico is not in a revolutionary situation, however sharply economic class lines may be drawn, as evidenced by the fact that lynching victims originate from class backgrounds little different from those of their executioners.

The victims are often petty thieves, itinerant vendors, and asocial peasants. Some of their presumed criminal activities are serious - rape, kidnapping, or murder, but others involve petty thefts or minor assaults. When the poor lynch the poor rather than attacking police stations, as occurred in a well-publicized case in Tres Arroyos, Argentina, in 1989, or collectively looting trains of the wheat or corn that they cannot afford to purchase, they reproduce both social relations that oppress as well as a stigmatized discourse on poverty that differentiates the "honorable" poor who bear their suffering from the "thieves, rapists, and murders" who prey on them.

The discourse differs little from that of the "culture of poverty" wielded by dominant groups. Finally, some lynchings, particularly those based on accusations of child theft, are the product of community fears and suspicions fed by press reports of children kidnapped for sale to adoption agencies or for use as organ transplant donors. Such fears find a rational basis in the disappearance of approximately 20,000 Mexican children annually.

As a judgment, lynching is singular and final. The accusers deny the accused the right to a defense and make no effort to scale the punishment to the crime. The one punishment is death. Without entering into a full-scale analysis, I believe that the target of lynching is transformed into a metonymical representation for all that is wrong-the assaults, rapes, thefts, and homicides that have gone unpunished because of the ineptness, corruption, or collusion of the authorities. By lynching, communities (or segments of them) substitute for the state, occupying the social niches that it has abandoned, but doing so in a way that merely inverts and in that way preserves the violence to which they themselves have historically been subjected. If lynching is a metonym for the numerous acts of violence suffered by thousands of workers and peasants, it is a metaphor for a "utopian" state, now transformed and purified through the "just" action of civilians.

Because it is enacted following the commission of a crime, lynching can have only minor preventive impact as a function of the spectacle of the beaten, broken, and occasionally burned body of the victim. Significantly, lynching is a popular inscription of the death penalty that most Mexicans, including the leadership of all major political parties, oppose. Each "lynching" of a Mexican citizen in Texas or Florida, following his or her passage through the "bourgeois system of injustice," engenders a national day of mourning in Mexico. It is ironic, then, that some Mexicans who oppose the death penalty when carried out in the United States enact it with growing regularity in Mexico under conditions in which the accused is denied due process.

However, popular justice does exist in Mexico in more organized and relatively democratic forms. For instance, on the coast and in the mountains of Guerrero, the social space abandoned by the state is being occupied in another manner. In 1995, residents of the marginalized rural municipalities of Malintepec and San Luis Acatlan responded to thefts carried out by armed gangs working the unpaved roads in an area in which "the police are rarely seen" by forming a 480-member armed police force to provide a 24-hour patrol. The Mexican Army briefly trained this unpaid, constabulary force in the handling of arms and the state governor donated 20 rifles to them.

The size of the force and its diverse constitution (members of three different ethnic groups and numerous grass-roots organisations) hopefully will check its being converted into a paramilitary force for exploitation by any individual or political party as occurred in Chiapas. The most interesting aspect of the popular patrols concerns the manner in which they enforce communal law. In Rio Iguala, chicken thieves pay a 50-peso fine, serve two nights in the local jail, and donate two days of unpaid communal labor. The fine triples with the theft of a turkey - 150 pesos, six days of unpaid work, and six nights in jail, and climbs steeply with larger animals. Rio Igualans punish goat theft with a fine of 400 pesos, plus 16 days of work, and 16 nights in the lockup, while the penalty for the theft of a horse, cow, or mule is a year behind bars.

Several points merit mention. First, the organisation represented a broad community initiative, as opposed to one impelled from the state capital or from Mexico City. It is an initiative with antecedents in the historical struggles against regional political bosses that gave birth to a variety of producers' organisations that, however undercapitalized, provide their members with a marginally better income than they obtained when the marketing of coffee and other products was monopolized by a few powerful figures. As Aviles notes,

> In the course of that struggle there formed the social organisation that today collects coffee and sells it under their own brand name, bottles honey, secures loans, and has even participated in electoral struggles: the Light of the Mountain Ejido Union, the Coffee-Corn Social Solidarity Society, the Regional Peasants Union of the Lower Coast and Mountains, 500 Years of Indigenous Resistance, the Community Supply Council, and the Council of Indigenous Authorities. In this case, state authorities ceded considerable social control to local interests.

INTERNATIONAL MIGRATION

Migration represents another survival strategy on an altered social field of power. With few exceptions, migrants seek the opportunity to earn an honest wage; they are much more likely to be the victims of avaricious coyotes, rightwing gangs, exploitative bosses, and corrupt Mexican cops and officials than victimizers. In migrating north, millions of Mexicans place themselves, however partially and temporarily, in social fields beyond the surveillance of the Mexican state. In the process, they often learn new things about themselves, their country, and its government; often they share these understandings with other Mexicans, both in the United States and on recurrent or permanent returns to Mexico.

International migration is not an exclusive product of Neo-liberalism. However, the growing incidence of migration from Puebla, Oaxaca, Guerrero, and other states outside the historic sending areas of western Mexico coincides with the economic crises of the 1980s and 1990s.

For instance, Zapotitlan de Salinas, a rural community in Puebla's southern Mixtec area, had no history of U.S. migration before 1984 when the first migrant left for "El Norte." By August of 1998, about 30% of the community's adults had made at least one trip to the United States. U.S. migration began in 1979 in Xoyatla, a rural community of the municipality of Tepeojuma; in less than a generation, 50% of the adult population had acquired international migratory experience (72% of the males and 28% of the females), mostly to the New York City metropolitan area.

By mid-1998, that area had become the temporary or permanent home to approximately 200,000 Mexicans, of whom approximately half originated from Puebla, proof of the immense importance of social networks in the migrants' choice of destination, as well as the extent to which similarly oriented networks had developed around the state. The moneys and goods remitted or brought back by migrants have, in many cases, reconfigured rural communities economically and reshaped them socially and culturally.

Transport, housing, clothing styles, language, and customs - in short, the entire panoply of what anthropologists think of as "culture" - have been affected by migration. In some cases, such as in Tecuani, migrant labor forms the community's economic base and a well-organized group of migrants in New York uses their control of precious migradollars to exercise considerable influence over community affairs. To the degree that social fields span two countries, it is probably legitimate to speak of "transnational communities" that transcend a single social location by employing technological advances to "annihilate space by time".

Even where transnational communities have not consolidated, migration often has profound effects on local social and economic relations. Half the businesses and 85% of the vehicles purchased by 50 households interviewed in Xoyatla were the product in whole or in part of migradollars. Xoyatlenses also invested migradollars to restore the church, and both mayordomias and family rituals (birthdays, baptisms, weddings, etc.) have become much more elaborate because of the availability of U.S.-earned income. However, as Rivermar points out, labor migration has also sharpened socioeconomic divisions within the community. Access to migradollars is unevenly distributed among households, and those with little or no access have little possibility of meeting the rising standards of consumption driven upward by more successful migrants. Even if able to maintain a nominal level of well-being, they suffer relative status deprivation.

Historically, many rural Mexicans viewed children's education as the principal route to upward mobility for the household. Parents and siblings often made impressive personal sacrifices to assist a younger member of the family through preparatory (high school) and, ideally, normal (teacher training) school. Parents with a teacher son or secretary daughter could rest reasonably assured that they would be cared for in their old age. However, the economic crisis has resulted in reduced access to higher education and has devalued its utility. Currently, rural schoolteachers earn a meager salary that hardly provides for their own maintenance, much less support for members of their extended families.

In Puebla, at least, several hundred rural school teachers annually request year-long leaves of absence from the state Ministry of Education in order to migrate temporarily to the United States, where they hope to work and save enough money to construct a home, purchase a car or truck, start a small business, or meet some other pressing need.

Their university or normal school degrees are worth little in the United States, where Mexican architects, engineers, and schoolteachers find themselves employed in the same restaurant, janitorial, and landscaping jobs as peasants and workers with little or no formal education. Reichart long ago identified a "migration syndrome" in which U.S.-bound migration achieves such prominence that it becomes incorporated into local value systems as an important and desired goal.

At young ages children begin to emulate their elders and look forward to their initial migration experience as a rite of passage to adulthood.

Education becomes secondary, especially where poorly educated migrants can, if fortunate and thrifty, earn many times more than much better educated non-migrants. In short, where migration has reached some undetermined critical mass, it contributes to changes in the educational and economic fields by constituting an alternative (and more likely, given the current crisis) route to economic success. Thus, in Zapotitlan, Edgar Lazama (personal communication) points out that a developing norm shared by youth and their parents is that young people complete secondary school, thus obtaining the minimum educational qualification required for many domestic jobs before migrating.

Rural dwellers in Puebla and elsewhere display enormous tenacity and much creativity in inventing new ways to preserve their most cherished values and standards of comportment in the context of rising international migration.

Yet in remaining the same, it is obvious that they also must change. International migration introduces stresses and strains as well as opportunities, products of its impact on local economic, educational, political, and religious fields of social relations. Weakened by the very neo-liberal economic policies that it promotes, the Mexican state has ceded control of social space in rural and urban areas.

Subjects formed before the crisis discover that internalized responses do not lead to desired outcomes (because the social fields in which they are implemented are distinct from those in which they were formed), paving the way for alienation, frustration, failure, or, alternatively, resistance and adaptation.

Some people respond with creative resistance, as the Zapatista Rebellion and the proliferation of human rights and citizens' organisations make clear. I have mentioned a few such progressive responses: the Morelos citizens' groups that forced out Governor Carillo and the communal police of coastal Guerrero. Most people, however, distrustful of government and skeptical that social organisations can bring about change, pursue individualized as opposed to collective coping strategies. International labor migration, overwhelmingly to the United States, is one of the most important of these.

Migrants have the advantage of earning dollars during a period of high domestic inflation and regular, steep devaluations of the peso, reflected almost immediately in rising prices of the increasing number of foreign products that stock the shelves of commercial outlets in the city and countryside.

Yet many people lack the social networks, the start-up capital, the knowledge, the energy, or the will to seek their fortune, even temporarily, in the United States. Though the vast majority of people seek to employ household economic strategies - working longer hours and reducing consumption - to survive, other formerly complaisant citizens flout legal codes to obtain "by means of violence" that which "society denied them." Moreover, as crime increases and impunity of wealthy and powerful violators continues, more Mexicans, distrustful of authorities who many view as complicit with criminals, take the law into their own hands.

Lynchings and vigilante justice are increasing, growing numbers of people carry firearms in public, and a public debate has opened around the advisability of instituting the death penalty (for crimes other than treason) and lowering the legal age of adulthood from 18 to 16, which would mean the consignment to adult prisons of many youthful offenders.

Finally, it bears mention that each of these responses is inscribed, as are economic relations generally, in transnational relations. Most of the firearms that enter Mexico originate in the United States, where lax gun laws make it easy for almost any adult to purchase a pistol or rifle. As is well known, the United States is the principal market for narcotics (as well as for stolen babies).

By contrast, labor migrants to Los Angeles, New York, and elsewhere are key players in flexible accumulation, preserving domestic industry by working for Third World wages and, through their work in restaurants, green grocers, landscaping firms, and janitorial services, servicing the accommodated managerial and professional classes that constitute part of the remaining "core" work force of multinational corporations.

At least one author has even argued that, along with other migrants, the arrival of approximately 200,000 Mexicans to New York contributed to the reduction of crime there:

They didn't arrive in New York as criminals. They found work, often the worst available, and they worked hard and insisted that their children take advantage of the educational system and behave themselves.

The Korean grocer worked too much to allow an adolescent criminal to steal apples from his fruit stand; he pursued the thief with a hatchet. The immigrants served as good examples for many other young Americans.... They began to provide New York with more social cohesion.

5

Integrating Globalisation into the Social Work Curriculum

While there has been discussion about the true relevance of globalisation to social work, the evidence of practice worldwide and the burgeoning literature indicate that social work is now truly a global profession. Clearly, we are now entering a period in which our profession embraces both international practice and also a more complex global understanding of social problems and solutions. In this chapter we expand upon the idea of an internationalized curriculum employing a global and holistic conception that fully embraces the complexities of the transactional nature of social work and its ecological perspective. An integrated curriculum addresses demographic, cultural, social, political, economic, environmental and psychological causes and consequences of globalisation attends to the consequent ethical responsibilities and the necessity of intercultural competence to promote social justice and human rights.

FROM INTERNATIONAL TO GLOBAL

There are different definitions of international social work and some usages of the term have been restrictive to practice, or used to "denote the exchanges that take place between social workers". Also, social work scholars have used the term in a comparative model and policy approach or international profile presentation focusing on the roles of social workers in other countries. However, more broadly, Healy defines the outcomes of "internationalisation" as being "(1) improved social work practice; (2) more humane and socially oriented public policies at the national and global levels; and (3) enhanced status for the profession of social work through its increased visibility".

While Healy consistently integrates a broad global perspective in her international social work discussion, we suggest adding a fourth more explicit outcome: an increased understanding of the complexities and human costs and benefits of a globalized and interdependent world with rapidly changing social, technological, and economic systems. We present this fourth outcome as a way of moving beyond more traditional conceptions of international social work towards a globalized social work perspective which captures the nuances of multiple and interacting world systems. This approach is consistent with Singer's view that "the term "globalisation" rather than the older "internationalisation" moves us past the era of growing ties between nations towards something beyond the existing conception of the nation-state".

It moves us to a fuller understanding of the effects of social, economic and environmental policies in one part of the world have on people in many other places. Asamoah, Healy, and Mayadas point out that the term global is also often used interchangeably with international, however global is broader as it "refers to a mode of thinking about the planet as a whole and the interactive effects of social phenomena, linking domestic and international concerns in a seamless web". There are multiple usages of the term globalisation, many of which explore the positive and more frequently the negative aspects of the phenomena.

Our discussion relies upon the International Federation of Social Workers (IFSW) definition that honors a "seamless web" of world systems. Incorporating culture and shared place, the

IFSW summarized globalisation holistically with a strong connection to people and cultures and highlighted the intersection of the profession and globalisation:

> Globalisation is the process by which all peoples and communities come to experience an increasingly common economic, social and cultural environment. By definition, the process affects everybody throughout the world. A more integrated world community brings both benefits and problem for all; it affects the balance of economic, political and cultural power between nations, communities and individuals and it can both enhance and limit freedoms and human rights. Social workers, by the nature of their work, tend to meet those who are more likely to have suffered the damaging consequences of some aspects of globalisation.

For this discussion, it is impossible to explore all the concepts of globalisation offered by economists, international development scholars, sociologists, social workers, and others. We present a set of core concepts relevant to the social work curriculum. Our following curriculum discussion builds upon these concepts and presents recommended content and practical teaching strategies to integrate globalisation issues into courses in social policy, community practice, human behaviour in the social environment, and sustainable development. Ethical issues related to globalisation are also explored, incorporating the concepts of human rights and social justice into considerations of human oppression and freedom.

SOCIAL POLICY

Kahn and Kamerman remind us that social policy has never been purely national in nature. Comparative international social policy has a well-established history in the field of social work with multiple methodologies. In advanced social policy courses, students can be assigned comparative social policy activities using indicators such as the Human Development Index, to encourage global thinking and critical analysis. Rotabi, Weil, and Gamble present a course assignment in which students focus on a social problem, such as child labor and trafficking or fair housing, and identify policies in the United States and two other countries, one of those countries being a developing nation.

Students present the different policies, relevant social indicators, the Human Development Index of each country, and they also answer a series of comparative questions including a discussion of the underlying values of equality and liberty. Also, students are asked to identify relevant United Nations human rights declarations or codes, such as the Convention on the Rights of the Child, and their application in each country presented. When students identify that one particular country has far superior social indicator data, they also present relevant social interventions (i.e. State provided health care in Europe and Canada).

This assignment provides students with an opportunity to apply a Human Rights Framework to social problems. Students also have the opportunity to explore the social interventions that result from a variety of social policies, including underlying concepts such as capitalism, liberalisation, socialized community care, social justice, human rights, inequality, and interdependence.

COMMUNITY PRACTICE

Community Practice courses offer a wealth of opportunities to engage students in active learning experiences connecting practice methods and skills with global practice issues and with the effects of globalisation on human migration and populations at home. Community practice involves discrete and complementary methods: organizing, development (i.e. micro-enterprises and women's cooperatives in Bangladesh, India, Kenya, and Columbia, planning, and local to global change strategies.

These methods have become central means of working with vulnerable populations responding to the multiple impacts of globalisation in their home countries. Likewise community practice is evolving as an important approach in countries that have received refugees from war torn areas, those who have had to relocate because of natural disasters, and those who have become internally displaced or cross-boarder migrants as a result of civil warfare.

The increased movement of populations and the effects of changing economies indicate that social workers throughout the Global South and those working in North America and Europe as well, need to give serious attention to these methods of developing immediate and long term mutual support, assisting community groups in organizing for their own welfare, strengthening social capital, building infrastructure and social structure through community development and in longer term social and community planning and social reform focused on increasing the abilities of peoples to exercise human rights and build more socially just communities and governments.

The social development and empowerment perspectives on human, community and economic capacity building provide an overarching framework for practice designed to strengthen vulnerable, low-wealth communities. Advanced macro courses in community practice can draw on a wealth of literature that: (a) documents practice methods and theory for community development; (b) presents asset development interventions; (c) reports on civic engagement worldwide; (d) presents models of social planning with communities and (e) describes means for empowering and organizing vulnerable or displaced groups. Abundant literature also focuses on relevant theory and policy approaches that form significant aspects of the knowledge base for such interventions.

In a course at the University of North Carolina, Chapel Hill on "Community Practice and Planning" students investigate and role play similarities and differences in engagement with and facilitation of community development processes founded in mutuality and interdependence with diverse populations in local and international settings.

Assignments include having each student study an organisation/agency involved in community practice in the U.S. and investigate examples of the same model in other nations based on web and literature searches. Commonalities and differences are critically analyzed for issues of intercultural competence, indigenous leadership approaches, facilitation issues (lack of gender equity, strong traditional hierarchies, etc.) building or re-building reciprocity in community engagement and methods of community-led needs assessment, planning and implementation of projects.

Following adult learning principles, students also take responsibility for class projects teaching each other culturally appropriate skills for working with diverse groups and relevant strategies for working with groups in other nations and with immigrant and refugee groups to organize communities, create development, educational and economic projects (Southeast Asian Women's Association and others), and devise appropriate means for evaluating local projects.

These assignments engage students in active learning, facilitation, and coaching/teaching strategies to assist them in working with community groups in ways that are focused on mutual learning, reciprocity, North/South and East/West dialogues, and transnational practice responses to globalisation abroad and at home. They are able to investigate the transferability of programs from South to North and to consider professional responsibility in working with migrant and disenfranchised groups in a developmentalist and empowerment focused model that emphasizes strengthening human rights particularly equal rights for women and girls) and righting historically unjust practices.

Students are expected to explore and compare a range of community practice models and interventions from local programs in different nations to global NGO development activities (e.g. Oxfam; UNICEF; Soros Foundation). In community practice courses that focus on issues of globalisation, students are able to sharpen their basic practice skills in facilitation, coaching, community development, program development and evaluation, and to hone skills and interests in specialized areas from work with photo-voice projects and revitalizing community culture among refugees, to inner-city and rural economic, social and sustainable development projects. In their international comparisons, students consider the following learning strategies: (a) analyzing the effects of different political/economic structures and related policy directions (gender equity; expanding rights for previously disenfranchised groups, etc.); (b) investigating cross-national and cross-faith issues related to cultural competency; (c) learning and applying empowerment theory and practice and supporting broader participation where strict patriarchy and class hierarchies have promoted policies of exclusion, and (d) documenting practice projects that support participatory planning and evaluation, and inclusive community-led change to support positive human and economic development.

Concepts critical to mastering skills and methods of community practice include: mutuality, community and indigenous leadership, intercultural competency, human and community capacity building, and basic ethical principles of the worth and dignity of the individual and the realities of human interdependence within communities and across the globe.

HUMAN BEHAVIOUR IN THE SOCIAL ENVIRONMENT

Theories of human behaviour presently emphasized in micro-level human behaviour in the social environment (HBSE) are selected for their empirically based foundations. This approach may privilege Western positivistic values over more constructivist or indigenous approaches to understanding human development that have stature in many cultures. A global perspective in teaching HBSE will encourage students to integrate disparate practice implications arising from theories of human development linked with these contrasting paradigms.

Transactions between the person and environment within and across micro, mezzo, and macro systems occurring across the life span are at the core of the HBSE curriculum. To capture adequately these dynamic processes, along with the changing nature of world economic, social, and technological systems, concepts of interdependence, responsibility, and reciprocity should be emphasized. These terms provide the impetus for a critical analysis of the consequences for individual, family, and community development of macro economic policies which promote globalized interdependent but inequitable economies that allow multinational corporations to abrogate civic responsibility.

The role of work and employment for individuals and families across the life span can be linked with core concepts of globalisation such as capitalism, multi-national corporations, and empowerment and students can be engaged in critical and comparative analysis of opportunities and outcomes. The social cognitive theory of human development, which characterizes self-efficacy beliefs as a motivating force for human action, links individual development with human agency and collective action. Each individual's life work is reflective of our common human identity, creativity and human agency but is also significantly impacted for many across the globe by neo-liberal economic policies which constrain opportunities for education, advancement, and employment.

Developmental consequences of foreign outsourcing of major US industries like textile manufacturing can be contrasted with those promoting corporate social responsibility such as the standards for business practices promoted by the fair trade movement. As a link to HBSE content on individual development the role of older women in women's collectives both in the US and abroad can be examined in parallel as a strategy to teach the bio-psychosocial benefits of intergenerational social engagement and productive engagement in later life. Older women in the US engaged in volunteerism create fair trade artisan markets in churches, or business enterprises such as Ten Thousand Villages. Women in developing countries who use their expertise as artists, craftsmen and lay health advisors are promoting sustainable livelihoods for their families and communities. Both groups of women are engaged in activities known to promote their health and successful aging.

Case examples can also illustrate the links between natural resource extraction in developing nations, environmental and social consequences of extracting and manufacturing raw materials into globally traded commodities, and their subsequent use and/or abuse in developed nations. Three examples are the global trade in sugar, coffee, and cocaine. Instructional activities should address educational opportunities for children, employment prospects for working age adults, and health and well-being of individuals and families in both the nations where the resource is extracted and manufactured and in those where it is primarily consumed.

Exploration of transnational family relationships brought on by migration in response to poverty, oppression, or disaster adds another layer to an HBSE focused analysis of globalisation. The exchange of economic remittances is one expression of interdependence and responsibility in transnational families. Exchange of bi-lateral aid across borders has been thought of as an expression of economic interdependence and a tool to promote responsible development across nations, or, alternatively, as a reflection of capitalistic exploitation and imperialism.

Other global events that lead to migration provide a fruitful resource for the HBSE curriculum. Topics include, unfortunately the short and long-term impacts of war, disasters, terrorism and human rights violations which often result in the movement of large numbers of refugees across borders. Other global events include educational innovations, changing health care practices, and cultural norms related to gender and age, and spirituality. A more difficult task for the HBSE instructor is to link globalisation in a coherent format across the course. HBSE is frequently organized along developmental trajectories (childhood, young adulthood, old age, etc.).

By comparing and contrasting developmental trajectories across the life span in collectivist and individualist oriented cultures numerous opportunities to integrate aspects of globalisation emerge. Child rearing and family care giving practices can be compared along with family rituals and spiritual practices associated with pregnancy and birth and developmental milestones such as menarche, menopause, and death and dying. An individualistic vs. collectivistic comparative approach leaves room for both the positivistic, empirically grounded theories of human development and more constructivist understandings. Educators employing this teaching strategy with US students are also exposing people who tend to be more individualistic in nature to the collectivistic orientation experienced by many peoples across the globe. Teaching that encourages students to reconcile the 'good' with the 'bad' of globalisation in the HBSE curriculum can promote cultural competence.

SUSTAINABLE DEVELOPMENT

Sustainable Development is a process as well as an outcome. The World Commission on Environment and Development defined it as "development that meets the needs of the present without compromising the ability of future generations to meet their own needs". Estes introduced social workers to the theories that inform sustainable development and its usefulness as a concept in understanding human development and social work practice. Understanding the meaning of sustainable development enlarges social workers concept of person-in-environment by incorporating human relationships with other species and with natural ecosystems as well as relations with social and institutional systems.

When social workers help people as individuals, families, or community groups to develop livelihoods that can be economically, culturally, and socially satisfying without contaminating or permanently eliminating the earth's resources they are working in sustainable development. A social worker who understands that we are all mutually dependent upon the earth's forests, fisheries, arable land, clean air, and potable water, practices from a global perspective. Mutuality, the idea that all people in the world have common needs for the earth's resources, helps students move directly to discussions of social justice, and how we decide what is fair in terms of consumption, production, growth, and development.

One way to help students connect personally with the ocal to global development relationships is to ask them to do a test that calculates their ecological footprint. The ecological footprint is a calculation of the number of acres a person needs to maintain their current lifestyle. The result helps students see that residing in an industrial country makes them contributors to the greatest proportion of environmental pollution, no matter how many vegetables they grow or how often they ride their bicycle to school.

A deeper exploration of how other cultural traditions have embraced the earth's resources helps students to gain perspective on the perceived superiority of the western positivist knowledge base and quickly disabuses the simplistic idea that "all we have to do to save the earth is decrease the fertility rate in the Global South". Vandana Shiva, renowned for her work in India and throughout the world to expose cultural theft, violence against women, and natural resource privatisation, describes in Earth Democracy how cultural diversity, a reverence for all life, and interconnection and interdependence of cultures is the only way to ecological sustainability. Wangari Maathai, winner of the Nobel Prize for Peace in 2004, has worked in Kenya for more than thirty years "to mobilize communities for self-determination, justice, equity, poverty reduction and environmental conservation, using trees as the entry point".

Winona LaDuke, provides American Indian perspectives on sacred lands, water, rice, horses and medicine in her collection of stories from indigenous North American communities. Student assignments with lots of freedom for incorporating the concept of sustainable development in their personal and professional development and in the ethical practice of social work expand social work knowledge in the areas of human behaviour, policy, practice, and research.

A student doing field practice in a local school, for example, could help the school do an audit of toxic cleaning materials, help develop student groups to celebrate and appreciate cultural diversity (especially for schools with significant immigrant populations), help to grow vegetables in the schoolyard for school snacks or lunch, help teachers develop resources for recycled school supplies, and help the school administration plan for ways to reduce energy consumption. Such projects, drawn from real student experiences, can be evaluated using Maureen Hart's Sustainable Development Indicators, helping students further understand the difference between traditional social and economic indicators (e.g. "the unemployment rate") and sustainability indicators (e.g. "diversity and vitality of the local job base"). Gaining experience in the understanding and practice of sustainable development helps students internalize concepts of social justice, responsibility, mutuality, and cultural competence.

EXPLORING SOCIAL WORK VALUES AND ETHICAL PRINCIPLES

An important component of the concept of globalisation is the idea of nation state decline in an emerging world-wide, neo-liberal economic system. Multinational corporations are the power brokers in this emerging world system creating a dynamic that has been called "turbo capitalism" and "predatory capitalism". As Singer points out, this shift from a nation-state orientation to that of a global system "needs to be reflected in all levels of our thought and especially in our thinking about ethics". Consideration of world-systems ethics provides students with an opportunity to explore the philosophy of ethics in a broader context than the traditional social work conceptions provide.

Ethical discourse within a human rights framework is an important classroom activity and encourages students to consider universality and cultural relativism as they grapple with examples of oppression related to globalisation. An integrated curriculum encourages students to actively apply the UN Declaration of Human Rights and associated conventions (i.e. Convention on the Elimination of All Forms of Discrimination) across courses as they consider societal ethics at home and abroad. Explicit human rights codes help students have concrete discussions about social justice and challenge students to apply their own conceptions of equality and liberty on a global scale.

Specific discussion as it relates to professional social work standards would draw upon Section 6 of the US National Association of Social Work (NASW) Code of Ethics: "The standards [in this section] explicitly highlight social workers' obligation to engage in activities that promote social justice and the general welfare of society from "local to global levels"". Local responsibilities in a global system are an important concept for American social work students and often, when learning within a globalized social work curriculum, they experience consciousness rising about the inevitable conflicts between our capitalistic system and global social justice.

Exploration of ethical principles and standards on a global level provides US students with an opportunity to become familiar with the International Federation of Social Worker's (IFSW) and the International Association of Schools of Social Work (IASSW) Ethics in Social Work, Statement of Principles. The IFSW/IASSW statement provides guidelines for professional conduct but leaves the primary responsibility for specifics of professional conduct to national organisations. The statement, however, makes very clear that all social workers everywhere must use the principles of human rights, human dignity and social justice as the guiding principles for their work, and must have knowledge of the seven United Nations conventions that outline basic human rights.

By its very nature, globalisation moves us from a nationalistic and localized conception of reality to a world-systems perspective. This represents a paradigm shift requiring new and holistic education strategies. The globalized social work perspective builds upon the more established international social work conceptions and moves beyond what has been simply called "broadening the mind" to a more transactional way of thinking which has been called "global mindedness". A globalized perspective also more fully incorporates conceptions of interdependence, responsibility and reciprocity, and cultural competence.

6

Sociological Rational Choice Theory

In the last decade rational choice theory has gained influence and visibility in many of the social sciences and in related disciplines such as philosophy and law. To appreciate just how rapidly its influence has spread, consider political science, a discipline in many respects similar to sociology. According to one estimate, the proportion of articles based on rational choice premises published in the American Political Science Review rose from zero in 1957 to nearly 40% in 1992. Job candidates specializing in rational choice now command a hefty premium in American political science departments. Given its own disciplinary history, which is often characterized in relentlessly holistic terms, sociology would appear to be a most unpromising terrain for the spread of rational choice ideas and methods.

Indeed, resistance to the approach has been notable. No American sociology department currently specializes in rational choice; only one even offers its graduate students a concentration in it. No jobs are listed for specialists in the area. This is in contrast to the situation in Western Europe, particularly in the Netherlands, Germany, and Sweden, where rational choice is considerably more institutionalized. Yet many sociologists, like the character in Moliere's Bourgeois Gentilhomme who was startled to learn that he was speaking prose, unwittingly rely on rational choice mechanisms in their own research. Signs of the growing acceptance of sociological versions of rational choice can be found in the establishment of the journal Rationality and Society, and in the regular proceedings of lively sections devoted to the approach in both the American and the International Sociological Associations meetings.

Some of the skepticism about rational choice among sociologists arises from misunderstanding. One criticism of rational choice focuses on the lack of realism in its assumption that we calculate the expected consequences of our options and choose the best of them. A vast body of social research reveals that people often act impulsively, emotionally or merely by force of habit. Think how agonizing decisions about jobs, spouses, and children can be. Were people the informed and calculating agents that rational choice theorists assume them to be, such decisions would not be particularly wrenching? Since these choices often take an emotional toll, it is easy to conclude that the theory is implausible. This conclusion, however, rests on a common misconception about the nature of rational choice.

The theory does not aim to explain what a rational person will do in a particular situation. That question lies firmly in the domain of decision theory. Genuine rational choice theories, by contrast, are concerned exclusively with social rather than individual outcomes. Given that each individual acts rationally, will the aggregate outcome therefore be "rational" or desirable? Not necessarily. Regarded as stable equilibrium, in which agents have no incentive to deviate from their course of action, given others' behaviour, social outcomes can be both unintended and undesirable. The overgrazing of the commons is a classic example of this dark side of Adam Smith's invisible hand.

Unlike decision theory, rational choice theory is inherently a multilevel enterprise. At the lower level, its models contain assumptions about individual cognitive capacities and values, among other things. At the higher level, rational choice models also contain specifications of social structures. These social structures serve both as the social and material context for individual action, and as new structures (Y) resulting from the actions of individuals whose behaviour is described by the lower level assumptions. Since norms and other kinds of institutions enter the models both as contexts for and as outcomes of action, rational choice theories do not rest on premises pertaining exclusively to individuals.

A second criticism of rational choice focuses on its motivational assumptions. Rational choice theorists regard both individual values and structural elements as equally important determinants of outcomes, but for methodological reasons their empirical applications typically place greater emphasis on social structural determinants. In consequence, rational choice explanations often are consistent with those of other general perspectives, such as structuralism and network analysis that are usually regarded as lying well within the sociological mainstream. One source of this methodological predilection lies in concerns about measurement.

Values and other internal states are far more difficult to measure than structural constraints, which are external to individuals. Measuring values from the verbal responses to direct survey questions is problematic. Some progress in measuring values is being made, however.

For example, matching models offer one means of measuring individual values indirectly without relying on peoples' responses to questions about their own internal states. The treatment of values in rational choice theory is due not only to methodological considerations; it is also a reaction to the complexity that is inherent in the multilevel nature of the theory. To reduce this complexity to more manageable limits, rational choice theorists assume some model of individual action, often one based on subjective-expected utility theory. They disagree about the most appropriate model, however. And so rational choice is more a rubric or a family of theories than a single all-encompassing one.

Perhaps the most important division separates "thin" and "thick" models of individual action. Thin rational choice models are unconcerned with the particular values (or goals) which individuals pursue. These models are based on a small number of strong assumptions: for example, that whatever an individual's values may be, they must be stable and transitive (if someone prefers a to b, and b to c, they must prefer a to c). Rational choice theories based on thin models - such as those usually found in economics and social choice theory - are highly universalistic and to that extent resemble theories in physics and biology concerning the optimal behaviour of atoms and organisms.

Thick models of individual action, advocated long ago by Max Weber, are substantively richer, for they countenance some aspects of intentionality. Since people have reasons for what they do, their behaviour is predictable only if we know what motivates them. Thick models therefore specify the individual's existing values and beliefs. There are several means of doing so, but the most popular strategy has been to assume that individuals seek maximum quantities of exchangeable private goods such as wealth and, arguably, power or prestige.

Wealth is commonly valued because it can be exchanged for a multitude of other goods in the marketplace. Thick models allow that individuals also value non exchangeable goods - that some people live for the music of Mozart, and others for the thrill of horse racing. Indeed, the models assume that for any given individual, idiosyncratic values of this sort can outweigh the common one. Hence, without knowing each person's unique value hierarchy, individual behaviour is unpredictable. As the size of groups' increases, however, these idiosyncratic values tend to cancel each other out. In many circumstances the remaining common value permits quite accurate behavioural predictions at the collective level.

Some rational choice theories specify other common values that individuals pursue, such as uncertainty reduction, local status, and distributive justice. Other rational choice theories are beginning to model the processes that might be responsible for the formation of these common values. Contrary to some perceptions, thick rational choice theories do not necessarily assume that individuals are selfish agents. These theories can postulate any individual values at all, not excluding complete altruism. What is required is merely that individuals are self-interested, not selfish.

Thin models are substantively empty. They can be made consistent after the event, therefore, with nearly any kind of behaviour. Thick ones - such as those postulating wealth-maximisation - often are just plain wrong. To the degree that the idiosyncratic values are not distributed randomly in a population, explanations based on the pursuit of exchangeable private goods such as wealth, power, and prestige will fail. Since outcomes may be partially a function of individual motivations, predictions made on the basis of thick models can be mutually inconsistent, and such inconsistencies can only be resolved on the basis of empirical evidence.

That decision theorists can routinely invalidate subjective expected utility theory is also troubling, even if they have yet to formulate an alternative superior to it. All told, the mechanisms of individual action in rational choice theory are descriptively problematic. Is a theory of higher-level outcomes invalidated by the inaccuracy of its lower-level mechanisms? Rational-choice theorists deny that it is. Not all sociological reservations about rational choice derive from misunderstanding, however. Above all, rational choice is a theory-driven enterprise: Many authors seem to value formal proofs of theories more than the confirmation of these theories on the basis of rigorous empirical tests.

Advocates often argue on its behalf, with not a little hauteur, by asserting that rational choice is the best available general theory in the social sciences. Since theories ultimately are judged by their capacity to account for empirical observations, the criticism that many rational choice theories are either false or remain untested cuts close to the bone. The appeal of rational choice in sociology is unlikely to increase substantially until the approach provides demonstrable empirical payoffs in a wide variety of substantive areas. In what follows, we review a sample of empirical applications of rational choice in sociology published in English since 1988, when the last survey of the contributions of rational choice to macro sociology appeared.

Whereas most of these are explicitly derived from rational choice premises, we also discuss several theoretically unmotivated studies that report findings consistent with rational choice. Inclusion of this latter category of studies may be questioned. After all, if such studies can be carried out without reference to rational choice, then why is the theory necessary? One answer is that rational choice provides a heuristic framework that permits the diverse findings in all of these fields to be unified. Another is that it aids in making the logical links between different theories more explicit. Finally, readers should be aware that this essay is not a survey of sociological rational choice in its entirety, for it ignores the purely theoretical developments that continue to make up the bulk of research in this field.

RECENT EMPIRICAL APPLICATIONS OF SOCIOLOGICAL RATIONAL CHOICE

Many critics readily concede that rational choice may be appropriate for the analysis of voluntary exchanges in the *Gesellschaft*, which constitutes the traditional terrain of economics. However, they contend that it can shed little or no light on social relations in the *Gemeinschaft* - those involving the family, religion, and gender. For this reason, we begin our review with recent applications in these areas.

THE FAMILY AND DEMOGRAPHY

The family was once thought to fall outside the purview of rational choice because this primordial institution engenders hot motivations - love and hate - rather than cold benefit/cost calculations. In a number of influential writings, Becker questioned the wisdom of dividing social relations into separate domains, each requiring its own distinctive analysis. Following his lead, rational choice now is routinely applied to individuals' family decisions. Two recent programmatic statements in this sub area resonate strongly with rational choice. The concept of "family adaptive strategies" captures the notion of choice under constraints (with the family as the unit of decision-making) in life course studies in sociology.

Likewise, Smith calls for a multilevel analysis of fertility. Many of the findings in the empirical literature are entirely consistent with rational choice theories. For example, Lloyd and South show that, net of individual characteristics, men's transition to first marriage is strongly influenced by the structural constraints they face, in the form of the availability of prospective partners in the local marriage market. South and Lloyd demonstrate that the aggregate divorce rates fluctuate with the structural opportunities available to spouses; the quantity and quality of potential new marital partners in the local marriage market significantly increase the risk of marital dissolution.

This substantiates Becker's suspicion that men and women continue to search for mates even while they are married. Together, these studies indicate that marriage and divorce are subject to the same external opportunities and constraints as exchanges in the market. Other research exemplifying how structural factors shape individual behaviour and social outcomes in includes Brewster's study of community effects on adolescent sexual activities; Lee *et al*'s analysis of the neighbourhood effects on residential mobility; Hoem's demonstration of the impact of legal changes on marriage rates in Sweden; and Hoem's findings concerning the effects of legal incentives on childbearing.

In contrast to marriage and divorce, standard microeconomic explanations of parenthood in the postindustrial age have not fared so well empirically. Prior to industrialisation and the implementation and enforcement of child labor laws, having children made ample economic sense to parents. But why do individuals in the post-industrial age continue to have children when their net economic benefit for doing so is negative? Friedman *et al* propose a theory of uncertainty reduction to account for parenthood in advanced industrial societies. They argue that children in the postindustrial age serve as a means to reduce uncertainty for women and couples, and they predict that those who face greater uncertainty in their lives and/or lack alternative means to reduce uncertainty are more likely to become parents.

This theory has been largely supported in its first empirical test. Once people decide to have children, when do they stop? Yamaguchi and Ferguson explain rates of stopping and spacing childbearing by assuming that parents derive higher value from having children of both sexes than from having those of a single sex. Thus they predict that parents with two boys or two girls are more likely to have a third child than are parents of a boy and a girl, and the conclusions of their analysis of census data are consistent with this prediction.

In addition to its contributions to the study of fertility, rational choice has also been applied to migration. Jasso and Rosenzweig study immigration to the United States as a matching process. On the one hand, potential immigrants must decide to emigrate from their countries of origin and choose a country of destination. On the other, host countries evaluate potential immigrants on a set of criteria and decide whom to welcome. Successful legal immigration takes place only when there is a match between the self-selective immigration decisions of foreign-born persons and the eligibility-conferring decisions of the host nations. Immigration therefore is a process of matching between two sets of actors, each attempting to achieve goals and operating under constraints created by the other.

Because migration should entail some loss of social capital, parental support ought to be crucial for the life prospects of children subsequent to family migration. Hagan *et al* analyze the mobility histories of Toronto families and find support for Coleman's expectation that the negative effects of migration are more significant in families with uninvolved fathers and unsupportive mothers.

RELIGION

Religion is another subject once deemed unpromising for rational choice analysis. This has not prevented the development of a lively rational choice literature about it, however. The rational choice approach to religion draws a close analogy between religion and the market economy. It conceives of a religious economy consisting of religious firms and religious consumers. Religious firms compete against one another to offer religious products and services to consumers, who choose between the firms. Stark and Bainbridge extend this analogy and offer a large number of propositions concerning the religious economy. They argue, for example, that the more pluralistic a religious economy is, the higher the level of religious mobilisation.

To the extent that there are many religious firms competing against each other, they will tend to specialize and cater to the particular needs of some segments of religious consumers. This specialisation and catering in turn increase the number of religious consumers actively engaged in the religious economy. This proposition has been confirmed in a number of empirical studies. A positive correlation between pluralism and religious mobilisation and commitment has been found in 17 Western nations, in 45 Catholic nations (finding an inverse relationship between Catholic monopoly and Catholic commitment), in 150 largest US cities in 1906, in 942 towns and cities in New York State from 1855 to 1865, and in 284 municipalities in Sweden.

Further, just as state regulation makes for inefficient business firms; state regulation of religion also makes for inefficient religious firms and dampens the mobilisation of religious consumers. It is well known that strict churches are strong and growing in the contemporary United States, whereas liberal ones are declining. For Iannaccone religious experience is a jointly produced collective good. Thus members of a church face a collective action problem.

Strict churches, which often impose costly and esoteric requirements on their members, are able to solve this problem by weeding out potential free riders, since only the very committed would join the church in the face of such requirements. Finke and Stark use this theory to account for the winners and losers in the history of the religious economy of the United States. Consistent with the notion that religious experience is a collective good, Iannaccone *et al* show that churches that extract more resources from their members (in the form of time and money) tend to grow in membership.

GENDER

Although critics have claimed that rational choice is oblivious to gender distinctions, and therefore is unable to account for female behaviour, here, too, there is disconfirming evidence. Thus Brinton explains persistent gender inequalities in Japan partly as a function of parents' (mostly mothers') calculated decisions to invest more in their sons' education than in their daughters'. Due to the absence of a reliable social security system and the continued importance of a patrilineal family system, Japanese parents are financially dependent on their sons in their old age. This gives parents an interest in raising financially secure sons.

By contrast, daughters will be incorporated into other families. Brinton also explains the disparity in educational attainment between Japanese men and women in rational choice terms. Japanese employers tend not to hire university-educated women because they have very few years left to work for the company before they invariably retire to get married at around age 25. University-educated women thus represent poorer investment prospects for the company than women with high school or junior college education who leave school at an earlier age and also can be hired at lower wage rates.

Given these constraints imposed by the employers, most Japanese women choose not to pursue a university education. In a study that addresses occupational specialisation by gender, Cowen, an economist, seeks to explain why so few women have become famous painters in history. His evidence shows women were discouraged from pursuing careers in the visual arts by the constraints of marriage and childbearing. Supporting Hechter, and later Friedman *et al*, Treas demonstrates that a "collectivized" financial arrangement among married couples (joint bank accounts without separate ones for husbands and wives), which increases the financial dependence of the spouses on their marriage, is strongly associated with more stable unions.

The general conclusion of Treas's study of married couples' financial organisation is that principles of transaction cost economics accurately describe the choices of both husbands and wives. Treas and Giesen's analysis of a national probability sample from the National Health and Social Life Survey shows that, while men are more likely to have extramarital affairs than women, identical considerations of opportunities, costs, and benefits underlie both men's and women's decision to engage in illicit sex. Mackie offers an intriguing explanation for the varying fates of two institutions affecting women in less developed societies.

Whereas female genital mutilation persists in Africa despite modernisation, public education, and legal prohibition, female footbinding lasted for a thousand years in China but ended in a single generation. Mackie argues that each institution is a self-enforcing convention maintained by interdependent expectations on the marriage market. Footbinding in China was overturned by the establishment of associations of parents who pledged not to footbind their daughters nor let their sons marry footbound women. Such pledge associations have not been established in Africa, however, and female genital mutilation persists there.

ORGANISATIONS

At least since Coase, rational choice analyses of organisations have proliferated. Since most of the research on capitalist firms is conducted by economists, it is not reviewed here. However, some sociologists have also made contributions. Thus Petersen analyzes the earnings of 63,000 salespersons in 178 department stores and finds that those who work under output-related payment systems (and receive either straight commission or salary plus commission) earn considerably more than those who work under non-output-related payment systems (and receive straight salary alone). Workers in the former system earn more because they are individually rewarded for working harder, while those under the latter system do not because they have no incentive to work harder.

Hedstrom combines rational choice with network analysis to explain the spatial diffusion of labor unions in Sweden from 1890 to 1940. Individuals' decisions to form a labor union are influenced not only by their expectations of what others will do, but also by their knowledge of what others in their immediate network have done in the past.

As anticipated, both spatial properties of the network and its density turn out to be important determinants of the speed and success of labor union formation. Bruderl *et al* explain career mobility in a large West German company in terms of the organisational structure and hierarchies, and Greve similarly explains job mobility in Norway in terms of organisational diversity.

Haveman uses the characteristics of the industry and organisational ecology at the meso level to account for individual careers and job turnover at the micro level, which then aggregate to tenure distributions at the organisational level. Her work therefore exemplifies the multilevel causal structure (albeit meso-micro in this case) typical of rational choice theory. Abell studies industrial producer cooperatives in Tanzania, Sri Lanka, and Fiji and concludes that the key to their success lies in support organisations.

While agricultural and commercial sectors have distinct capital advantages over the industrial sector in these developing nations, these established sectors have no compelling incentive to promote cooperatives. Abell and Mahoney examine similar cooperatives in India, Peru, and Senegal and note that one of the determinants of their success in these countries is the solidarity, whether exogenously or endogenously produced, of cooperative members. Other rational choice sociologists focus on non capitalist firms and on unconventional organisations like urban and criminal gangs. Walder's analysis of Chinese factories focuses on the attainment of compliance in a communist system.

Although workers in capitalist firms usually are motivated both by firm-internal sanctions and by pressure from the labor market, the latter source of incentives was largely unavailable in China at the time of Walder's study. Instead, motivation was provided by much stronger dependence and monitoring mechanisms than those typically found in capitalist firms. Workers in China depended on factory leaders for the satisfaction of a broad range of social benefits that could not be satisfied elsewhere. Dependence was further increased by workers' inability to switch jobs. Nee accounts for the relative success of private firms over their state and collective counterparts in the transitional economy of China in terms of the former's transaction cost advantage over the latter.

In contrast, Walder attributes China's rapid industrial growth under its transitional economy to the higher efficiency of public firms, especially those run by local governments, which face different financial incentives and constraints than the central government. Two notable qualitative contributions to the literature on organisations are Gambetta's analysis of the Sicilian Mafia, and Jankowski's ethnographic study of urban street gangs in three American cities.

For Gambetta, the Mafia is a firm offering private protection in a society where state protection often is unreliable. (Jankowski's gangs also offer protection for the residents of low-income neighbourhoods who are not well-served by police.) Because the Mafia lacks legitimacy and cannot guarantee its products, it must first convince potential customers of their quality. Gambetta interprets seemingly bizarre aspects of the Mafia - its arcane rituals, obscure symbols, and blood ceremonies - as attempts to make credible commitments to customers and rivals alike.

CRIME AND DEVIANCE

Deterrence theory has long been identified as an application of rational choice. With Cornish and Clarke, rational choice theories of crime emerged to explain criminal behaviour as a function of expected reward and punishment, weighted by the subjective probability of detection. Jacobs' interviews with 40 active crack dealers show that their behaviour and their interpersonal strategies are jointly determined by their desire to maximize profit from their sales and to minimize the possibility of arrest by undercover narcotics officers.

The dealers, who mostly interact with anonymous clientele, employ perceptual shorthand on unfamiliar clients; these are observational and testing techniques to detect deception on the part of the clients. Horney and Marshall's analysis of data collected from incarcerated adult offenders of major felonies confirms that the criminals' subjective perception of the risk of detection is realistically updated by their own experience in the particular crime; those who commit the crime often without getting caught lower their expectation of detection while those who are caught most of the time subsequently increase their perception of risk.

Recently, rational choice perspectives on crime have converged with the routine activity approach. Both distinguish between criminality (the decision to become involved in a particular form of crime) and crime (an actual criminal event), and explain the latter in terms of opportunities - the simultaneous presence of criminal target and absence of risk of detection. A distinctive thrust of rational choice theories of crime is their conception of criminality as a function of higher expected material returns from criminal activities relative to those from conventional pursuits.

Williams, Jankowski, and MacLeod all provide ethnographic accounts to show that teenagers in low-income neighbourhoods make deliberate decisions to pursue criminal activities because few legitimate alternative means to make as much money are available to them. Jankowski notes that, in some chronically poor neighbourhoods, gang membership has become a family tradition, and many parents actively encourage their children to belong to the same gangs to which they themselves belonged when they were younger, much as parents with Ivy League educations encourage their children to attend their alma maters. Pezzin argues that economic incentives and opportunity costs exert a powerful influence on criminal career duration and desistance choice.

Her analysis of the National Longitudinal Survey of Youth shows that future expected criminal earnings have a strong negative effect on the decision to terminate a criminal career among youths between the ages of 16 and 22. Since the effect of the availability of legal income-generating activities is just as strong as that of perceived cost of punishment, Pezzin argues that the carrot may work just as efficiently as the stick in shortening the length of criminal careers. Pampel and Gartner provide a multilevel explanation for variations in homicide rates in 18 advanced industrial nations. Other researchers stress the need to include institutional factors in the explanations of crime. Hechter and Kanazawa use Hechter's theory of group solidarity to explain the low crime rates in contemporary Japan.

They argue that the higher dependence of the Japanese on their groups and their higher visibility within the groups increase their conformity to social norms. They reject cultural explanations of low crime rates in Japan by showing that China and South Korea, which share many cultural characteristics with Japan, have higher crime rates, and that the same mechanisms of dependence and visibility work to induce conformity among American auto workers in Japanese transplants factories. Petee *et al*'s finding that the deterrent effects of informal sanctions are the strongest among communities characterized by higher levels of integration is also consistent with Hechter's theory, which predicts that compliance to norms is a multiplicative function of the dependence and the efficiency of social control.

Finally, one of the most influential modern theories of crime and deviance, Hirschi's control theory, has a strong rational choice flavor. This theory explains juveniles' propensity to engage in delinquency in terms of preferences ("attachment," "belief"), opportunity cost ("commitment"), and resource scarcity ("involvement"). Nagin and Paternoster, among others, provide empirical support for control theory.

COMPARATIVE-HISTORICAL SOCIOLOGY

Many have claimed that the scope of rational choice theory is limited to the capitalist era, for previous social formations were much less individualistic. However, rational choice historical sociologists have accounted for variation in state autonomy and policy implementation in absolutist societies on the basis of dependence and control mechanisms. Thus Kiser suggests that the most autonomous early modern monarchs had independent resources and faced the weakest monitoring (legislative and judicial) institutions. Kiser *et al* show that in the case of war - a policy that rulers tended to favor more than their subjects - high ruler autonomy resulted in more frequent war initiation in early modern Western Europe.

Even the most autonomous rulers must delegate authority to agents if they are to implement policies, however. Hence, agency theory ought to cast light on the causes and consequences of tax administration. For instance, when the ruler's monitoring capacity is poor, tax farming should be a more efficient means of providing state revenue than bureaucratic administration because it gives agents stronger incentives to collect taxes and surrender them to rulers. Supportive evidence is found both in early modern Prussia and Imperial China. In a similar vein, Adams explains the failure of the Dutch East Indies Company, and contrasting success of the English East Indies Company, in terms of the problems that the European owners faced in controlling their agents in Asia.

The Dutch company collapsed when colonial servants saw better alternative opportunities offered by the English company, and the Dutch owners were not able from afar to stop their servants' defection. Explaining major institutional shifts is one of the great challenges of historical sociology. Both of the popular perspectives in historical sociology - structuralism and cultural analysis - would appear to face insuperable difficulties in accounting for institutional change endogenously.

One such institutional change is the subject of Friedman's recent study. Until the late nineteenth century, in all Western societies the custody of children after their parents' divorce or separation was presumptively and routinely awarded to their fathers.

Then, between 1880 and 1920, in all of these countries presumptive custody shifted from the father to the mother. Due to rising divorce rates, these states faced the prospect of having to support a large number of divorced women on welfare. In order to avoid this expenditure, Friedman argues, they transferred the custody of children from fathers to mothers, making fathers responsible for the financial welfare of their children. Divorced fathers' child support payments also secondarily contributed to the economic welfare of their former spouses, the custodial mothers. By this means, all Western countries avoided supporting divorced women and took responsibility only for the education of children.

POLITICAL SOCIOLOGY

Although collective action is an abiding concern of rational choice research on politics, much of the effort has been theoretical and therefore falls outside of the purview of this review. There are notable exceptions, however. In an impressive study, Brustein seeks to explain the rise of the Nazi party in interwar Germany. Hitler's rise is often ascribed to his party's manipulation of emotional voters susceptible to ressentiment, but Brustein argues that the popularity of the National Socialists was due to their strategic adoption of policies that appealed to the pocketbook interests of a large and socially heterogeneous part of the electorate.

One of his intriguing conclusions is that Hitler had to conceal his anti Semitism in order to gain popularity among blue-collar workers. Brustein's theory is strongly supported by his analysis of data on more than 42,000 Nazi members who joined the party between 1925 and 1933. Survey data collected and analyzed by Opp *et al* reveal how the macro outcome of the successful protest movement in East Germany in 1989 was an aggregate result of the values, incentives, and network ties of Germans at the micro level. These individuals' decisions to participate, in turn, were influenced by macro level political conditions. In contrast, Shlapentokh accounts for the absence of collective protests in Russia in the face of deteriorating social and economic conditions in 1992-1994 in terms of individuals' expectations that such collective action would not be successful.

STRATIFICATION AND MOBILITY

Human capital theory long has been the principal rational choice approach to stratification. A vast sociological literature on labor markets compares its merits to those of status attainment and structural perspectives. However, a new rational choice approach to stratification has been developed. Logan employs a two-sided logit methodology to model employment outcomes (the matching of workers to jobs) as a function of explicitly rational choices made by workers and employers under structural constraints.

The jobs that employers supply function as the constraints within which workers make their choices, given their preferences; the supply of workers functions as the constraint within which employers make their choices, given their preferences. Further, the preferences of the employers for certain types of workers create the constraints for the workers, and the preferences of the workers for certain types of jobs create the constraints for the employers. Logan's analysis of General Social Survey data showcases the utility of this new method. Until 1967, secondary schools in Ireland charged their students tuition fees, and these costs were thought to be barriers to educational attainment for children from working-class families.

However, when these tuition fees were eliminated by the educational reform of 1967, access to secondary education did not become more egalitarian. Raftery and Hout argue that, due to the high employment rate and high wages in the Irish economy in the late 1960s, the opportunity costs of continuing education (in the form of forgone wages) were high, relative to the cost of tuition fees, now eliminated. Thus, it did not make much economic sense for Irish children of working-class families to continue formal education and postpone full-time employment, even in the absence of tuition fees, and the educational reform failed to have the intended effect. Breen and Whelan's analysis concurs with Raftery and Hout.

Walder provides a macro-meso explanation of stratification among organisations in a socialist economy, and he tests it with survey data gathered in a large Chinese industrial city. Budgetary resources of the local government and its dependence on a work organisation jointly determine how much revenue the local government extracts from the organisation. The level of revenue extraction by the government determines (at the meso level) the organisation's abilities to provide benefits to its employees, which then aggregates (at the macro level) to inequalities among organisations. Walder's explanation of organisational stratification in China is therefore another example of the multilevel causal structure of rational choice theory.

RACE AND ETHNIC RELATIONS

Most of the rational choice research in this area has been theoretical, with relatively few empirical applications. Clark, however, finds empirical support for Schelling's theory that slight differences in residents' preference for the racial composition of their neighbourhood quickly lead to extreme segregation. Nee *et al* contend that the structure of ethnic and ethnically mixed economies in Los Angeles is a function of the economic opportunities and constraints that Asian immigrants face as well as of their skills and qualifications.

While most Asian immigrants prefer to work outside of their ethnic enclaves to take advantage of higher pay and better working conditions, many are unable to do so because of their lack of occupational and language skills. One means of upward mobility available to immigrants of little occupational and language skills is entrepreneurship. Sanders and Nee demonstrate that the self-employment status among Asian and Hispanic immigrants is strongly facilitated by human capital (foreign-earned formal education) and financial and social capital available from their family members. Those with spouses and other family members who can contribute to their business are more likely to succeed as entrepreneurs than are single immigrants.

Split labor market theory can explain how ethnic and racial antagonism arises, but it cannot account for interracial solidarity. Brown and Boswell use Heckathorn's theory of group-mediated social control to address the possibility of interracial solidarity or strikebreaking under split labor market conditions. Their qualitative comparative analysis of the Great Steel Strike of 1919 largely supports their predictions. Chai's theory of ethno genesis seeks to explain the location of ethnic boundaries in developing societies. The theory proposes a link between cooperation and altruism in small, rural communities.

Then it predicts how these altruistic preferences, in conjunction with structural factors and rational behaviour, generate boundaries for larger-scale ethnic collective action. The theory is applied to the creation of new ethnic groups among the Pan-Igbo in Nigeria, the Luba-Kasai in Zaire, the Pan-Malays in Malaysia, and the Muhajir in Pakistan. Group process researchers mostly concentrate on the dynamics of dyads and small groups. Research in this tradition began with Emerson's seminal analysis of exchange relations in dyads, which was later extended to exchange networks.

Currently there is a debate about the determinants of dyadic cohesion among self-interested rational actors. On the one hand, Kollock argues that when the outcome of an exchange is uncertain, individuals make commitments to particular exchange partners in order to reduce uncertainty. On the other, Lawler and Yoon's theory of relational cohesion maintains that individuals experience positive affect from successfully negotiated and completed exchanges. Then self-interested actors develop affective commitment to particular exchange partners, even in the face of more attractive offers, in order to consume this positive affect from continued exchange with the same partner.

Sometimes research on group processes has clear macro level implications. Orbell and Dawes' "cognitive miser" theory explains social welfare, order, and efficiency at the macro level in terms of dyadic interactions at the micro level. Their theory argues that intending cooperators are more likely to play dyadic Prisoner's Dilemma games than intending defectors, when they have the option not to play. Then the outcomes of most completed games are mutual cooperation, whereby the players enjoy the fruit of cooperation, which aggregates to order and economic surplus at the macro level. Their laboratory experiment confirms the theory's crucial hypothesis that intending cooperators are more likely to choose to play than intending defectors.

The problem of cooperation and public goods provision is usually conceived of as an n-person Prisoner's Dilemma game. In contrast, Diekmann's "volunteer's dilemma" game captures the problem of cooperation in situations where there is a potential diffusion of responsibility. The public good in the volunteer's dilemma is produced by a single volunteer (with the effect of additional volunteers completely superfluous), and there is no pure dominant strategy; players are better off defecting if there is at least one cooperator, but better off cooperating if there is none.

The volunteer's dilemma points to the utility of sociological rational choice theory in that the use of a strictly game-theoretic solution - a mixed Nash equilibrium strategy - leads to highly inefficient outcomes. An optimal level of cooperation requires communication and coordination among actors, which is fostered by social norms. The experimental evidence shows that subjects do not employ strictly game-theoretic solutions.

MEDICAL SOCIOLOGY

Whereas medicine has been an important site for the application of behavioural decision theory, rational choice is in its infancy in medical sociology. Thoits, however, calls for more emphasis on human agency, and on the deliberate choices that individuals make, in the study of stress and depression. Her analysis of panel data shows that individuals are often able to solve potential problems in their lives (and thus are not affected by them), and that only those they fail to solve lead to psychological symptoms.

Although Pescosolido's "social organisation strategy" framework ostensibly is critical of rational choice, it is entirely consistent with the version of rational choice presented in the present essay. Her analysis of individuals seeking medical help specifically incorporates network structures and uses network ties and information gathered from past interactions as resources and social capital.

Broadhead and Heckathorn conceive of AIDS prevention as a collective action problem. They use agency theory and Heckathorn's theory of group-mediated social control to argue that peer-driven intervention programs are more effective in combating AIDS. Extensive ethnographic data support their contention.

Sociological rational choice is an inherently multilevel enterprise. It seeks to account for social outcomes on the basis of both social context and individual action. In this respect it often differs, at least in emphasis, from other (thin) versions of rational choice theory that are employed in much economic analysis and game theory. Sociological rational choice is beginning to make empirical contributions to a broad range of substantive topics in the discipline. While applications of rational choice in subfields like politics, labor markets, formal organisations, and criminology by now are traditional, the approach has also begun to make empirical advances in areas formerly regarded as inhospitable, such as the family, gender, and religion.

At the same time, a growing number of theoretically uncommitted empirical researchers are testing rational choice theories - sometimes unwittingly - in their own domains. These studies will reveal much about the scope and limits of rational choice theory. Invariably, their findings will strengthen certain versions of rational choice theory at the expense of others. Beyond the crucial task of subjecting existing rational choice theories to empirical tests, we discern three future directions for developing sociological rational choice theory. To better explain social outcomes arising from individual action, rational choice theorists must begin to understand the origin and the nature of values that motivate human behaviour.

Values - and the preferences derived from them - are one of two major categories of determinants of individual behaviour in rational choice theory, the other being institutional constraints. Rational choice has been mute on the origin and nature of individual values. This silence has been justified under the *dictum de gustibus non est disputandum*. Due to the difficulty of arriving at valid and reliable measures of internal states, rational choice theorists usually impute values to actors by assumption. The typical value assumption has been wealth maximisation because wealth is highly fungible. Thus actors who may hold various idiosyncratic values can be expected to pursue wealth as a means to achieve their divergent goals.

Yet some research also has advanced atypical value assumptions, including uncertainty reduction, local status, distributive justice, and regret-dissonance reduction. Even if we know what values and preferences actors hold, their decision-making mechanisms are contested. Hence the study of decision algorithms is a second promising field of inquiry. Subjective expected utility maximisation theory, the foundation of most macroscopic rational choice theories, posits that actors are forward-looking maximizers. Based on the available information and their best estimates of what the future holds, actors assign subjective probabilities to various future states of the world and make their decisions according to these subjective probabilities.

However, critics have pointed out that this forward-looking process of decision-making is cognitively too demanding for most human actors. Others have proposed alternative decision algorithms. Macy argues that individuals are backward-looking adaptive learners who adjust their decisions on the basis of the past outcomes associated with their choices, and he provides experimental evidence supporting his contention. In contrast, Heckathorn argues that individuals sometimes are sideways-looking cultural imitators whose decisions emulate those made by their neighbors who are doing well. In his view, whether actors are forward-, backward-, or sideways-looking depends on the nature of available information about the future.

If genuine and accurate information is available about the future, then actors will assess the subjective probabilities of various states of the world as predicted by the subjective expected utility maximisation model. If the past is the best predictor of the future, then actors will be backward-looking. If the future is best known by observing who is doing well in the present, then actors will be sideways-looking imitators. The ultimate challenge for sociological rational choice theory is explaining the emergence of institutions.

Unlike values and preferences, institutions are intersubjective and therefore more easily measurable. So far this has not led to concerted research on institutional emergence, however. Still, a handful of forays have been made. Contributions to Hechter *et al* begin to tackle the emergence of a small handful of institutions, and Coleman provides one framework for understanding how norms emerge among actors with specific interests and resources. Logan's two-sided logit model offers a promising new way to trace the origins of institutional constraints for actors to their exchange partners' preferences. And Chai and Hechter propose an elementary model for the emergence of the state and of social order. However, an endogenous theory of institutional emergence remains a distant goal at this time.

7

Social Exclusion and Social Solidarity

The changes affecting the poor were changes in kind as well as degree, in quantity, in ideas, attitudes, beliefs perceptions, values. They were changes in what may be called the "moral imagination". Since the mid-1970s, the advanced capitalist democracies have been undergoing a process of profound economic restructuring. As a consequence, new social problems have emerged that appear to challenge the assumptions underlying Western welfare states. While universal social policies still insure against risks predictable from a shared life-cycle, career pattern, and family structure, a standardized life course can no longer be assumed. More and more people suffer insecurity, are dependent upon "residual" means-tested programmes, or are without any form of social protection. In the countries of the European Union, 50 million people live below a poverty line set at one-half the national median income; 16 million people (10.S per cent of the workforce) are officially registered as unemployed, of whom more than half have been unemployed for over a year.

How are we to understand these developments? As Himmelfarb noted, earlier economic and social upheavals brought about a shift in the "moral imagination", giving us the concepts of "poverty" and "unemployment". Similarly, today's transformations are giving rise to new conceptions of social disadvantage: the "underclass", the "new poverty", and "social exclusion". This chapter traces the evolution of the term "exclusion" over time, notably but not exclusively in France. It focuses on definitions of the term indicating its numerous connotations, and distinguishes three paradigms within which social exclusion is embedded (solidarity, specialisation and monopoly), presenting the theory underlying each, with clarificatory remarks. Finally, the economic dimensions of the three paradigms are discussed. In conclusion, questions regarding the significance of exclusion in politics and social policy are raised.

THE EXCLUSION DISCOURSE

Exclusion became the subject of debate in France during the 1960s. Politicians, activists, officials, journalists and academics made vague and ideological references to the poor as les exclusion. However, the exclusion discourse did not become widespread until the economic crisis. As successive social and political crises erupted in France during the 1980s, exclusion came to be applied to more and more types of social disadvantage and the continual redefinition of the term to encompass new social groups and problems gave rise to its diffuse connotations.

The identification of exclusion as a social problem occurred just as France was belatedly completing its system of standard social provision and as postwar economic growth was slowing down. The coining of the term is generally attributed to Rene Lenoir, who was then Secretary of State for Social Action in the (Gaullist) Chirac Government. He estimated that "the excluded" made up one-tenth of the French population: the mentally and the physically handicapped, suicidal people, aged invalids, abused children, drug addicts, delinquents, single parents, multi-problem households, marginal, asocial persons, and other "social misfits".

All were social categories unprotected under social insurance. Since the mid-1970s, France has introduced numerous policies designed explicitly to combat exclusion of these sorts so that today, the handicapped and single mothers, for example, tend to fall outside both the rhetoric of exclusion and the purview of commissions on "integration" and "insertion". During the 1970s, the French Left also began to distinguish between objective and subjective exclusion. The latter, drawing upon the existentialism of Jean-Paul Sartre and the participatory ideology of Catholic social action, referred to alienation and the loss of personal autonomy under advanced capitalism.

In stressing subjective exclusion, the discourse moved away from political expressions of class conflict towards the struggles of mass urban and social movements. Exclusion meant being treated as an object - a condition which could apply to virtually any individual or group. If exclusion and "insertion" were used as ideological terms during the 1970s, economic recovery from the oil crisis soon made it clear to the public that some were being excluded from economic growth. As Lionel Stoleru observed, poverty was a problem that economic growth could not resolve. Thus, during the late 1970s, the excluded referred to "the ones that economic growth forgot".

By the early 1980s, the use of the term "insertion" in political discourse shifted from a focus on the handicapped to young people leaving school without the adequate skills to obtain a job. Bertrand Schwartz, who wrote a report, *L'insertion professionnelle et sociale des jeunes*, for Prime Minister Pierre Mauroy in 1981, headed a new policy for locally based programmes for the "insertion" of young people into employment. Over the next decade and a half, and after street demonstrations by young people protesting against reforms of church schools and education, universities, and minimum wages, the State instituted a wide variety of "insertion" policies to help young people in difficulty.

By the mid-1980s, both the Right and the Communist opposition were blaming the Socialist Government for rising unemployment and what was being called "the new poverty". In symbolic politics, the power to name a social problem has vast implications for the policies considered suitable to address it. Thus, in response to the opposition's emphasis on the new poverty and inequality, the Government took to speaking of "exclusion". The term referred not only to the rise in long-term and recurrent unemployment, but also to the growing instability of social bonds: family instability, single-member households, social isolation, and the decline of class solidarity based on unions, the labour market, and the working-class neighbourhood and social networks.

There were not only materials but also spiritual and symbolic aspects to this phenomenon. As I will show, this exclusion discourse drew upon the rich Republican rhetorical tradition of France to describe the difficulty of establishing solidarity between individuals and groups and the larger society. The prototypical definitions of social exclusion can be found in the publications of the Commissariat General du Plan (CGP) [general planning commission] which has recognized the State's responsibility to nourish "social cohesion". The current Planning Commissioner, Jean-Baptiste de Foucauld, argues that preventing exclusion requires a conception of social justice different from the one underlying the postwar social consensus which simply insured the population against predictable risks.

The welfare state must bind itself to the ethical and cultural values that define citizenship not only in the form of rights, but as a particular relation to "the other". A more personalized, participatory welfare state should rest on new principles of social cohesion, sharing, and integration. This new citizenship "enables us to reconcile our tradition of solidarity with the rise of individualism". In another CGP account, exclusion is used as a metaphor for the "social polyphony of post-modern society", for the lack of communication between individuals and groups or for their mutual incomprehension which prevent them from negotiating on mutual recognition and a sense of belonging.

The long review by Martine Xiberras of the sociological literature upon which this diagnosis was based defined exclusion as the result of a gradual breakdown of the social and symbolic bonds - economic, institutional, and individually significant - that normally tie the individual to society. Exclusion entails a risk for each individual in terms of material and symbolic exchange with the larger society. In the terms of Durkheimian rhetoric, exclusion threatens society as whole with the loss of collective values and the destruction of the social fabric.

So in this particular case, integration means solidarity, that is, the ability to re-establish mutual recognition by all parties in society. For the regulating State, this would mean the ability to handle the expression of a multitude of beliefs and values. The emphasis on "insertion" and integration as the appropriate responses to exclusion is reflected in the titles of a wide variety of new social programmes introduced in France during the 1980s. For example, the social activists who advocated the revenu minimum d'insertion (RMI) [minimum income for social integration] adopted the Republican rhetoric of "solidarity", "cohesion", "social bonds", and a "new social contract" in Jean-Jacques Rousseau's sense.

One analyst, after claiming to strip away the multiple and ideological meanings of "insertion", then went on to define it as a form of regulation of the social bond and a response to a perceived threat to social cohesion. The discourse was so compelling that, by the 1988 presidential campaign, the electoral manifestos of both Right and Left included proposals for a minimum income to promote "insertion ". However, subsequent political crises served to expand the meanings of exclusion and "insertion". Since in Republican France the Nation and the State are one, *les exclus* came to mean the "pariahs of the nation", in the words of Paul-Marie de la Gorce.

Political and social developments in the 1980s in which the term exclusion came to acquire further nuances of meaning include the rise of xenophobia, open political attacks on immigrants and restrictions on their rights; the consequent emergence of new anti-racist movements like SOS-Racisme and France-Plus, which mobilized mass demonstrations; and the ongoing public debate about integration and Republican values occasioned by some Muslim girls wearing headscarves at their state, non-denominational schools. In January 1990 came the establishment of the Secretariat General a l'Integration [general secretariat for integration], an indication of the sense of crisis in French Republican values.

Finally, exclusion encompassed the issue of the banlieues, the deprived outer suburbs. It became possible to associate the related rhetorics of integration of immigrants, youth problems, and economic exclusion in a spatial sense after a series of violent incidents in suburban housing estates during the 1980s and early 1990s. Residents of these deprived suburbs were increasingly described as "excluded". Through ongoing state decentralisation and reform of social and housing services, policies to combat juvenile delinquency, the neighbourhood social development programme (DSQ), and the creation in 1991 of a fully-fledged Ministry for Urban Affairs, the State sought to combat "urban exclusion".

Again, programmes were couched in Republican terms: *prets locatifs aids d'insertion* [housing loans to assist integration], *fonds de solidarite logement* [solidarity housing funds], and programme development-solidarite [solidarity and development programme], to name but a few. From France, the discourse of exclusion rapidly spread across the rest of Europe. In 1989, the Council of Ministers of Social Affairs of the then European Community passed a resolution to fight "social exclusion" and to foster integration and a "Europe of Solidarity". The European Commission's 1994 White Paper, Growth, competitiveness, employment, called for fighting exclusion and "the poverty which so degrades men and women and splits society in two". Today, Denmark, Germany, Italy, Portugal, France and Belgium in particular, have introduced new institutions to take action on social exclusion.

US President Clinton himself took up the rhetoric of exclusion in late 1993 when, speaking of inner city problems, he remarked, "It's not an underclass any more. It's an outer class. "But an attentive ear discerns some differences of meaning across the Atlantic. In October 1994, the President remarked, "to rebuild a society that has been pressured both in our inner cities [and] our isolated rural areas is going to take a concerted effort that starts with parents, churches and community groups and private business people and people at the local level. The Federal Government cannot be the salvation of that. We have to rebuild the bonds of society."

DEFINING EXCLUSION

Given the varied usages of the term, one might justifiably ask what precisely is meant by exclusion. The remainder of this chapter seeks to answer this question by distinguishing three paradigms within which the notion of exclusion is embedded. By all accounts, defining exclusion is not an easy task. One European Union document conceded that "it is difficult to come up with a simple definition". Similarly, a recent review of sociological theories of exclusion concluded:

In fact, observers agree on only one point: the impossibility of having a single, simple criterion with which to define exclusion. The numerous surveys and reports on exclusion all reveal the profound helplessness of the experts and responsible officials. Indeed, the CGP in France, although responsible for designing and evaluating policies to combat exclusion, also recognized how difficult it is to define the term and to synthesize existing theories. The CGP's Commission on Social Cohesion and the Prevention of Exclusion concluded that:

Every attempt at establishing typology is inevitably reductionist, and all the more so in cases of excluded population groups or those facing exclusion. The factors bringing about exclusion - whether originating in individual, family or socio-economic circumstances - are numerous, fluctuate and interact in such a way that, often, they end up by reinforcing each other.

Thus, exclusion appears to be a vague term, loaded with numerous economic, social, political, and cultural connotations and dimensions. Despite attempts at official definitions,... in the end, the notion of exclusion is permeated with both sense and nonsense and is liable to misinterpretation; after all the concept can be made to express pretty well anything, including even the pique of someone who cannot get everything he wants.

Clearly, the expression is so evocative, ambiguous, multidimensional and elastic that it can be defined in many different ways. Yet the difficulty of defining exclusion and the fact that it is interpreted differently according to context and time also can be seen as an opportunity. The discourse of exclusion may serve as a window through which to view political cultures. This chapter argues that exclusion is polysemic, i.e. it has multiple meanings and therefore requires extensive semantic definition. The different meanings of social exclusion and the uses to which the term is put are embedded in conflicting social science paradigms and political ideologies.

Thomas Kuhn describes a paradigm as "a constellation of beliefs, values, and techniques and so on shared by the members of a given community". Paradigms "specify not only what sorts of entities the universe does contain but also, by implication, those that it does not". In effect, they are ontologies that render reality comprehensible and that mingle elements of what "is" and what "ought to be". When paradigms conflict, practitioners speak from incommensurable viewpoints using the same language to mean different things. In what follows, I introduce three paradigms of social exclusion and indicate how each accounts for economic disadvantages like poverty and long-term unemployment.

EXCLUSION IN FRENCH REPUBLICANISM

Whereas poverty and inequality have become accepted concepts in social science, it is more accurate to consider the term "exclusion" as a "keyword", in Raymond Williams' sense, in French Republican discourse. It not only originated in France, but is deeply anchored in a particular interpretation of French revolutionary history and Republican thought. From this perspective, "exclusion" is conceived not simply as an economic or political phenomenon, but as a deficiency of "solidarity", a break in the social fabric.

The moral discourse of "social solidarity" rejected both liberal individualism and political representation (or citizenship) as sufficient bases for defining social integration. Rather, it sought a "third way" that would reconcile individual rights with state responsibility and socialist rejection of exploitation. The concept of "poverty" which originated in the United Kingdom was discredited in France by its association with Christian charity, the ancient regime, and utilitarian liberalism. Socialists incorporated "poverty" into the broader category of "inequality", making it a labour issue. Republicans, however, rejected both liberal individualism and socialism in favour of the distinctively "social" idea of "solidarity", which legitimized the Third Republic.

Seeing the State as the embodiment of the General Will of the Nation and the moral duties of citizens, Republican solidarity justified the establishment of public institutions to further social integration. Under that banner, French "social policies became parts of a more general rationalisation of collective authority". In France, social security did not result from working-class struggles or from the overwhelming rise in poverty and urban misery, as it did in the United Kingdom. Rather, social reform expressed the perfection of Republican democracy and the collective responsibility for any citizen suffering from the failures of the State. The idea of social solidarity allowed the State to assume responsibility for social aid. In the Revolutionary rhetoric, equality meant that the Republic must promise citizens subsistence or assure them a right to work. In return, assisted citizens have a duty to work and to participate in public life.

Solidarity mingled notions of Catholic charity with Revolutionary rhetoric on fraternity and nineteenth-century working-class mutual aid. In contrast to traditional Christian charity, solidarity had a philanthropic or humanist element based on compassion, equality, and a more secular morality. Coined by Pierre Leroux and propagated by Leon Bourgeois, the term solidarity was more humanist than it was organic in its reconciliation of the feeling of belonging to the collectivity with the demand for individual fulfilment. Thus, solidarity had both a subjective aspect in individual experience, borrowed from liberalism, and an objective component, grounded in socialism and expressed in principles of social and political organisation.

The mutual aid movement contributed the notion that solidarity comes from the society, justifying social protection policies. From the sentimental vision of the social bond as sympathy, solidarity developed into a logical, secular moral system of rights and duties underlying future social policies. The work of Emile Durkheim was "the climax of a long intellectual struggle to demonstrate the interdependence of social solidarity". Indeed, reconciling the needs of State and society was a constant preoccupation of nineteenth-century French political philosophers. Since that time, the Republic sought to create a "social bond" (lien social) with the poor, a bond which is central to the Republican concept of solidarity.

In Revolutionary thought, the social bond created a "quasi-contract uniting the individual to the species and to the collectivity of his peers". Rousseau, who coined the term lien social of the Manuscrit de Geneve, saw the social bond as natural and, hence, communitarian. The Law and the General Will would bring about a distinctively "social" conviviality that went beyond formal, civil or legal equality. As Rousseau argued in The social contract, the State is composed "of morality, of custom, above all, of public opinion". Over time, Republican solidarity came to encompass cultural as well as political criteria of citizenship.

Indeed, the State defends the superior interests of the Nation - the General Will - over those of the communes and ethnic groups. According to Republican values, *les moeurs republicaines*, individual citizens are less bearers of rights than participants in a communal civil life, a public life of fraternity. Such moral unity and equality demanded abolition of feudal representative bodies that competed with the State for citizens' loyalty and in fact oppressed individuals. Throughout the nineteenth century, the laws on association were a major preoccupation in France until the passage in 1901 of the law on associations which created public bodies that shared the legal and moral authority of the State in return for registering and then submitting to state regulation. The law officially recognized religious and voluntary associations partly in order to control and relegate them to the private sphere.

Whereas social integration under the old regime rested on the Estates (les etats), the State (l'Etat) became th e new basis for social integration. This "Jacobin" State - strong, unitary, centralized, egalitarian, universalist, and secular - actively sought to assimilate regional, national, and religious cultures into a single, distinctive conception of citizenship and national civilisation. The State incorporated mediating institutions in order to reconcile and synthesize separate interests and memberships. The term "social bond" is most fully discussed in Durkheim's Division of labour in society where the term "solidarity" specified two sorts of social bond, the organic and the mechanical, that morally regulated individual behaviour. Solidarity referred to distinctively "social" relations, in contrast to political or market relations. Thus, Durkheim rejected liberal, individualist, utilitarian, or "Anglo-Saxon" notions of the social contract, in which social relations are economically motivated, commercial, and competitive, the State is minimal, and interested free exchange and cultural and political pluralism are valued.

THREE PARADIGMS

In contrast with these distinctive French Republican conceptions, challenges to Republican ideology and the adoption of exclusion discourse in other national contexts imparted meanings to the term more properly considered within other paradigms of social disadvantage. For example, liberal reconstructions of exclusion concentrate on various forms of discrimination, isolation, and the cross-cutting or cumulative personal characteristics of excluded individuals which are often generalized into the idea of an "underclass". The European Union increasingly uses an evolving, social democratic notion of exclusion based on T. H. Marshall's idea of social citizenship, recementing the term to notions of inequality and the discourse of social rights.

For this reason, the threefold typology of the multiple meanings of exclusion presented here distinguishes between different theoretical perspectives, political ideologies, and national discourses. Based on different notions of social integration, I call these types the solidarity, specialisation, and monopoly paradigms. Each paradigm attributes exclusion to a different cause and is grounded in a different political philosophy: Republicanism, liberalism, and social democracy. Each provides an explanation of multiple forms of social disadvantage - economic, social, political, and cultural - and thus encompasses theories of citizenship and racial-ethnic inequality as well as poverty and long-term unemployment.

All three paradigms are cast into relief when contrasted with conservative notions that present social integration in organic, racial, or corporatist terms and with neo-Marxist conceptions of the capitalist social order which deny the possibility of social integration to begin with. Exclusion not only varies in meaning according to national and ideological contexts. Another reason it is difficult to define is that the empirical referents of the idea of exclusion are not always discussed in that terminology. The concept - if often conflated with the new poverty and inequality, discrimination and the underclass - is also expressed in such terms as superfluity, irrelevance, marginality, foreignness, alterity, closure, disaffiliation, dispossession, deprivation, and destitution. This means that exclusion must also be analysed "onomasiologically ", defining the same concept with reference to more than one term. Identifying the many synonyms of exclusion makes it possible to delimit the term conceptually and empirically.

The multiple, often contradictory, connotations and synonyms of exclusion transform it into an "essentially contested concept", in that the proper use of it "inevitably involves endless disputes". Essentially contested concepts are usually appraisive, complex, open in meaning, and explicable in terms of their parts, so that selecting from among the mutually exclusive meanings of exclusion necessarily entails the adoption of particular values and world views. Prior to recasting social exclusion as a general phenomenon or a scientific concept transcending national and political contexts, the values underlying its usage should be made explicit in order to clarify the implicit objectives of anti-exclusion policies.

Indeed, the use of the term exclusion to denote the changing nature of social disadvantage in the West may have important political implications. On the one hand, by highlighting the generalized nature of the problem, the idea of exclusion could be useful in building new broad-based coalitions to reform European welfare states.

On the other hand, exclusion discourse may also ghettoize risk categories under a new label and publicize the more spectacular forms of cumulative disadvantage, distracting attention from the general rise in inequality, unemployment, and family dissolution that is affecting all social classes. In fact, by recasting the rationale for social solidarity, it may inadvertently undermine consensual support for older welfare state schemes, much as distinguishing the unemployed from the poor created two-tiered welfare states in the United Kingdom and the United States. Thus, just as the idea of exclusion reflects different notions of social integration, solidarity, and citizenship, it can also serve a variety of political purposes.

EXCLUSION AND INTEGRATION

Those unfamiliar with the term exclusion often ask the question "exclusion from what?" since virtually any social distinction or affiliation excludes somebody. In the United States, for example, the term calls to mind exclusionary immigration policy, exclusionary zoning, and exclusionary social clubs. But, by comparison with France, the English-speaking countries use the rhetoric of exclusion relatively rarely. Yet consider just a few of the things the literature says people may be excluded from: a livelihood; secure, permanent employment; earnings; property, credit, or land; housing; the minimal or prevailing consumption level; education, skills, and cultural capital; the benefits provided by the welfare state; citizenship and equality before the law; participation in the democratic process; public goods; the nation or the dominant race; the family and sociability; humane treatment, respect, personal fulfillment, understanding.

At the heart of the question "exclusion from what?" lies a more basic one, the problem of social order during times of profound social change in society. Just as the ideas of poverty and unemployment emerged from the great transformations of earlier centuries as did the first sociological accounts of social order to address them, so under contemporary conditions the notion of exclusion calls for an account of social inclusion. In this case, theories of "insertion", "integration", "citizenship", or "solidarity" provide points of reference, making it possible to identify three paradigmatic approaches to exclusion: solidarity, specialisation, and monopoly.

SOLIDARITY

In French Republican thought, as mentioned, exclusion occurs when the social bond between the individual and society known as social solidarity breaks down. Adumbrated by Rousseau and exemplified by Durkheimian sociology, the "social" order is conceived as external, moral, and normative, rather than grounded in individual, group, or class interests. A national consensus, collective conscience, or general will ties the individual to the larger society through vertically interrelated mediating institutions. The approach lays heavy emphasis on the ways in which cultural or moral boundaries between groups socially construct dualistic categories for ordering the world.

Like deviance or anomie, exclusion both threatens and reinforces social cohesion. The inverse of exclusion is thus "integration" and the process of attaining it, "insertion". In a Durkheimian sense, this implies assimilation into the dominant culture; however, most recent uses of the term are post-modernist in that they incorporate multicultural notions about how the basis of solidarity is reconfigured, as the dominant culture adjusts to the minority culture as well as the reverse.

This paradigm draws heavily on anthropology, sociology, ethnography, and cultural studies generally. It focuses attention on the exclusion inherent in the solidarity of nation, race, ethnicity, locality, and other cultural or primordial ties that delimit boundaries between groups. Yet applications go beyond analyses of Republican citizenship, ethnic conflicts, and deviance to include discussion of cultures of poverty and long-term unemployment and of trends toward "flexible specialisation" in political economy.

SPECIALISATION

In Anglo-American liberalism, exclusion is considered a consequence of specialisation: of social differentiation, the economic division of labour, and the separation of spheres. It assumes that individuals differ, giving rise to specialisation in the market and in social groups. It is thus individualist in method, although causation is situated not simply in individual preference but also in the structures created by cooperating and competing individuals markets, associations, and the like. Liberalism thus conceives of the social order, like the economy and politics, as networks of voluntary exchanges between autonomous individuals with their own interests and motivations.

Specialized social structures are comprised of separate, competing, but not necessarily unequal spheres, which lead to exchange and interdependence between them. Social groups are voluntarily constituted by their members, and shifting alliances between them reflect their various interests and wishes. This gives rise to cultural and political pluralism. Liberal models of citizenship emphasize the contractual exchange of rights and obligations and the separation of spheres in social life. Thus, exclusion results from an inadequate separation of social spheres, from the application of rules inappropriate to a given sphere, or from barriers to free movement and exchange between spheres.

Because of the existence of separate social spheres, exclusion may have multiple causes and dimensions. The same individual may not be excluded in every sphere. Nor are social spheres and categories necessarily ordered hierarchically in terms of resources or value. Specialisation protects liberties and may be efficient, as long as excluded individuals have the right to move across boundaries. Individual freedom of choice based on diverse personal values and psychological motives for engaging in social relations should give rise to cross-cutting group affiliations and loyalties contributing to the integration of society.

To the extent that group boundaries impede individual freedom to participate in social exchanges, exclusion is a form of "discrimination". However, group and market competition and the liberal State's protection of individual rights impede the operation of this form of exclusion. In social science, liberal individualism is often reflected in methodological individualism which treats group characteristics as individual attributes. Liberal individualism underlies neo-classical economics, theories of political pluralism, rational and public choice theories, and mainstream sociology. It encompasses two streams of thought: libertarian or neo-liberalism and social or communitarian liberalism.

MONOPOLY

Finally, the third paradigm, influential on the European Left, sees exclusion as a consequence of the formation of group monopoly. Drawing heavily on Weber and, to a lesser extent, Marx, it views the social order as coercive, imposed through a set of hierarchical power relations. In this social democratic or conflict theory, exclusion arises from the interplay of class, status, and political power and serves the interests of the included. Social "closure" is achieved when institutions and cultural distinctions not only create boundaries that keep others out against their will, but are also used to perpetuate inequality. Those within delimited social entities enjoy a monopoly over scarce resources. The monopoly creates a bond of common interest between otherwise unequal insiders. The excluded are therefore simultaneously outsiders and dominated. Exclusion is combated through citizenship, and the extension of equal membership and full participation in the community to outsiders.

These processes of social closure are evident in labour market segmentation. The particular boundaries of exclusion may be drawn within or between nation-states, localities, firms, or social groups. Whatever the nature of the boundary, the overlap or coincidence of group distinctions with inequality - "the barrier and the level", to adopt Gobelot's terms - is at the heart of the problematique of this paradigm.

CLARIFICATION

A number of remarks are in order, before applying these paradigms to the question of economic exclusion set in the context of these paradigms. The paradigms are, of course, ideal types - in reality, different societies and cultures define "belonging" in their respective ways. For this reason, defining exclusion with reference to its opposite can pose its own problems. This is not simply because social integration necessarily coexists with exclusion, both being relative concepts. If this were the only issue at stake, the relationship between exclusion and integration might seem to be zero-sum, by definition. In fact, only the monopoly paradigm posits that integration makes it easier to exclude others - through greater social control or state power. Rather, the problem with considering the reverse of exclusion is that such a concept implies that a clear political consensus exists within nation-states as to the nature and bases of citizenship, integration, and membership of society.

On the contrary, that fighting exclusion means different things to different people. Moreover, at various times, national debates have emphasized some aspects of exclusion and not others:

Sometimes the emphasis is on migration and refugees (e.g. Belgium, Germany), sometimes on long-term or extremely long-term unemployment and exclusion from the labour market (e.g. Denmark, France, the Netherlands); or on the problem of low income (Portugal). Discussion is sometimes directly linked to specific policy-making, as is the case with the guaranteed minimum income (France, Spain) or it can be part of a more general consideration of the functions of the welfare state (United Kingdom: Citizens' Charter) or be used in policies discouraging the passivity engendered by certain forms of social protection (Denmark, the Netherlands, United Kingdom). It is sometimes fuelled by campaigns run by associations or the media, which focus on particularly visible problems or those which in any case catch the public eye, such as the homeless (France, United Kingdom), drugs (Italy), child labour (Portugal), and inner-city crisis (France).

Although the cultural embeddedness of the concept of exclusion makes the development of legitimate cross-national indicators more difficult than those of the development of similar indicators for measuring poverty or unemployment, the paradigms do illuminate the reasons underlying the contested and selective meanings of the term. Choosing one definition means accepting the theoretical and ideological "baggage" associated with it.

Second, as is appropriate for a sociological analysis, each of these paradigms presents exclusion as a social relationship between the included and the excluded. That relationship may derive from social action, from the activity of excluding, thereby calling attention to the actors responsible. But does exclusion refer only to a change in the condition of those who were integrated, or can it refer to the constant condition of excluded people who wish to be included? In so far as exclusion is a process, analysts should specify its beginning as well as its end.

Observers who insist that exclusion is only a dynamic process (rather than an identity or a condition) miss the structural outcome of the process. The institutionalisation of exclusion may create a social boundary or a permanent division between the "ins" and the "outs". It may take the form of social distancing over time or of social distance at any one point in time. The action of exclusion becomes structural when it is repeatedly confirmed through social relations and practices. Turnover among the individuals who are excluded does not alter the structural existence of the social boundary. Indeed, its social reality is confirmed when movement across the boundary provokes reactions like distancing, fear, or new legal barriers.

Collective reactions like these properly belong in any study of exclusion. To be sure, the excluded themselves need not constitute a social group with common consciousness, goals and activities. In fact, the very differentiation and isolation of the excluded may be responsible for their collective inability to demand inclusion on their own. In this respect, as in others, social exclusion can also be a condition. Nevertheless, exclusion should not be confused with social differentiation per se. If the existence of social groups necessarily implies the existence of boundaries, it is less clear that every difference or distinction implies exclusion.

Exclusion may be based on virtually any social difference, but the extent to which differences produce exclusion depends on such issues as the permeability of boundaries, the extent to which membership is freely chosen, and whether, as in John Rawls's principle of difference or Adam Smith's division of labour, distinctions have any social benefits. Indeed, some marginal or deviant individuals may not want to be included; they can deliberately choose to be social drop-outs. These issues should be explored rather than defined out of the scope of scrutiny.

Third, exclusion can be viewed macro-sociologically or micro sociologically. Achille Weinberg and Jean-Claude Ruano-Borbalan distinguish between macro and micro causes in contrasting exclusion from "above" and "below".

"Top-down" perspectives may view exclusion as an employment crisis or as a crisis of ineffective immigration and social policies or as a crisis in the integrative social institutions of the nation generally. They emphasize macro-sociological phenomenona like modernity, cosmopolitanism, and individualism, or increasingly global, mobile labour markets, and technological innovation. In contrast, local and communitarian "grass-roots" perspectives cast exclusion as a crisis of community solidarity and social regulation, with micro-sociological processes of assimilation, downward mobility, or social isolation as a person is gradually excluded from a job and other social relations.

Fourth, the distinctions between paradigms should not be confused with institutional classifications, like types of welfare state. Institutions are historical accretions that bear the imprint of past conflicts between ideologies and paradigms. To say, for example, that the French Republic institutionalized Republican ideas implies that during a given period of institution-building a popular coalition was formed around a particular ideological consensus. However, other coalitions contested these ideas and, to the extent that they too had influence, the law, the welfare state, and other social institutions incorporated their different ideas as well.

Fifth, all three paradigms must be distinguished from organic approaches to social integration. The solidarity, specialisation, and monopoly paradigms of social integration fall within the spectrum of mainstream sociological thought which attributes greater scope and autonomy to civil society relative to the State and market than do other paradigms. Indeed, the discipline of sociology (and its central concern with integration) developed to provide an alternative explanation of the social changes brought about by the democratic and industrial revolutions to those offered by utilitarian liberalism and socialism, as well as reactionary thought.

However, where democracy and industrialisation came late, as in Germany, Italy, the Iberian Peninsula, and many less developed countries, other less sociological conceptions of social integration took hold. In some places, traditional conservative, pre-industrial, and corporatist notions of integration degenerated into justifications of authoritarianism and fascism. In the postwar era in particular, Christian Democracy and societal corporatism tempered organicist thought with recognition of individual rights and tolerance of ideological and religious rivals. Indeed, some analysts classify France in this category, merging Republican ideology with Christian Democratic or neo-corporatist thought.

Finally, some "plural societies" developed a form of stable consociational democracy in which elites compromise and check one another's power on behalf of distinct social segments. These alternative notions of social integration took hold in both European and Third World contexts. Organic models of social integration are often contrasted with liberal and Marxist paradigms, whose pitfalls - extreme individualism or extreme collectivism - they seek to avoid. Yet, like those paradigms, organic models are empirical, normative, and methodological; they describe social reality, provide conceptions of what a good society should be, and offer a selective strategy of analysis.

Although organicism is often considered conservative, these paradigms may in fact call for state intervention to restructure the established society and institute changes in the pursuit of social justice. Thus, organicism and Catholicism in a context of entrenched privilege may actually be radical. What most distinguishes organic approaches is less their politically conservative or centrist tendencies than their seeking to construct a social order based on groups, be they functional, regional, or primordial (on ethnic, religious or linguistic bases). Within this broad range of thought, three streams can be identified: Christian Democratic (societal or neo-corporatist); state corporatist; and consociational. Although they differ in the emphasis they accord to individual rights and group autonomy, all reflect to some degree the principles of "community" and "subsidiarity".

The vision of a harmonious community is classically expressed in Leo XIII's encyclical, *Rerum Novarum*, in which it is denied that class conflict is necessary. Liberalism and capitalism encourage class struggle because of insufficient state intervention, while socialism entails an overreaching of the State into autonomous spheres. Subsidiarity is the term used in Catholic social thought for the notion that "it is an injustice, a grave evil, and a disturbance of right order for a larger and higher organisation to arrogate to itself functions which can be performed efficiently by smaller and lower bodies".

While Protestant Reform churches speak of "sovereignty in one's own circle", thereby emphasizing the separate and exclusive (if limited) responsibility of the individual and small group, the Catholic formulation stresses "the inclusion of these small units of society in greater wholes, within which, however, they have a sphere of autonomy on which they have a right to insist. The responsibility for what can be done at lower levels must not be allowed to gravitate to the top". Christian principles of social integration imply a particular perspective on the issue of exclusion. On the one hand, the State has the responsibility to ensure personal development and thus social, political, and civil rights for all.

On the other hand, the inequality inherent in horizontal pluralism is also justified. Thus, if the pre-labour-commodification "corporatist-statist legacy" - feudal paternalism, patronage, and clientelism; corporativism of cities, guilds, and friendly societies; and Bismarckian statism - justified the earliest welfare states, it also shaped the tendency of Christian Democratic welfare states to preserve differentials between social classes, occupations, and status groups as well as to support the traditional family. Thus, this paradigm recognizes the exclusion of those not organically integrated into the various smaller, autonomous units of society that make up the greater whole - families, communities, classes, nation-states, and so on but is less cognizant of gender and economic inequality as causes of exclusion.

By contrast, Roman law recognized no individual freedom of association. The only legal organisations were those officially recognized by the State on the basis of *lex specialis*, or "privilege". Thus, the State legitimately shapes the structure of civil society so that functional parts are integrated into an organic whole. In return for a corporate charter, associations have an obligation to the State to perform a public service. In this, organic statism differs from Republicanism. Indeed, in the second preface to the division of labour in society, Durkheim rejected state corporatism because controls on worker and other associations made them part of the official administration, restricted meaningful participation, and implied coerced integration rather than integration through the collective conscience.

Several weaknesses in the organic-statist model produce what might be called "social exclusion ". First, there is no clear justification for recognizing some groups rather than others. For example, the paradigm privileges functional groups over groups based on primordial (e.g. ethnic, religious, regional, or linguistic) identities, which are thus excluded. Second, it is unclear why vertical functional associations, with elite representatives, are privileged over horizontal, decentralized, participatory and membership organisations, like community groups, which can be considered as excluded.

Third, if functional groups are indeed granted autonomy, there is little to prevent some groups - particularly those with the initial hold on power from gaining control over others, thus undermining the presumption of organic harmony. This inequality in civil society can also produce social exclusion. Finally, while the State's concern with the integration of parts of society can lead to top-down control of functional groupings, undermining their autonomy, dependent States may find it difficult to integrate multinational capital within national corporatist structures. In such a case, workers in the export sector would be "excluded" from bargaining rights.

In sum, unlike liberalism, Christian Democracy is "personalist" rather than individualist and, unlike socialism, is "pluralist" rather than collectivist. Similarly, consociationalism, by checking the power of majorities, guarantees groups the autonomy to run their internal affairs within nation-states. And corporatism (organic statism, to use Stepan's terminology), rests upon official state recognition or " chartering" of mediating associations which are thus centrally coordinated and controlled for the public good, which contrasts strongly with their free, competitive, interest-based operation in liberal pluralism or their suppression under command socialism.

Finally, each paradigm addresses more than one dimension or aspect of exclusion: economic, sociological and interactional, cultural and political. Thus, the paradigms cut across the social sciences. This interdisciplinary approach differs from prior classifications of theories of exclusion, which focus on conditions in one country, usually France, or on one discipline, especially sociology. Although each paradigm includes theories drawn from economics, political science, and anthropology, and also stress sociological theories because the concepts of exclusion and integration are central to that discipline.

Even when social exclusion is defined in global terms, research tends to be more sectoral, focusing on a specific population identified as being at risk of exclusion. Thus, empirical studies of exclusion may draw on more than one paradigm, although they tend to emphasize one over the others. The research literature on exclusion includes studies of the following specific social categories: the long-term or recurrently unemployed; those employed in precarious and unskilled jobs, especially older workers or those unprotected by labour regulations; the low paid and the poor; the landless; the unskilled, the illiterate, and school drop-outs; the mentally and physically handicapped and disabled; addicts; delinquents, prison inmates, and persons with criminal records; single parents; battered or sexually abused children, those who grew up in problem households; young people, those lacking work experience or qualifications; child workers; women; foreigners, refugees, immigrants; racial, religious, and ethnic minorities; the disenfranchised; beneficiaries of social assistance; those in need, but ineligible for social assistance; residents of rundown housing or disreputable neighbourhoods; those with consumption levels below subsistence (the hungry, the homeless, the Fourth World); those whose consumption, leisure, or other practices (drug or alcohol abuse, delinquency, dress, speech, mannerisms) are stigmatized or labelled as deviant; the downwardly mobile; the socially isolated without friends or family.

These absolute and relative social disadvantages may occur simultaneously. Indeed, the extent to which these dimensions overlap is a frequent subject of research on exclusion. Some find very weak correlations between the types of exclusion. But others conceive of exclusion as the accumulation of such disadvantages, as the last stage in a process of social disqualification. For example, those born into certain groups, with a particular upbringing, education, family or work history may in a sense be doubly or triply excluded. However, the disproportionate representation of people with these social characteristics among the "excluded" does not imply that these characteristics determine whether any given individual is excluded. One needs to examine the incidence of these attributes in the included population as well. Some individuals with such characteristics do make their way into secure, well-paid employment, stable families, political participation, and the like. Provided turnover is ensured, there need be no "hard-core " group of excluded people.

ECONOMIC EXCLUSION

The three paradigms may be illustrated with theories addressing the economic dimension of exclusion. Although the discipline of economics is less prone to paradigm conflicts than the other social sciences, it still has a number of "schools" which differ along the lines already delineated. In so far as economists address "social exclusion", as distinct from poverty, inequality, or unemployment per se, it is probably more precise to say these are schools of political economy.

Readily available quantitative indicators of poverty and unemployment, and job statistics are often used in discussions of economic exclusion. In the United States, where there has been low-wage job growth, the focus has been on poverty and the underclass, whereas Europe has emphasized long-term unemployment. But on both sides of the Atlantic, the development of new socio-economic indicators has highlighted the novelty of the concept of social exclusion. The new measures not only offer insight into new thinking, but reflect existing paradigm assumptions as well.

Because the paradigms provide three different ways of linking economic and social concerns, social scientists other than economists have addressed the economic dimensions of exclusion. Thus, one can also glean analyses of economic exclusion from the literature on the underclass, the culture of poverty, and informal economies.

SOLIDARITY

As mentioned, the French idea of solidarity drew upon the nineteenth-century working-class mutual aid movement and syndicalism. Through this influence, assumptions central to the solidarity paradigm can be found in the flexible specialisation school of political economy.

In addition, the French regulation school shares with the flexibilisation school several important components of Republican and Durkheimian thought, especially the role of institutional, legal and normative regulation. However, I shall show that regulation theory more properly belongs in the monopoly paradigm, which treats exclusion more narrowly as either a social control mechanism or a barrier to competition. In any case, both schools of contemporary political economy depart from the liberal specialisation paradigm's assumption of self-regulating markets.

As is typical of the solidarity paradigm, the "flexible specialisation" approach rejects the assumption of classical political economy that the economy is separate from society. Flexible specialisation rests upon "microregulation" - compatible institutions that instigate and coordinate innovation - in which family, school, and community ties are tightly intertwined with economic organisation. Flexibility refers to the continual reshaping and rearranging of the components of the productive process, while specialisation reflects limitations on the possible rearrangements and the ends to which they are put.

Unlike liberal specialisation that does not recognize constraints on economic organisation beyond those of markets (e.g. transaction costs), flexible specialisation is grounded in social solidarities. Productive decentralisation and the "reinvigoration of affiliations that are associated with the pre-industrial past" enable relatively autonomous, skilled workers to deploy modern technology successfully. However, organisations and communities of flexible specialisation have boundaries that limit entry, and "outsiders... cannot be permitted to lay claim" to local public services or the system will be overburdened.

Relationships fostering cooperation and coordination beyond the workplace wed politics to markets. A system based on honour and pervasive trust is the foundation of community institutions that temper but do not eliminate economic competition. "The recognition of common interests and mutual obligations does not guarantee that all members of the community are treated equally". Indeed, limited competition on the basis of products rather than labour costs promotes innovation, productive flexibility and, thereby, economic growth. Thus, the approach differs from the liberal specialisation paradigm in restricting competition and from the monopoly paradigm in promoting group boundaries and accepting moderate inequality.

Because it focuses on the advanced industrialized countries, the implications of flexible specialisation for Third World economic development are ambiguous. On the one hand, developing countries may be specializing in mass production, while the advanced countries shift to flexible specialisation. However, small-scale enterprises, community norms, and informal economies might provide the basis of flexible specialisation in the Third World, as well.

Despite its strong Marxist orientation, the French regulation school contains elements that recall the solidarity paradigm. Key to the regulation school is the concept of "regimes of accumulation ", stable configurations that wed economic institutions to social regulations and norms. Such regimes are governed by institutionalized rules and social conventions which constrain collective and individual behaviour. Regulation adjusts production to social demand so that there develops a relative compatibility between income distribution and growth in the means of production and consumption. Another key concept for this school is the rapport salarial, one that also recalls the solidarity paradigm's social bond: this refers to the legal and institutional conditions regulating the use and reproduction of wage labour under capitalism. Wage relations differ according to the production norm, labour process, organisation, consumption norm or way of life.

For example, the Fordist regime of the post-war Golden Age was based on a social pact which gave corporations control of mass production in return for high wages to fuel mass consumption. Unlike an earlier regime of competitive capitalism, Fordism administered the economy through Keynesian economic policy, collective bargaining, Taylorism, and economies of scale. However, there are differences of opinion within the school as to the likely course of global capitalism since the crisis. It is not clear whether the emerging regime will pursue high-quality employment in a post-Fordist regime of flexible regulation or revert to a competitive strategy of externalizing market uncertainties through low-quality, low-wage jobs subject to numerical flexibility. Most regulation theorists do support the further development of a social pact within the European Union.

Regulation theory has also influenced post-Marxist thinkers like Andre Gorz, who advocate work sharing and the development of socially productive and democratic activities outside the capitalist workplace. French "insertion" policies, however, epitomize the solidarity approach. The minimum income for social integration (RMI) was based on the idea that "insertion" is a form of regulation of the social bond and a response to a perceived threat to social cohesion. Thus, in return for a minimum income, beneficiaries must sign a contract agreeing to pursue either a "social" or an "employment" activity, be it a subsidized job, training, community activity, or a personal project that enhances the ability to form social relationships and function in society.

These functions are also the aim of French schemes for deprived young people as well as many urban revitalisation schemes. Even schemes officially directed at "insertion" through economic activity combine social and business rationales. The *entreprises d'insertion* (enterprises established for the purpose of helping the excluded to rejoin society through work), for example, draw upon an older tradition of the crafts guilds and conceive of the work group as a community with social as well as economic functions.

Although the flexible specialisation and regulation schools both emphasize historical contingency, national variation, and institutional and normative regulation, there remain important differences between them. Regulation theory tends to emphasize macroeconomic phenomena, the form of competition, and employment or class relations, which the flexible specialisation school considers too deterministic. Rather than seek a new international economic regime, the latter school emphasizes the microeconomic and holds that many different types of political economy may coexist.

Moreover, a careful reading of the regulation school indicates that it is best classified under the monopoly paradigm, especially when the framework is applied to developing countries. For example, Alain Lipietz argues that Fordism, the postwar intensive regime of accumulation based on mass consumption, rested upon a "monopolistic mode of regulation". A network of institutions stabilized the growth in workers' income and created "monopolies in a productive structure that allows the big firms of leading sectors to administer their prices independently of fluctuations in demand". By exporting mass production goods, the regime also "excluded" less developed countries from capital accumulation.

However, the contradictions setting off the crisis of Fordism produced a series of changes in the developing world. First, "bloody Taylorisation" integrated Third World labour into competitive, exploitative mass production. Then, in the 1970s, attempts at import substitution and the growth of internal markets allowed a form of "peripheral Fordism" to take hold, especially in the newly industrialized countries. However, the collapse of Fordism and Keynesianism encouraged monetarist policies that withdrew investment capital and exacerbated the indebtedness of less developed countries. In sum, Western advantages in the world economy were preserved by maintaining forms of monopolistic regulation.

As the discussion of the monopoly paradigm will show, the regulation school's approach dovetails with labour market segmentation approaches to productive flexibility. However, economists are not the only ones to address the issue of economic exclusion from the perspective of the solidarity paradigm. Recall that the solidarity paradigm sees exclusion as a necessary by-product of group solidarity, cultural cohesion, and hence, social ties. It draws upon Durkheimian thought in which Republican concepts like social bond, organic solidarity, moral density, and collective conscience play a central role.

The Durkheimian school of sociology concentrates on the problem of human solidarity, particularly moral and normative integration that entails classification of people and ideas into sacred and profane, conforming or deviant. This tradition influenced cultural anthropologists who emphasize the binary oppositions or dualisms inherent in symbolic representations. For example, in Natural symbols, Mary Douglas introduced a distinction to explain how cultural codes control individual behaviour and social organisation. "Group" refers to the external boundaries that differentiate collectivities from "the outside world". "Grid" refers to the other internal distinctions and delegations of authority used to limit social interaction.

Cross-classifying these two dimensions provide a classification of individual behaviour in daily interaction and the ways in which social institutions constrain and channel individual behaviour. In this view, the moral order divides the world into categories which are continually recreated by primordial sentiments, essential identities, and institutional enforcement of the norms and values that define group boundaries. The cultural solidarity approach to exclusion is based upon primordialist/essentialist, rather than constructivist, instrumentalist, or materialist approaches to culture.

The primordialist school maintains that, unlike class and interest group conflicts, cultural conflicts have a peculiarly intensive, affective or emotional nature because they touch on primordial identity. Cultural boundaries enclose a social space behind walls where social life is orderly and people feel they "belong" and are "safe". Outsiders thus threaten this social order. They may provoke a reaffirmation of in-group solidarity or, if the bases of group solidarity expand to encompass those once considered as outsiders, inclusion and integration can be achieved. Essentialism may also underlie the cultural solidarity of excluded or minority groups who demand self-determination, cultural autonomy, separatism, political decentralisation, or multiculturalism.

While the essentialist approach is most frequently used to analyze ethnic, racial, linguistic, religious, and other forms of cultural exclusion, it can also be applied to those excluded for economic reasons.

For example, Godfried Engbersen *et al.* applied Mary Douglas's group/grid framework to the question of whether the long-term unemployed in the Netherlands have developed a monolithic culture. Cross-classifying cultures by group and grid, they arrive at five ways of life among the unemployed: egalitarian, hierarchical, individualistic, fatalistic, and autonomous. Hence, Engbersen *et al.* conclude there are in fact multiple cultures of unemployment and not a monolithic Dutch "underclass."

Exclusion was most evident in the fatalistic culture of unemployment, which Engbersen *et al.* consider a sort of "culture of poverty". Older, poorly educated persons were more likely to experience an isolated, dependent existence - a "shrinking of the social and geographic world they lived in". Long-term unemployment led to:

> ...exclusion from social institutions and networks and had made them completely dependent on the Government... The negligible success on the labour market, the high social costs that continual job-seeking behaviour entails and the reduction or disappearance of social frameworks can all serve to account for this shift from conformist to retreatist behaviour, and the longer the unemployment lasts, the more this is the case.

It is important to note that proponents of the solidarity paradigm often reject the term underclass. For example, one CGP publication explicitly translates *les exclus* as outsiders in Howard Becker's sense of deviants, rather than as underclass. Nevertheless, as the Dutch study illustrates, the literature on the underclass does touch upon the issue of exclusion. It might appear that some "conservative" theories of the underclass fall within the solidarity paradigm, given their strong emphasis on the deviant behaviour of the poor and their use of dominant consensual values as a point of reference. Empirical studies that use single motherhood, school-leaving, or welfare receipt as "behavioural" indicators of the United States underclass essentially treat the poor as deviants.

For example, Ken Auletta says the underclass "generally feels excluded from society, rejects commonly accepted values, suffers from behavioural as well as income deficiencies. They don't just tend to be poor; to most Americans their behaviour seems aberrant."

The reference to mainstream culture is also found in the work of David Ellwood, a major proponent of American welfare reform in the Clinton administration. He has argued that the proposed reform embodies the contradictory American values of individual autonomy, the virtue of work, the primacy of family, and community. Because Americans want all of these, policy has reflected the trade-offs found in three "helping conundrums": security vs. work, assistance vs. family structure, and targeting vs. isolation. Ellwood finds exclusion in the third conundrum - the more services are targeted at the most needy,

> ... the more you tend to isolate the people who receive the services from the economic and political mainstream... Targeting can label and stigmatize people... When people see the most support and services going to those who are doing worst, it appears to the non-poor and possibly to the poor that the needy live by different rules than does everyone else... Targeting tends to isolate politically the "truly needy" from the rest of society. This implies that welfare reform should reflect the consensual values underpinning social solidarity.

However, truly conservative underclass theories more appropriately fall within the organic paradigm of social integration. They assume that preserving the moral order is a state responsibility and that policy should coerce people into appropriate behaviour. Just as some members of the British Conservative Party have recently been proposing a "Back to Basics" ethic, American neo-conservatives have been insisting on "family values", sexual probity, and the individual responsibility to work. For example, Lawrence Mead argues that the idleness of the underclass reflects moral failure, not insufficient job creation, so the State should force able-bodied citizens to participate in workfare programmes.

To become full citizens, the poor must balance their entitlement to social support with the exercise of moral obligations. In contrast, Charles Murray, who is conventionally considered a conservative, more properly belongs in the specialisation paradigm because he views joblessness as a rational, self-interested reaction to the work disincentives in welfare policies. As the next section indicates, liberal theories of the underclass attribute persistent poverty and unemployment to perverse welfare state effects, market imperfections, or supply-side and human capital variables. These concerns differ from the moral emphases in the organic and solidarity paradigms.

SPECIALISATION

It is banal to note that liberalism underpins neo-classical economics. In the specialisation paradigm of separate spheres, markets work best when States and institutions intervene least. Generous government income supports create perverse work disincentives that engender long-term dependency. The traditional solution to poverty and unemployment is to create jobs and raise productivity by lowering wages and eliminating rigid employment regulations.

It is no accident that both liberal political economy and the idea of "poverty" emerged from the Great Transformations of late eighteenth-century Britain. Just as exclusion is now being distinguished from poverty, so during this earlier period of dramatic social change did new distinctions set the poor apart from the rest of society? This new concept of poverty, culminating in the Poor Law reforms and exemplified by the workhouse spread quickly, especially to the United States. It is the origin of the principle of "least eligibility" in means-tested schemes, one which continues to stigmatize recipients as undeserving or morally unworthy.

These early liberal assumptions are also reflected in measures of poverty as such. The narrow conception of poverty is reflected in the myriad thresholds of absolute poverty used by Western governments to determine eligibility for means-tested schemes. Not only are poverty lines often pegged to subsistence levels, but income support levels are pegged to minimum wages so as to eliminate w ork disincentives and preserve union-negotiated wage standards.

While the distinction between the undeserving and the industrious poor persisted, over time further distinctions were refined with which to measure the poor. By the end of the nineteenth century, persons suffering from the effects of economic dislocation came to be distinguished from undeserving paupers who rarely (if ever) worked, lived on alms, and lacked direction and self-respect. The "respectable poor" were distinguished from the "residuum". During the 1880s in the United Kingdom:

> For the first time unemployment became a political issue, perceived as a problem distinct from poverty, caused by factors other than moral failings, deserving of public sympathy and remedial action by the State... Much attention was subsequently focused on the need to separate the efficient unemployed, who could and should be helped into the labour market, from the "unemployables" or "inefficients" who should be removed from it.

If early mutual aid associations and social insurance schemes served the "aristocracy of labour" and excluded the unskilled and casual worker, workers of all kinds were soon covered by universal welfare state schemes. With the rise of this Anglo-American "social liberalism", rights to social insurance were legitimated on the basis of contributions made during employment. Unlike means-tested schemes, insurance implied an obligation of the able-bodied to work when economic conditions allowed. Thus, liberals still insist that even contributory unemployment coverage be accompanied by job search requirements and policing against fraud. Pauperism was slowly restricted to a small segment of the poor unable to work - the Fourth World, as Father Wresinski, a French activist priest, has called them. Since the poverty addressed by means-tested benefit schemes came to be regarded as a residual problem, its meaning gradually narrowed to denote simply an insufficiency of income.

Yet, the liberal conception of exclusion does not reduce it to an economic phenomenon any more than do the other paradigms. Because individuals have diverse personal values and psychological motives for engaging in social relations, specialisation arises not only in the market but also among social groups. Specialized social structures are comprised of separate, competing, but not necessarily unequal spheres which lead to exchanges and interdependence between them. Much as market competition erodes discriminatory practices, individual freedom to choose group affiliations and competition between groups for members create cross-cutting loyalties that break down tendencies toward social closure.

Conversely, exclusion results from "discrimination", that is, from the inappropriate exercise of personal tastes or the enforcement of group boundaries that individuals are not free to cross. Thus, it may have multiple causes and dimensions, depending upon the social sphere in question. Yet not all social differences are the consequence of deliberate exclusion or discrimination. Unlike organic models reliant on a strong State, liberalism allows for voluntary deprivation. Simply granting rights to assistance does not mean that free individuals will choose to accept it. As long as there is free access to information and people are not shamed, stigmatized or coerced, the take-up rates of welfare benefits may vary widely. The liberal State is under no obligation to bring the excluded in.

Nor do specialisation and interdependence of separate social spheres necessarily imply social inequality. Liberalism considers social differentiation to be a horizontal dimension of social structures, rather than a vertical one. Like the division of labour, specialisation may have positive outcomes: economies of scale, skill enhancement, reduced transaction costs, diversification of choice, and the preservation of liberty. On the grounds of efficiency or freedom, liberals may justify social distinctions that the other paradigms may consider exclusionary.

For example, efficiency wage models assume that some firms find it profitable to pay above-market wages because they raise worker productivity more than enough to offset additional labour costs. If higher wages increase the cost of losing a job and lower the costs of supervision, recruitment, and training new workers, then shirking and turnover can be reduced and work effort increased. Thus, firms with high monitoring costs (such as large corporations) might find it easier to trust their workers when they reward them amply. Efficiency wages may also improve workers' morale and loyalty to the firm because they are perceived to be "fairer" than market wages. Indeed, industrial wage differentials are related to job tenure and quit probabilities.

To some, this may suggest workers in high-wage industries are earning rents that they do not want to lose. Indeed, inter-industry wage dispersion rose between 1970 and 1987, partly because workers in more productive industries enjoyed increased rents. Thus, from a monopoly perspective, exclusion would appear to benefit "insiders". Yet, efficiency wage models also show how excess labour supply can become a structural feature of the labour market in equilibrium. Over and above the wage effects of union threats, minimum wage laws, large firms' internal labour markets, or "imperfect" competition produced by other institutions, long-term structural unemployment may be consistent with market efficiency.

In so far as exclusion constitutes "discrimination" - the drawing of inappropriate group distinctions between free and equal individuals which deny access to or participation in exchange or interaction - it is construed as an individual experience. In social science, liberal individualism is often reflected in methodological individualism which treats group memberships as individual attributes. In contrast to the solidarity paradigm, these studies do not emphasize the dualism between insiders and the excluded but, rather, perceive the latter in all their rich diversity.

Neo-classical labour economists often associate the duration of poverty, dependency on welfare, and unemployment with the personal characteristics of the poor rather than with economic or political conditions. These "supply-side" studies, based on survey analysis, usually find that the poor, unemployed, or underclass population is socially heterogeneous. For example, the Centre for the Study of Costs and Income (CERC) found that no single characteristic (e.g. difficulty in childhood, living in a single-parent household) could be identified as the principal cause of poverty or receipt of RMI in France.

Most scholarly research in the United States, United Kingdom, the Netherlands and Germany reports that those unemployed for at least a year are also socially heterogeneous. Because there is so many turnovers among the unemployed over time, long-term unemployment affects virtually all categories of French workers. The National Institute of Statistics and Economic Studies (INSEE) found that those unemployed for under a year are no different socially from newly hired workers.

While those unemployed on the way to becoming excluded tend to be older, to lack qualifications, skills, or experience, and to be more likely to have an immigrant background or handicap, even these individual characteristics do not predict well who will regain employment. Sometimes, even school-leavers are hired in preference to their experienced and educated elders. An additional reason why some categories of worker remain unemployed longer is that hiring is based not only on whether the worker's skill fits the job, but also on whether the worker will integrate into the work group. Indeed, a wide range of social characteristics may be hindrances to regaining employment. In addition to cyclical and seemingly permanent unemployment, France faces a problem of recurrent unemployment - *chomage d'exclusion* - in which many move back and forth between idleness, internships, training courses, and short-term jobs.

In contrast to labour economists, sociologists have a long research tradition on the social psychology and behaviour of the unemployed on which to draw. These micro-sociologists found that unemployment is usually experienced as humiliating, causing the jobless to withdraw from friends and family. For example, Newman's study of downwardly mobile Americans identified both general and particular responses to unemployment. Most workers felt anger, dismay, and a sense of injustice, as if a social contract had been broken.

Unemployment challenged personal identities, disrupted the life trajectories of entire families, and undermined cultural values, like loyalty and the work ethic. Managers, with their individualist, meritocratic creed, tended to blame themselves, whereas workers who share their sense of identity with others in a union or a community, tended to blame outside forces for unemployment. Groups based on a shared experience of unemployment helped the unemployed retain some dignity, as well as providing an explanation for their fate. Nevertheless, a common sense of victimisation did not overcome feelings of helplessness.

Even French sociologists who use solidarity rhetoric have treated exclusion as a process of individual disaffiliation or disqualification. The longer people are unemployed, the more personal problems they develop, the more they appear unemployable to potential employers, and the more discouraged and isolated they become. The defining characteristic of exclusion is thus gradual withdrawal from face-to-face social relations. The micro-sociological causes of exclusion are located in the individual's immediate social environment, life course, or personal attributes.

One sees in these studies an emphasis on individual characteristics, micro-sociological interaction, and psychological effects, even if they are considered as outcomes of economic restructuring. Indeed, it is no accident that micro-sociology and "the curious importance of small groups" arose in liberal America. In these studies, exclusion is neither a problem of macro-social integration nor an absolute categorical condition resulting from having crossed over some boundary line. Rather, it is a multidimensional process that individuals undergo. In a person's life trajectory, exclusion occurs at different paces and in different social spheres. For example, Serge Paugam defines exclusion as a process of "social disqualification" that occurs in three consecutive stages: fragility (under/unemployed but retaining links with society), dependence on social aid (discouraged from working but filling other social roles), and then complete breakdown of social bonds.

At each stage, people renegotiate their identities and may find a way of regaining their previous status. But if individuals travel the full course of disaffiliation, they lose most of their social ties - job, housing, relations with the social support system, and the most elementary form of solidarity, a stable family. Accumulating handicaps and failures, they come to feel useless, uncared for, hopeless, and may turn to drugs or alcohol or become hostile to the welfare system. Without social relations of any kind, they lack the resources to find a way back into society.

Robert Castel also argues that there is a dynamic, three-stage process running from full integration through precarious, vulnerable employment and fragile relations to disaffiliation or exclusion. Castel argues that although the new poor are socially heterogeneous, the overrepresented social categories share a particular mode of dissociation of the social bond that he calls "disaffiliation". It is an effect of the conjuncture of two vectors, one economic, the other social.

The first axis runs from integration (stable employment) through forms of precarious, intermittent, or seasonal occupations to the complete loss of work which he calls "exclusion". The second axis runs from "insertion" in stable socio-familial networks of sociability to total "isolation". When cross-classified, these dimensions identify a zone of integration (guaranteed permanent work and solid relational support) which assures social cohesion, and a zone of disaffiliation (the absence of work and social isolation) which provides little or no cohesion. Between the two extremes is a zone of vulnerability in which work is precarious and relations are fragile. Although integration in one sphere may compensate for exclusion in another, vulnerability puts one at risk of both kinds of exclusion.

For example, 77 per cent of RMI beneficiaries lack jobs and 76 per cent lack a stable marital relationship. Thus, "insertion" measures must go beyond distributing aid to filling the social void caused by disaffiliation. Apart from changes in the structure of employment, changes in other institutional spheres socially isolate the economically excluded. First losing a job or re-employment on a temporary, short-term basis means losing job-related social insurance coverage. Receiving means-tested assistance that was formerly reserved for the permanently excluded entails a loss of status as well as of income.

Second, the decline of organized labour, ideological politics, and the break-up of working-class neighbourhoods has eroded class solidarity. In deprived outer suburbs, many young people do not form stable relationships and immigrants cannot assimilate; in the ghettos, the young have no positive role models, clubs or centres of their own. The decline of shared values and practices in daily life also weakens financial and social support from neighbours. Third, while school should be a vector of social cohesion, many young people drop out of school because they feel excluded.

One's own home can amount to a ghetto the family have no money. Indeed, job and family instability have led to more single-parent families and to more people living alone. In sum, exclusion is a series of breaks in the web of belonging that leave individuals stranded in a "social no-man's-land". As in the other paradigms, these French sociological studies consider exclusion to be a process both economic and social. However, they focus on the individual's experience. The analysis posits the existence of separate spheres, and individuals are located along multiple dimensions which do not necessarily intersect.

A similar approach was used by Jencks who rejected the idea of the existence of an American underclass, arguing that because trends in various social indicators have moved in different directions over time, disadvantages do not cluster in the same group of people. New and increasingly multi-dimensional ways of measuring the underclass consistently show that single parents, ghetto residents' school dropouts and people dependent on transfers constitute only a subset of the poor. Findings like these are moving social policy in an increasingly individualistic direction. Since each individual has a different combination of problems, assistance must be personalized and rendered comprehensively. Income support, medical and housing assistance, social services training, and subsidized employment are increasingly "packaged" to fit each individual's or household's needs.

The specialisation paradigm does not emphasize the individual and micro-sociological causes of economic exclusion only. Social liberals are cognizant of the effects of structural changes in labour demand on individuals' immediate social environments, and thus on their opportunities for social affiliation in a variety of separate spheres. The split between supply-side and demand-side theories parallels the division between classical and social liberalism. The latter is concerned with maintaining boundaries between separate spheres, including that between politics (with its equality of citizenship) and the market (with its inequality of resources).

In contrast to supply-side theoreticians who attribute poverty or unemployment to individual failings, most sociologists now accept that the new poverty and long-term unemployment have demand-side or structural causes perhaps exacerbated by liberal economic and social policies. The educational level of the Western labour force continues to rise, suggesting that supply-side policies will be ineffective in addressing these problems. Evaluations of French training schemes, for example, report that they do little to improve the job prospects of the trainees unless they are tied to enterprises. Even when the unemployed re-enter the labour market, new openings are almost all to jobs of short duration.

About half the figures of newly registered unemployed in France concern lost "precarious jobs". The trend is for jobs at all skill levels to offer little security. However, different social spheres offer different affiliations and resources. Family·and community ties may replace income for the long-term structurally unemployed. With access to productive assets (land, capital, credit), self-employment and self-support/sufficiency in food may be possible, incorporating the excluded into direct market exchanges, barter, and informal economies. The West has seen a rise in self-employment, self-help strategies, and household economies among the poor, a phenomenon once confined to developing countries.

One illustration of the liberal approach to informal economies weds network theories to the concept of "social capital". It builds on rational choice theory but rejects its extreme, individualistic premises of utility maximisation by assuming that individuals are socialized in micro-sociological settings. For example, James Coleman views the various forms of social capital - obligations and expectations, information channels, and social norms - as resources for action, increasing human and financial capital. Networks that attain social structural "closure" enhance the positive effects of particularistic obligations, expectations, and norms.

Larger households and resi dents of tightly-knit local communities have an advantage in maintaining consumption on these bases. By contrast, informal economies are less likely to work among the socially disaffiliated and the State may be the only recourse to the latter.

Such attention to the various institutions, groups, and spheres in civil society is characteristic of liberal paradigms in sociology and political science. Unlike the monopoly paradigm, these approaches do not privilege the market. Like the solidarity paradigm, they highlight the social embeddedness of economic activity, but do not assume that rank in one social sphere is always consonant with rank in the others. Indeed, social liberalism finds the roots of exclusion in the inadequate separation of spheres unenforced rights, or market failures which justify state intervention.

MONOPOLY AND LABOUR MARKET SEGMENTATION

The monopoly paradigm treats exclusion and unemployment as symptoms of group monopolies which generate inequality and severe economic exploitation. As Joan Robinson put it, "the only thing that is worse than being exploited is not being exploited". Powerful "status groups" with distinctive cultural identities and institutions use social closure to restrict the access of outsiders to valued resources. The overlap of group distinctions and inequality is at the heart of the problematique of this paradigm. Theories of labour market segmentation epitomize the paradigm's link between social closure and economic exclusion. Segmentation occurs wherever there are barriers to free competition between workers and/or firms. Many labour market barriers - from regulations to credentials - operate simultaneously. Like social closure in a more general way, labour market segmentation results in poverty and economic inequality.

Two theories dominated the first wave of segmentation research. First, in institutional economics, Peter Doeringer and Michael Piore identified the "dual labour market" which distinguished between primary and secondary labour markets based on both job quality and worker characteristics. To explain why some groups could not gain access to highly paid, secure employment, they proposed the notion of the "internal labour market" that insulates primary workers from external market competition. Early dual labour market theories assumed that the secondary labour market operates like a classic competitive market, but that non-price criteria, such as the racial origin of workers, ration good jobs in the primary labour market.

Similarly, some firms can use union membership promotion from within and other institutional restrictions on mobility to limit access to in-house jobs. Second, complementing the neo-institutional approach, neo-Marxist economists portrayed the segmentation and stratification of labour markets as mechanisms to divide and control labour under conditions of partial unionisation. Worker power produces higher wages in unionized segments, while the disproportionately female and minority secondary and subordinate labour markets serve as a reserve army of labour.

Although these early studies were criticized on theoretically methodological and empirical grounds, they shared the assumption that, contrary to competitive or human capital theories of wages, jobs vary in the compensation they offer to equally productive workers. Compensation of all (kinds - wages, promotion opportunities, fringe benefits, or risks of unemployment - can serve as monopolized resources. Since the supply side is controlled, these theories reason, a persisting differential must result from the rationality of firms. If wages remain higher, there must be institutional or "non-price" barriers to mobility, access, and competition from unemployed or otherwise employed workers. Such exclusion rations jobs and creates queues. Thus, high unemployment may in fact be compatible with productivity and economic growth.

The second round of labour market segmentation studies improved upon methodology and provided strong evidence for the theory. Some of the most compelling empirical substantiation for the theory was the evidence provided by some American economists of large and enduring inter-industry wage differentials between equally productive workers. Yet, current economic segmentation theories differ as to the particular mechanisms responsible. For example, "insider-outsider" models start from the same premise as efficiency wage models.

However, reasoning from union behaviour, they argue that the turnover costs of replacing incumbent workers with the unemployed increase the bargaining power of organized insiders who, by threatening to quit, can demand higher wages. Since insiders can cost employers more than they would gain by hiring outsiders, the acceptance of lower wages by outsiders is insufficient to give them access to good jobs. Both the erosion of skills and the stigma employers attach to "outsiders" make it more difficult to re-enter the labour market after a spell of unemployment, particularly if it is a long one. The empirical support for this model is that high-wage industries have lower quit rates.

Where monitoring and turnover costs are more important in some sectors, industries or firms than in others, one would expect to find labour market segmentation. Some jobs will pay higher wages to increase productivity and will be rationed. Occupants of "good jobs" who do not need added incentives will still collect "rents" because those jobs will be scarce relative to the number of workers wanting them. In neo-classical theory, this excess labour supply for good jobs should drive down primary sector wages, enabling workers to attain access through intersectoral mobility. Instead, it produces a labour queue of either the unemployed or workers in "bad" jobs. Labour market queues also support the theory of statistical discrimination.

In sum, labour market institutions and institutional demand-side variables can be seen as the source of group monopolies and social exclusion, which in turn cause wage inequality. Because of non-universal coverage, attempts to reduce inequality through collective bargaining and labour legislation may have inadvertently created new bases of exclusion. For example, there is an incentive to shift work to small firms, the self-employed, or part-time and temporary employees who evade or are exempted from compulsory welfare contributions and taxes, paying compulsory benefits, or respecting standards on hours and safety. Rules on length of service also restrict the access of new labour market entrants to well-paid, protected jobs.

There may also be trade-offs between redistributive equity, in the form of social security contributions, and economic efficiency. Although negative income tax experiments suggest that substitution effects (that reduce effort) may be outweighed or at least offset by income effects (that increase effort), marginal (rather than proportional) taxation may exacerbate the trade-off. Assumptions about a decent family wage that underlie much labour legislation and collective bargaining may also have contributed to exclusion on the basis of sex and of household structure. The labour force influx of working women partly accounts for growth in part-time employment.

The European Union appears to have accepted the existence of these trade-offs. The Commission's 1994 White Paper, Growth, competiveness, employment, proposed collective mechanisms of " solidarity" between those with and without jobs, rich and poor, men and women, generations, regions, and neighbours:

Social protection schemes have - in part at least - had a negative impact on employment in that they have, in the main, tended to protect people already in work, making their situation more secure and consolidating certain advantages. They have in effect proved to be an obstacle to the recruitment of jobseekers or of new entrants to the labour market.

In addition to this "dual standard of treatment working to the detriment of the jobless," the Commission deemed labour market rigidity to be "the root cause of what are relatively high labour costs". Those in employment have enjoyed the fruits of economic growth while the unemployed are excluded. Of the 10 million new jobs in the European Union created between 1990 and 1993, only 3 million were taken by the registered unemployed; the rest absorbed new entrants or re-entrants. In countries where a large youth cohort has bloated the labour supply, there may indeed be a trade-off between wages and employment.

Yet, the higher wages produced by group monopolies may also have created incentives to shift employment to more competitive sectors. Indeed, these processes underlie some theories of the informal economy. In both developed and developing countries, employers and the self-employed evade legal regulations in order to lower the cost of production. This makes them attractive as subcontractors for larger, even multinational, corporations. Obviously, differential sectoral labour costs are only one reason for the rise of precarious informal employment and subcontracting. Others are greater market uncertainty and the economies of scale derived from specialisation. Nevertheless, the monopoly paradigm emphasizes the contribution of regulatory barriers to sectoral segmentation and, thus, economic exploitation and exclusion.

As the French regulation school points out, similar processes may account for the increasing "numerical" flexibility in Western labour markets. Global competition has increased the pressure to cut labour costs through quantitative flexibility, hiring and firing workers with fluctuations in demand. Indeed, in OECD countries like France and Germany, growth was almost exclusively in part-time employment. As good jobs in high-wage sectors are automated or subdivided into more low-wage jobs in less regulated, more competitive sectors, employment growth may be decoupled from its historic association with rising wages and greater income equality.

The problem is not only a consequence of low-wage job growth, however. With technological innovation, the relative wage return to higher education has been rising in most advanced countries, resulting in greater income inequality. Differential access to firms, or jobs within firms introducing internal, "qualitative" flexibility - where jobs and profits are more tied to capital investment, reorganisation, teamwork, and retraining than to the cost of labour inputs - may itself generate a new basis for labour market segmentation and exclusion in the future. Job security and benefits as well as wages may be traded off for employment. In sum, there is a tendency towards dualism among those who do have jobs. as well as between those in and those out of work.

This example of "dual closure" illustrates how segmentation theories account for economic exclusion within the framework of the monopoly paradigm. Any labour market barriers to or shelters from competition that persistently raise wages for some workers at the expense of others effectively exclude the latter from access to some forms of compensation or employment conditions. Whether justified on grounds of efficiency, merit or for political or institutional reasons, exclusion may result from differential access to high-wage countries, high-wage industries, or firms and jobs with internal labour markets and "flexible specialisation ".

Since informal social contacts and place of residence often channel some groups into such firms and industries, socially isolated or minority groups may find themselves at a disadvantage. Thus, not only material and legal, but also cultural and geographic boundaries restrict access to valued resources, giving insiders a form of monopoly and power over outsiders. The monopoly paradigm sees culture as a form of domination: by including some, it necessarily excludes others. While the solidarity paradigm stresses culture's essentialism and the specialisation paradigm sees culture as an autonomous sphere of valued beliefs and practices, the monopoly paradigm's deconstructivism sees culture as "interested", i.e. protecting material advantages.

Any form of exclusion necessarily entails inequality. For this reason, perhaps British writers' discussions of economic post-Fordism often conflate it with cultural post-modernism: both advocate relaxing rigid social boundaries. The monopoly paradigm treats the subject of informal economies as another aspect of sectoral segmentation. The formal/informal split is yet another expression of exploitative core/periphery relations. Although social contacts and community ties, coupled with free time, may help all the economically inactive to enlarge their social world through participation in the "household economy" and local voluntary activities, the opportunity to engage in informal economic activities is differentially distributed among the unemployed.

In the monopoly paradigm, the unequal power underlying group monopolies can be mitigated, if not eliminated, by inclusive citizenship or social rights. The social democratic formulation of citizenship as "full and equal participation in the community" draws explicitly upon Marshall's classic formulation. The gradual extension of civil, then political and, finally, social rights bestows an equal status and the equal rights and duties with which that status is endowed. Although, capitalist societies are inherently unequal and conflictual, social citizenship in a redistributive welfare state and "a direct sense of community membership based on loyalty to a civilisation which is a common possession, would "abate" economic inequality.

Over time, European social democrats adopted Marshall's rhetoric of citizenship to support an egalitarian programme of decommodification, class compromise, and material redistribution through the expansion of universalist welfare states. They contrasted citizenship with inequality. The distinction between the monopoly and solidarity paradigms is clearly illustrated by the European Union's shifting discourse of exclusion. Initial discussions used the French Republican sense of the term. For example, the Community Charter of the Fundamental Social Rights of Workers adopted by the (then) European Community's Heads of State declares that "... in a spirit of solidarity, it is important to combat social exclusion". However, the European Commission's report, Towards a Europe of solidarity, already shifted towards rhetoric of social rights:

... social exclusion refers. in particular, to inability to enjoy social rights without help, suffering from low self-esteem, inadequacy in their [sic] capacity to meet their obligations, the risk of long-term relegation to the ranks of those on social benefits, and stigmatisation which particularly in the urban environment, extends to the areas in which they live.

The subsequent European Commission report on the subject explicitly used Marshall's notion of social citizenship:

Here we define social exclusion first and foremost in relation to the social rights of citizens... to a certain basic standard of living and to participation in the major social and occupational opportunities of the society.

The Final Poverty 3 Programme report also noted this passage and itself concluded that exclusion "implies the denial (or non-realisation) of social rights".

Many European social scientists are now analyzing the underclass in terms of a Marshallián understanding of exclusion. In the rare cases in which the term exclusion is used in this context in the United Kingdom, reference is usually made to Marshall's three-pronged conception of citizenship and its role in combating inequality. For example, the Child Poverty Action Group used the rhetoric of exclusion to argue that the poor are excluded from full citizenship and participation in the society and, thus, are often excluded from public consciousness as well.

A contrast with the liberal perspective highlights the monopoly paradigm's incorporation of inequality into the notion of exclusion. In line with Marshall, the monopoly perspective defines the underclass as "that group of people who are not fully citizens because they are not able to participate in certain basic social activities" and "are excluded from the mainstream of society... Against this, it can be argued that members of the underclass exclude themselves by refusing to make the best of their opportunities". The paradigms thus differ on the question of who is responsible for exclusion.

Most British thinkers on the question argue along the lines that "the idea of an underclass is a counterpart to the idea of social classes, and acquires its meaning within that same framework of analysis... they belong to family units having no stable relationship at all with the 'mode of production' - with legitimate gainful employment". Like poverty and the underclass, exclusion has class-based connotations in the United Kingdom. For example, Peter Townsend maintained that the poor "are, in effect, excluded from ordinary living patterns, customs, and activities". Frank Field noted that "the very poorest are separated, not only from other groups on low income, but, more importantly, from the working class".

The underclass is situated below the working classes, because their "roles place them more or less permanently at the economic level where benefits are paid by the State to those unable to participate in the labour market at all". Slowly, the monopoly model of citizenship is expanding beyond social class questions. Social democratic thought is just beginning to adjust to increasing diversity in styles of life and cultural values and to the political challenges posed by immigrant minorities, environmental movements, and long-term unemployment. British multiculturalist and post-modernist thinkers are increasingly using the notion of citizenship and equality of status to encompass the recognition of diversity, the inclusion of all groups, and the protection from stigma. Weberian references consonant with the monopoly paradigm can also be found: Lydia Morris, for example, concluded that the British underclass consists of those suffering from "status exclusion".

Even some American social democrats have adopted the monopoly paradigm's exclusion discourse. Lee Rainwater has argued that "the person living in poverty is not the Middle American: he has passed over an invisible border". Michael Harrington asserted that The Other America is invisible: "to be impoverished is to be an internal alien [without] links with the great world". Michael Katz provides an excellent example. First, he deconstructs the solidarity approach to exclusion in terms reminiscent of Marshall:

> We can think about poor people as "them" or as "us". For the most part, Americans have talked about "them ". Even in the language of social science, as well as in ordinary conversation and political rhetoric poor people usually remain outsiders, strangers to be pitied or despised, helped or punished, ignored or studied, but rarely full citizens, members of a larger community on the same terms as the rest of us.

Then he deconstructs liberal discourse: "Poverty in America is profoundly individual; like popular economics, it is supply side". Lastly, he casts exclusion and citizenship as issues of monopoly and inequality:

> For finally, the politics of poverty are about the processes of inclusion and exclusion in American life: who, to put the question crudely, gets what? How are goods distributed? As such, it is a question of race class, gender and the bases of power... Europeans today write about the "new poverty", which they understand in a similar way. They do not write very much about the underclass which highlights the peculiarly American tendency to transform poverty from a product of politics and economics into a matter of individual behaviour.

He blames the economic, spatial, social and cultural isolation of the inner-city black poor on exclusionary laws and practices of private employers, unions, and white workers. And like Marshall and social democrats, Katz calls for "finding ways to talk about poor people as 'us' that expand ideas of citizenship".

The dominance of the monopoly perspective on the Continent is also reflected in methodology. The European Union's statistical service, Eurostat, and the Luxembourg Income Survey adopted standardized comparative methods to measure poverty relative to average national income (equivalent expenditure). Relative poverty lines simultaneously incorporate absolute deprivation and inequality, "a barrier and a level". Moreover, many justify these measures with reference to Marshall's definition of citizenship, arguing that poverty must be measured relative to a society's normative standards of living or consumption levels. Without a requisite level of goods and services,... individuals cannot participate as full members of their society". Similarly, poverty may be considered in subjective terms, based on what most people in a society regard as the "decent" or "adequate" income necessary to "get by".

Relative poverty lines have been used for decades, but the term "new poverty" was introduced to maintain the distinction between those populations traditionally considered as the poor and those displaced by economic change.

Unlike the old poverty which reflected cyclical downturns, the new poverty, especially in the United Kingdom, was considered structural, grounded in a new economy that subjects all social classes to employment insecurity. This vulnerability to downward mobility created a relative poverty of deprivation, as many lose what they expected to have - a socially accepted or customary style of life. The term "new poverty" encompassed many of the same empirical realities as those that the French labelled "exclusion" phenomena.

Yet French observers insist on the distinction between "exclusion" and "inequality". For example, Touraine argues that the two phenomena follow different types of logic. Inequality occurs in an industrial society of production in which opposing classes are "integrated" because they confront each other face to face; whereas exclusion is a symptom of economic growth and social change in which social actors contesting the dominant power structure and culture are divorced from the economic and political system.

In the emerging postindustrial society, the social problem is no longer inequality, but justice and the rules of the game. Jean-Baptiste de Foucauld also argues that inequalities and exclusions are not the same, although both are rising and may have cumulative effects.

Unlike inequality, exclusion is associated with rising individualism and a changing market society which is divorcing actors from the system and separating productive and social demands. De Foucauld still sees inequality and exclusion through Republican eyes: despite their differences they are joined through the perspective of the need for social cohesion in a dynamic society. Thus, it is necessary to encourage both equality and justice, rather than trade one off against the other. Finally, it is worth noting that while participatory democracy is an essential part of the social democratic vision of citizenship, it is not directed towards a form of solidarity based on national consensus.

Rather than stressing participation as a duty of citizenship or integration in the republic or nation, both the Catholic and the Socialist Left advocate direct participation in local associations and social movements as a means of connecting the excluded to the larger society through organized opposition and challenges to powerful interests. Decentralizing power to localities and workplaces permits the excluded, whatever their group background, to pursue their common interests in inclusion and redistribution. Locally based "insertion" and integration policies should create "a political space of belonging". Integration is a project seeking to reconstruct an active citizenship. Participation in public life makes the struggle against exclusion political and launches a debate over the nature of new forms of solidarity and the terms of a new social contract. State intervention might thereby be legitimated.

EXCLUSION, POLITICS, AND SOCIAL POLICY

In this chapter I have presented three major paradigms of exclusion, each grounded in a different conception of integration and citizenship. In the solidarity paradigm dominant in France, exclusion is the breakdown of a social bond between the individual and society that is cultural and moral, rather than economically interested. Cultural boundaries give rise to socially constructed dualistic categories for ordering the world, defining the poor, the unemployed and ethnic minorities as deviant outsiders. However, by tying national solidarity to political rights and duties, Republican citizenship imposes an obligation on the State to aid in the inclusion of the excluded. By presenting itself as a "third way" between liberalism and socialism, Republican thought weds economic to social concerns through the notion of solidarity. Similar emphases can be found in new schools of political economy.

In the specialisation paradigm, exclusion reflects discrimination. Social differentiation, economic divisions of labour, and the separation of spheres should not produce hierarchically ordered social categories if excluded individuals are free to move across boundaries and if spheres of social life governed by different principles are kept legally separate. Cultural pluralism, like political pluralism, rests upon voluntary membership and group competition. Liberal models of citizenship emphasize the contractual exchange between individual rights and obligations and the tensions between the sphere of civil society based on liberty and a public sphere based on equality and democracy. Liberal assumptions are rooted in micro-sociology, which emphasizes small groups, and in neo-classical economics and other social sciences which are characterized by methodological individualism.

Finally, the third paradigm sees exclusion as a consequence of the formation of group monopolies. Powerful groups, often displaying distinctive cultural identities and institutions, restrict the access of outsiders to valued resources through a process of "social closure". The same process is evident in labour market and enterprise segmentation which draws exclusive boundaries between and within firms. At the heart of this paradigm is the necessary overlap of group distinctions and inequality, "the barrier and the level". Inequality is mitigated by social democratic citizenship which, in Marshall's formulation, entails full participation in the community.

However they are conceived, the empirical manifestations of rising deprivation in the advanced countries call into question the adequacy of existing welfare arrangements. The numbers of means-tested schemes designed to serve small constituencies are growing rapidly. The assumption underlying post-war social insurance schemes of a uniform life-cycle, career pattern, and family structure applies to a shrinking number of people. "New" types of social disadvantage are increasingly emerging as are demands that these newly identified social problems be addressed.

Once-quiescent beneficiaries are organizing politically under the banners of their various "demographic identities", are forming lobby groups, and are pressuring local government in the areas where they are concentrated. This "politics of consumption" is concerned less with transfers than with unpopular and residual social services (e.g., drug rehabilitation, assistance for refugees or immigrants, urban renewal programmes); as such it introduces distributive conflicts not only between productive and unproductive citizens, but between cultural groups as well. The demand for individualized, differentiated services for socially marginal groups also challenges the principle of universalism that once legitimated the postwar welfare states. This crisis in social policy requires a rethinking of the notions of citizenship and solidarity.

Although these manifestations of the phenomenon of "exclusion" have led to new social policy approaches, especially in France, any large-scale recasting of welfare state institutions will require a broad political consensus. It is useful to recall that the initial establishment of national welfare states was a process of "institutional searching" for political compromise. To achieve such compromises, it was necessary to formulate political ideas that blended pre-existing nation-specific norms and practices. As the paradigms illustrate, such ideas are still reflected in existing welfare state institutions.

Today, as new social problems call for major social policy reforms, the importance of new ideas to forge political consensus appear to be just as important. Does the notion of exclusion offer a formula with which to achieve the political compromises necessary to meet these challenges? As I have indicated, exclusion means different things to different people. Only at the extremes of the political spectrum is one likely to find people actually in favour of it. Given the multiple connotations of the term, it might provide a political opportunity to cement a broadly based alliance in favour of new social policies.

For example, the importance that French observers attach to distinguishing exclusion from other terms denoting social disadvantage suggests that the concept does have political significance. If we define exclusion as a thoroughly new, multidimensional phenomenon touching people at all levels of the social hierarchy in some respects or at some point in their lives, large, cross-class coalitions to combat it may become easier to build. Most people have suffered from some kind of rejection or misery in their lives, and apprehension about being excluded has become widespread. As the connotations of exclusion expand to encompass the dashing of extravagant aspirations, " in the end everyone will consider himself excluded from something".

For example, a survey conducted in France in December 1993 by CSA/La Rue, a newspaper sold by the homeless, found that 55 per cent of French adults and 69 per cent of young people aged 18-24 fear they will become "excluded" and three-quarters worried that someone close to them would. That feeling of vulnerability is not confined to France. The Families and Work Institute found that 42 per cent of American workers report their companies are reducing their workforces temporarily or permanently. Those near-majorities of respondents perceive a clear threat of exclusion - in the broad sense of a loss of social status - may account for the term's wide appeal and its even wider application.

Recent inflammatory remarks about immigrants by certain French politicians are nothing if not divisive and have mobilized the opposition. However, whether public apprehension and indignation will be sufficient to mobilize strong political support for new social policies in France remains to be seen. In the spring of 1994, demonstrations against inadequate provision for unemployed young people revealed a wide range of attitudes among the young - including a fear that their expectations of continuing a comfortable lifestyle acquired at home will not be fulfilled. If the common fear of exclusion may cement an alliance among those differentially placed in the social hierarchy, this may not prove sufficient to overcome other social cleavages.

Indeed, to the extent that exclusion is understood in the liberal, individualistic terms of the specialisation paradigm, it may become a euphemism for stigmatized, isolated, or scapegoated groups. Its meaning may narrow to those with multiple disadvantages. From this perspective, the university student protests against declining employment prospects may simply reflect a defence of their traditional prerogatives and a demand for protection from increasing competition. By identifying the victims of economic restructuring and the end of full employment, terms like exclusion, the new poor, or the underclass may even serve to justify majority resistance to redistributive taxation and expenditures.

Targeted social policies will then entail no sacrifice by the privileged and dualism will be reinforced. Thus, though the idea of exclusion could be useful to reformers who wish to point to the inadequacies of existing welfare states, conversely it may serve to distract attention from the overall rise in inequality, general unemployment, and family breakdown that is affecting all social classes. By ghettoizing risk categories under a new label and publicizing the more spectacular forms of poverty requiring emergency aid, policies to combat exclusion may make it easier to re-target money on smaller social categories, like the homeless or the long-term unemployed. It may even undermine the universal social insurance schemes that traditionally protected the working- and middle-classes. In sum, therefore, just as the idea of exclusion has many meanings, it can also serve a variety of political purposes.

8

The Scope of Ethics and Social Philosophy

There are two distinct ways in which we may regard the facts and problems of human nature. We may, on the one hand, treat them descriptively. We may collect and analyze all sorts of facts concerning human nature and make generalisations there from. We may formulate laws descriptive of the actual operations of human nature. Such is the procedure of psychology, the general science of human behaviour. Such is the procedure of sociology, the science of human behaviour in its social relations. Social psychology is really the key to sociology.

It is the description and interpretation of the individual's behaviour, as influenced by social contacts and in turn as determining his social attitudes. The distinction between individual psychology and social psychology is simply one of emphasis. In individual psychology the self's social contacts and attitudes are considered primarily as properties of the individual person. In social psychology the individual person is regarded primarily as the meeting point of Social relations. Both procedures are correct if not pushed to the point of excluding one another.

On the other hand, we may study human nature normatively. When we do this we are concerned with the facts of human behaviour, including, particularly, thoughtful behaviour, with special regard to the values, the ends, the goods or the ideals which man by his purposeful activity seeks to realize.

Ethics is commonly defined as the fundamental science of human values. It is the business of ethics to determine in the light of rational reflection what are the most comprehensive and best values, ends, goods, ideals which should guide man in his purposive activity. Now the business of ethics and social philosophy is pre-λminently with values, ends, goods; and philosophy is the systematic study of human values, therefore ethics is a philosophical science and an essential part of philosophy.

It is generally agreed that ethics or moral science, or moral philosophy, is the systematic study of the principles for determining the rightness and wrongness, the goodness and badness of human actions and motives and characters. It is likewise admitted that human conduct and characters fall under the categories of moral judgment, as right and wrong, good and bad, only in so far as conduct is the expression of voluntary deliberation or consciously willed action. The admission of the distinction between willed or voluntary action and involuntary action is the basic presumption upon which all ethical judgments depend.

If this distinction be invalid, if there be no real difference in kind between a mechanically determined action and a voluntary, a consciously self-determined action, then ethics falls to the ground. It becomes a pseudo-science, a systematic study of illusions. There are, then, no different meanings in judgments of ethical valuation, in speaking of good and bad and allotting reward and punishment, praise and blame than there are in applying oil to an engine or in cleaning or removing some of its parts. If man as a moral agent be not free in the sense of having the power of self-determining valuation and choice with respect to some of his acts, then it is not only idle, it is silly to talk of human responsibility.

Then the phrase, moral agent, is empty and misleading and leads to cruel discrimination. The concept of responsibility is worthless and mischievous. Voluntary conduct, conduct that is subject matter for ethical judgment, is conduct in which the end of the act is intended by the agent, chosen by him because it promises to satisfy some interest.

The end is valued or, as in the case of play or creative work, the means are valued as part of the end. A good act is good because it furthers experiences which have value for some one. A bad act is bad because it thwarts or destroys some experience of value. Value and good are identical from an ethical standpoint; unvalue and bad are likewise identical. A right act is one which promotes something good, some value for a self; a wrong act, one which hinders or destroys a good. So, too, with motive and intentions. To say that ethics is the science of human values is the same as to say that ethics is the systematic study of the principles of the good life.

It is the business of ethics to determine, by systematic reflection, what are the most comprehensive and inclusive standards for the guidance of human beings in determining the good or valuable experiences that they should seek. Ethics is concerned with the intrinsic value, or goods of life; in other words, with the valued acts, experiences or goods which are worth while for their own sakes, since they satisfy the deepest and most lasting cravings of selves. In contrast with ethical values, the economic and industrial values which lands, machinery, capital and money have are instrumental, since these things have value as instruments to promote human welfare. The enjoyment of beauty, love, friendship, understanding, scientific and scholarly knowledge and philosophic insight and religious communion seem to be the intrinsic values since they satisfy essential capacities of human nature.

Ethics is called a normative science since it deals with norms or standards of valuation for human conduct. It is contrasted with descriptive sciences, such as chemistry or psychology which analyzes, describe and correlate facts.

This distinction is useful if it be not misunderstood and misapplied. Ethics is descriptive, too, for it deals with facts-the facts of human conduct with reference to its valuations and aims or purposes. The natural sciences also involve norms. A discovery in chemistry may lead to a norm of behaviour in engineering, medicine or diet; a discovery in psychology to a norm in education or psycho-therapeutics.

VALUE OF ETHICS

But what need is there for a study of ethics; of what use is this so-called science? Cannot human beings determine what is good without the study of ethics? Our answer is that they cannot, in our present complex and sophisticated civilisation, determine what are the relative goods, what are the relative values of varying kinds of motives, aims and ideals of conduct without ethical reflection, whether or no they study ethics formally. The existence of communities of human beings, from a family to a nation, implies certain socially accepted and effective modes of regulating the impulses of the individual in relation to his fellows.

These are the mores, customs or folkways of social groups. In a custom-ridden community, the individual's acts are entirely regulated by the recognized and enforced code of the group. He must obey the customs. If he violates them, punishment is swift and sure. The code is backed by the group conscience and its supernatural guardians, In a complex modern civilisation, not only is the individual much freer in the choice of his aims, but he is actually confronted by a variety of different and often conflicting interests, aims, standards. Even if he wills to accept the accepted morals of some group with which he identifies his interests, he must at least take some attitude towards the morals of other groups.

If he be a union labor man he must take an attitude towards the open shop, non-union labor and the employer. If he become a Buddhist or Christian Scientist or a pacifist he must take some attitude toward the morals of other groups. Now, the central problem of ethics arises just here. How shall the individual be guided, in facing the various social claims which confront him, towards an intelligent and good choice? In a complex society composed of reflective individuals, the central problem of ethics is that of social obligations. How shall the individual adjust the various social claims upon him, made by community interests of different types, to one another and to his own individuality?

ETHICS AND SOCIAL PHILOSOPHY

If the central problem of ethics be what is stated above, no sharp distinction can be drawn between ethics and social philosophy. Since the key question of ethics is the relation between the individual's own preferences or interests or valuations and his obligations as a member of various groups or communities, it is impossible to attempt to solve ethical problems without a social philosophy. The heart of ethics is the heart of social philosophy. The central question is: How may the individual's life be ordered so that he can be a moral self as a member of the community of moral selves?

It is often said that ethics deals with the individual as the source and bearer of moral values, whereas social philosophy deals with the moral relations of individuals as members of society. But the individual, as the source and bearer of moral values, is already a member of social groups; He cannot be a human individual otherwise. And social groups consist of individuals in various relations of contact, cooperation, communion, conflict.

One may begin with the consideration either of the individual or of the group; but one can make no headway at all, and certainly one can reach no conclusion, if one remains where one begins. The individual is a subject of moral life only as a member of social groups. The group is a moral fact and as such it consists of individuals in interrelations of action and passion. Ethics, the doctrine of the good life, the comprehensive theory of human values, has a wider and richer scope than morals, the doctrine of right social relationships. There are super moral values. But super moral values have place only when the moral foundation has been laid. Human values include more than morals, but this more is built on morals.

The ethical agent is such only in relation to his fellows, and the social order is nothing more than the order of relations between individuals that are thus far members of one or more social groups. We may discuss the ethics of certain aspects of private life that do not easily lend themselves to treatment from the standpoint of social or group relationships-such as the ethics of an individual's aesthetic gratifications; or his tastes in clothes, food, drink, amusements or private hobbies. But even these modes of behaviour bring him into some relation to his fellows.

We may study the ethical principles of the social order without paying particular regard to the idiosyncrasies of its constituent members. But certainly an ethical theory of the social order which ignored the facts and claims of human idiosyncrasy would be a one-sided, and thus far unethical, social philosophy. In brief, the chief part of ethics is social ethics, and social ethics is but a concretion or specification of social philosophy. One might discuss actual problems of concrete social ethics without constantly lugging in his social philosophy or theory of social values, but one can never arrive at a rational solution of the concrete problems of social ethics without employing a social philosophy.

ETHICS AND SOCIAL PHILOSOPHY TO POLITICS, ECONOMICS AND JURISPRUDENCE

Politics is the comparative study of the definite types of political organisation and the distinction of the relative values of the different types. It is clear that the basic problems of politics can be intelligently considered only in the light of a social philosophy. Political philosophy, the theory of what the state ought to be, is a part of social philosophy. Any attempt to weigh the respective merits of the different types of political constitution presupposes on the part of the weigher a conviction in regard to the fundamental human values to which political organisation should be instrumental. Jurisprudence, or the philosophy of law, is simply the application of a social ethics or social philosophy to the facts and problems of the legal order.

Law is a means to a social end. Its principles consist of the ethical minima in conduct that can be formulated and enforced by the power of the state. Economics is the systematic study of the facts of the production and distribution of material wealth. Thus far it is purely a descriptive science. It is often treated as having a normative aspect. In this regard it becomes simply the application to the judgment of the actual economic order of the theory of social values. In other words, when one undertakes to judge the human or ethical values of the economic order one employs a social philosophy.

THE PROBLEMS OF ETHICS AND SOCIAL PHILOSOPHY

The fundamental problem of ethics and social philosophy has already been indicated. It is that of the right relation of the individual to the various social groups, and by consequence that of the right relations of these groups to one another. The first step to the solution of these problems will be to determine what are the salient characteristics of human nature in the raw; that is, of human nature before it has been socialized and moralized. The second step will be to determine in what ways and to what extent the development of individuality is and should be shaped by social influences.

The third step and the most important of all is to determine what ideal, that is, what standard of value or good in regard to the worth of the individual as a member of society, is most acceptable to reason. In other words, the central problem of social philosophy is the central problem of ethics-namely, what is the ethical criterion of the social order? What human values are to constitute the basis of our judgment of the social order? Our next problem will be to consider the general nature of society or of the community.

A solution of the aforementioned problem in total constitutes the general principles or foundations of the social order. The second part of ethics and social philosophy, the more concrete part, is applied social philosophy. It will consist in the consideration of the main types of social groupings or social institutions, in the light of the principles arrived at in the first part. The chief of these institutions are the family, the civic community, economic institutions, the state, law and justice, education, organized religion, and international relations. Finally we may consider the problem of the meaning and reality of social progress.

METHOD

The method to be pursued into an inquiry of this kind is the method of science-namely, an analysis of facts, and reflection upon the facts, for the purpose of generalisation from them. The facts with which we are concerned herein are biological, psychological and cultural. In other words, we shall consider; first, the actual nature of man as a conskis living organism with a special regard to his social relationships. Secondly, civilized man is a cultural being; in other words, his nature as a conscious organism is developed and molded through institutions and through the co-operating and conflicting activities of men and groups in his cultural history.

All the social institutions embody the cumulative results of the labors of the past generations towards the development of the cultural matrix in and through which the present living generation acts and is acted upon. The institutions of civilisation, imperfect though they be, embody humanity's attempts to establish patterns of social organisation through which the values, or goods, that are possible of achievement and enjoyment by man, may be realized and possessed. All human institutions are means for the satisfaction of man's persistent thirst for a lasting good. From the standpoint of ethics and social philosophy the most cardinal fact about man is that he is a being who sets up and tries to achieve values.

The family, the civic community, education and culture, economic activity, the political state and religious institutions are the foundations and scaffoldings for the home of values. Friendship, love, spiritual culture, the enjoyment of beauty and worship or communion with the highest-these are some of the principal forms of value in which the human soul seeks to quench its thirst for a lasting good. Throughout this work "spirit" and "spiritual" are used to designate all forms of mental activity, experience and aspiration which are not subordinated to physical and material ends. Pure knowledge, intellectual beauty, disinterested service, friendship and love no less than worship of the Highest, are forms of the realisation of spirit.

SOCIAL HUMANISM

The theory of self-realisation recognizes the necessity for self-denial, self limitation, self-sacrifice. The higher good is not attained without the sacrifice of lower goods. The young person who sets out upon the career of training himself for a learned profession or for the cultivation of artistic propensities must forego or postpone many joys; he must postpone marriage, he must forego many pleasant social activities. He may have to content himself with shabby clothing, poor food and little recreation. Every one who chooses a career shuts himself off from the possibility of satisfying a number of desires.

The scholar, for example, who elects the vocation of a teacher, must forego forever the pleasures of affluence, of popular fame and power and of much travel. No doubt he wins compensating joys, but Goethe's words, "Thou shalt renounce," are true of every one who elects to lead an honest and worthy life. Those who would serve worthily and win their own self-respect as well as the respect of others whose respect is worth having must renounce the fleshpots of Egypt.

The doctrine of self-realisation, in this respect, is identical with the Christian ethics. "He that will be great among you, let him be the servant of all, for the Son of Man came not to be ministered unto but to minister. He that seeketh his life shall lose it, and he that loseth his life for my sake and the gospel's, shall find it." This means that the way to self-realisation is the way of self-denial, self-limitation, and self-sacrifice.

Now, is it not a paradox to say that self-realisation is won through the sacrifice of self even to the uttermost? How can we say that the person who sacrifices a worthy career or foregoes marriage to devote himself to the care of a dependent parent or of his younger brothers and sisters is realizing self: How can we say that the captain who goes down with his sinking ship after the passengers have all been put in life boats, the men who died on the *Titanic* for the sake of the women and children, or the millions of soldiers who died in the mud and cold in the late War, in sacrificing themselves for their respective causes realized their true selves? Over some British graves in Flanders is the following epitaph: "That your to-morrow might be better these have given their to-day." The to-morrow has come, is it better?

In the meantime, those who gave their to-day are being forgotten. The world seems to have slumped back into a selfish and unintelligent scramble for bread and the circus. How did they realize themselves? For what far country did they sacrifice life? It is doubtful whether most who died in the War were conscious of the end for which they died. But this doubt would not invalidate the moral principle involved in their acts, if indeed permanent and objective values were realized by their sacrifice.

The men who, hating war and loving the life of the cultivated scholar, loving their sweethearts, wives, children and friends, yet went forth voluntarily from England, France or the United States, to die in the mud, to perish from shells, poison gas or trench fever, did not achieve self-realisation unless the spirit of man is immortal. Self-realisation through ultimate self-sacrifice is a contradiction in terms unless the spiritual essence of personality survives death. Thus the doctrine of self-realisation is not a complete and consistent theory on any other interpretation of the universe than the spiritual one which makes the natural order subservient to the spiritual order.

I cannot here enter into a discussion of the problem of immortality. There does not seem to be any conclusive empirical evidence of immortality. The so-called communications from the spirits of the departed to the living have still too dubious a character, and even if true, they do not shed any very encouraging light on the state of personality after the death of the body. The immortality of the personal spirit seems to me a postulate or implication of the doctrine that the moral standard consists in the realisation of the higher selfhood through the service of objective, social and cultural or spiritual values.

Its better to define the moral standard as consisting in the expression of the spiritual self or personality through the service of the objective, social, spiritual structures that are embodied in the cultural life of humanity -in the service of the communal life; in the family, the neighbourhood and community, the vocation and, through these, in the service of the nation and of the more universal interests of humanity that are embraced in the cultural and spiritual values embodied in education, literature, art and science.

May we not say that the individual who serves in any honest and thorough way the maintenance and improvement of the cultural life of humanity, of the progress and perpetuity of humanity's spiritual life, through any forms of activity by which that life is furthered, is obeying the highest moral standard? While he realizes himself as a distinct and permanent center of spiritual life, he expresses his true self in the furtherance of the good life in human society. The supreme moral standard then is: Whatsoever promotes the progress of human society through the achievement and conservation of spiritual ideals and values and their augmentation in the future. Whatsoever furthers progress now can do so only by ministering to the conservation and enrichment of the present spiritual order.

The condition of future progress is conservation of the fruits of progress up to the present. The living generation finds its values immediate to itself, but the living generation is a link in the chain of the generations.

It is the present bearer of the future of the race. Its task is to sustain and enlarge the social order, the heritage of spiritual culture, without which humanity lapses into barbarism. The supreme principle of the good is not mere individual perfection. It is the service of perfection, dedication to the progressive ennoblement of humanity. Thus the furtherance of justice, freedom, truth, culture in human society is a higher moral principle than the realisation of the life of the individual; the latter is fulfilled and expressed through the service of the former.

The efforts of a people in the control of nature, in education and culture, in the maintenance and improvement of their civilisation have their own immediate moral values-of honest work, integrity, justice, freedom and loyalty to great causes. These immediate moral values are in turn the conditions without which the moral values of human culture cannot be preserved and enriched for future generations. We labor and we die for the future generations, but our labors and our deaths are worth while as contributory factors in the continuing, spiritual movement of human culture-that is, they are worth while if the spiritual culture of man has a permanent place in the nature of things.

We must either assume the supremacy in the cosmos of a spiritual order which is in very truth, however imperfectly, embodied in the mental and spiritual development of the human race or we must accept the alternative that, ultimately, all is vanity that is done under the sun. All the values for which humanity has striven and in which it has found its deepest joy shall finally tumble into the abyss of utter nothingness.

Our choice lies between a moral nihilism for which the human race is a cosmic blunder, on the one hand, and on the other hand faith in the enduringness and supremacy of a psychical life which is progressively realized in the life of humanity, through the growth and fruition of personalities in fullness and harmony of action and experience; in understanding, fellowship, sympathy and the enjoyment of beauty and love. Nevertheless, whatever be the future of the individual or the race, these values are good in their own right as they are lived. Immediate value belongs only to living experience.

THE PRINCIPLE OF HUMANISM

In short, the fundamental principle of control in human conduct is the harmonious integration of the dynamic capacities or energies of human nature. Since it is the prime conditions of harmonious integration that the wider, deeper and more permanent interests of the self shall be preferred to the narrower, shallower and more transitory interests, the principle of harmonious integration involves a hierarchical organisation of interests. The values or conditions which arise from the satisfaction of interests constitute a scale or hierarchy, since some interests are wider and more permanent than others.

An act is good if it satisfies an interest and at the same time either promotes or does not hinder the satisfaction of interests that are at least equally wide and deep and equally permanent. A motive or intent is good if it aims at the satisfaction of an interest in the right way. An act is bad if it either thwarts an interest or, in the satisfaction of an interest, prevents the satisfaction of other interests that are at least equally wide and deep and permanent; or, still worse, wider and more permanent interests. In every case the criterion is this-how does the act or the intent to do the act contributes to the furtherance of the harmonious system of interests?

Our criterion involves subordination of the more isolated transitory and superficial interests to the more comprehensive, pervasive, permanent and deeper interests. It involves the principles of measure and proportion as guiding criteria which Plato stressed so much. Is our principle individualistic or collectivistic? It is both. It is collectivistic, inasmuch as we recognize that the harmonious integration and energizing of human interests can take place only through a community life that is organized and conducted precisely to further this end in all its members. The individual who will not contribute his part to the furtherance of the economic substructure and the cultural superstructure of a good community life defeats himself as well as thwarts the lives of others.

The aim of the community, as Plato said, should be not to make any one individual happy by him but to make all members as happy as possible. We can go further and say that the individual can not be made truly happy, as we have defined happiness or welfare, without regard to the social conditions of the common weal. The human individual is so constituted that it is impossible for him to realize and enjoy in a harmonious and continuous fashion the basic interests of his being except as a contributing member of the community life. "He that seeketh his life shall lose it, and he that loseth his life shall find it," is a profound psychological truth and a paramount ethical principle.

The individual who refuses to marry or embark on any other social adventure because of its risks fails to realize his true individuality. In order to be truly human we must, as Goethe put it, join a whole or make one. To this one may add in qualification that we do not have to make a whole, all we have to do is to take the whole in which we find ourselves, the life of the community, and make it a better instrument for the organisation of harmonious individuality on the part of its members. As a member of the family, as a friend, a comrade, as a contributor to the economic sustenance of the community, as a furtherer of its cultural wealth, the individual realizes his personality.

On the other hand, our criterion is individualistic, since it finds in the development and enjoyment of harmonious, intelligent, self-determining individuality on the part of all its members the true measure of the value of the community life. As one surveys the panorama of life one finds that increase of individuality on the part of its members is the true criterion of the place of any living species in the scale of evolutionary development. In the lower invertebrates there is commensal communities-plant and animal communities not made up of distinct individuals, but having common roots and branches.

In the societies of ants, bees and wasps, while the individuals are distinct organisms, they are wholly subordinated and merged in the life of the society. In the vertebrates, the individual, while he mates as an individual, is the creature of the instincts or emotions which rule the pack or herd. The same is true, though in lesser degree, of the more primitive human communities. The recognition of fuller scope for the exercise of self determining individuality in human societies first appeared through military rule, priest craft and the administration of customs and laws.

The ethical significance of democracy as a social creed and policy consists in this-it is the express recognition of the universal right of human beings to the development of harmonious individuality or self-determining personality. There is no inconsistency between democracy in this sense and genuine mental aristocracy. On the contrary the one implies the other, for the realisation of the fundamental aim of democracy requires leadership, guidance, initiative, and creativeness. The true aristocrats in a democracy are those who serve the universal aim of the realisation of individuality by the exercise of their super average powers.

The attainment and enjoyment of individuality is possible only through a community life rich in opportunity for the attainment by all its members, up to the limit of their capacities, of cultural goods. It is the function of exceptionally endowed individuals to enrich the cultural goods and to further their distribution to all who can assimilate and use them. The richer, the more vigorous and progressive the cultural life of the community the more various and manifold will be the enjoyment of harmonious individuality by its members.

SOCIAL FUNCTIONING: CONTAGIOUS BEHAVIOUR

We have been talking as if each person found out for himself the way in which he can function. Usually, however, the individual does not work out his own behaviour patterns; he picks them up from other people. behaviour is contagious - it is catching. This applies to bodily actions, to ideas, to emotions, and to purposes. It applies to physical functioning, to emotional functioning, to imaginary functioning, and to functioning on purpose. That people want others to share their experiences was pointed out; in this chapter we shall see that people crave also to share the experiences of others.

THE HUNGER FOR ACTION PATTERNS

Most people most of the time are hungry for action patterns. The healthy body is ready with surplus energy to do anything that is interesting. All that is needed is a good pattern on which to act. The physical or sub-social environment suggests many. But the social environment is vastly more fruitful of suggestions.

The normal child is apt to crowd as near as he can to any one who is doing anything interesting; the child keeps trying to participate, and says over and over: "Let me do it!" "Let me help!""Now it's my turn!" In adults this desire to take part in nearby activities is only a little concealed by manners and by unhappy past experiences of being snubbed.

Dr. H. K. Nixon undertook some experiments to discover what made people look into store window displays. The account in the *New York Times* for October 3, 1926, includes the following paragraph:

By the use of decoys it was found that interest could be stimulated -thus testifying anew to the validity of the old follow-the-leader influence. These decoys were a young man and a young woman of good appearance; they proved more effective as a magnet than did the window display alone.

CONTAGIOUS ACTION PATTERNS AMONG APES

Readiness to imitate interesting activities was characteristic of Kφhler's chimpanzees. The stunt of climbing an unsupported pole before it fell over, which was described, was invented by Sultan, but it was imitated by five other apes, one after another, including the heavy and clumsy Tschego. Even more complicated behaviour patterns were imitated by the chimpanzees from one another. One instance was the fad of fishing for ants:

At the height of summer a small species of ant forms a perfect plague in Tenerife. Wherever they pass, they form wide streams of moving brown, and this stream also poured itself along the beams around the wire-netting encircling the playground. The chimpanzee has a special taste for acid fruit, which he prefers to all others; and so he also relishes the acid flavor of ants. If he passes close by a board or beam covered with ants, he simply rolls his tongue along it and gathers them in! On the beam around the wire netting he could not pursue this primitive method, as the ant-stream was outside the wire netting.

So, first one of our animals, then another, and then the whole company, began to stick twigs and straws out through the meshes and drew them in immediately, covered with ants which were promptly devoured.... Probably the "play spirit" was as strong and stronger here than the special relish for ants; for there were enough places available where they could be enjoyed with one flick of the tongue, and, when "fashion" had taken a different turn, the most profuse hordes of ants were simply ignored. But while the fashion lasted, all our animals were to be seen, squatting side by side along the ants' pathway, each armed with straw or twig like anglers on the river's bank.

It became the reigning fashion to stab the fowls.... Between two mouthfuls of bread, a chimpanzee will sometimes hold his slice between the meshes of wire; a hen approaches to peck at the bread, but before she can do so, it is pulled back again. At one meal this joke will be repeated about fifty times.... Rana, the most stupid of all our chimpanzees, really feeds the hens intentionally.... She continues to hold out her slice, so that a hen can, and does, take several pecks at it in succession; she gazes in lazy benevolence at the fowl.... A third game is as follows: the fowl is attracted to the bars with a slice of bread, but in the very moment when she is about to peck, the free hand of the same chimpanzee (or of another beside him) thrusts a stick or - even worse - a strong pointed wire into her feathered body. When two chimpanzees take part in this (one as baiter and one as thruster) there has certainly been no previous agreement between them; circumstances decree that the momentary activity of each happens to suit the other; they realize it and continue their "collusion."

Spontaneous leadership through contagious behaviour occurred also among the apes. Tschego and Grande sometimes led dances:

One after another the rest of the group approach, join the two, and finally they march in an orderly fashion and in single file round and round the post. Their movements become animated; they no longer walk, they trot, and as a rule with special emphasis on one foot, while the other steps lightly; thus a rough approximate rhythm develops, and they tend to "keep time" with one another. They wag their heads in time to the steps of their "dance" and appear full of eager enjoyment of their primitive game. Variations are invented afresh with every occasion.... That the whole company was playing could not be doubted by any one seeing them, marching in a circle, one behind the other, the big animal stamping its foot violently at every step, or every other step, and the others exaggeratedly accentuating the marching movements.... It seems to me extraordinary that there should arise spontaneously, among chimpanzees, anything that so strongly suggests the primitive ring-dancing of some indigenous tribes.

CONTAGIOUS ACTION PATTERNS AMONG CHILDREN

Miss Verry has reported the following examples:

On the slide, the children already go down in various ways, head first, lying down and sitting up, and backwards. On the first and second day, Gertrude and Sylvester were the only children to slide in various ways. To-day five others went down backwards....

The children were kept busy with molding clay. Belle made a birthday cake, sticking it full of colored sticks for candles. The teacher remarked about it, and the rest of the children did likewise at once.... To-day, the children got out the beads again. Charles made a pen of some of the square beads, saying to the teacher, "This is my garage." The others then began to pile up the beads, making each his own tower or pen, instead of stringing necklaces. They would leave this occupation to slide or make a cake every few minutes....

Helen, who had pulled one lace through a hole in her card, began to drag it about the floor for a "wagon." Four others then spent the rest of their play period dragging cards about....

There was great variety in the ways of making the cakes; they were sometimes "baked" in special corners, or turned out of the pan, etc.; each child following a routine but adopting suggestions from what the other children were doing. A mother was in the habit of reading the *Atlantic Monthly* while she rocked her baby to sleep. The baby's sister took over the action pattern by rocking her doll to sleep, and although she was too young to read she insisted that she, too, must have an *Atlantic Monthly* to hold during the process.

It is scarcely necessary to call attention to the fact that adult human beings copy also from each other complicated ways of acting. The bobbing of women's hair, the new dances, the operating of radio sets, the working of cross-word puzzles, the use of new slang words - indeed anything which can be described as a fad or fashion - illustrates the fact that ways of acting are catching.

BEHAVIOUR EPIDEMICS VIOLATE INSTINCTS AND REASON

Not only pleasant and harmless ways of functioning but even painful, dangerous and self-destructive action-patterns - ways of behaving that seem to go directly contrary to "instincts" - have caused behaviour epidemics. For instance, in the middle ages a sect grew up called flagellants. They made a practice of walking down the street scourging their own naked backs until they bled. Great numbers of people caught this way of behaving. In the early centuries martyrdom became so fashionable that the church forbade people from seeking it purposely. behaviour patterns like wearing extremely tight corsets, binding the feet of girls as was once done in China, flattening the foreheads of babies by binding boards against them as certain tribes of

American Indians used to do, thrusting pieces of metal or wood through one's nose, lips, or ears, as certain African and American tribes have done, making deep scratches in one's flesh and rubbing irritating roots into the wounds so as to make ornamental scars, as the Australian natives have done, or tattooing words and pictures by painful processes as sailors and others do, indicate that pain is not a sufficient argument against imitating the behaviour of other people.

We are apt to think of the contagion of action patterns as being a matter of intellectual choice. Quite often, however, it is purely involuntary. Not long since it became usual for people in Bryn Mawr to start every third sentence or so with the words "I mean." The phrase was insignificant and not in the least clever, yet it was hard to avoid picking it up as a habit. Similarly, northern visitors to the south are likely to pick up unconsciously the southern accent.

MENTAL FUNCTIONING ALSO IS CONTAGIOUS

Not only bodily movements but also ideas are catching. Instances noted among the preschool children were as follows:

The teacher said, "I am a big bear and I'll catch you." Will shouted with pleasure and ran. Five other children joined in the run. The teacher dropped out in a few minutes, but for a long time the children would run up to each other saying, "I'm a bear." Will began to crawl after Myrle to his evident enjoyment. Myrle would run, Will after him, growling. Sylvia dropped on her knees and went growling after the two boys. The children would stop and slide, or play at the sand, then goes back to being "bear" all the morning.

Three days later Beatrice, Myrle, and Sylvia played "bear" up and down the slide. Sylvia began by calling "See, I'm a bear," and growling as she went down. "I'm a bear," Myrle said and also came down growling. Beatrice and Genevieve did the same. Then Sylvia came down saying, "I am a mouse." The children spent a long time sliding as various animals, but aside from making a uniform growling noise made no attempt at impersonation of the different kinds they made believe to be. The teacher was used as an audience for this game....

After each child had been down the slide a time or two, Helen, apparently from some inner impulse, shouted, as she went down, "All aboard for Iowa City." At once six other children joined, shouting "All aboard for X" (fitting into the sentence whatever town they happened to think of). Wilma went slowly to the slide and tried it once, but did not shout; then she went back to her sand. During the war some publicity man changed the title of a photograph of a factory where animal bodies were reduced to soap and the like, so as to indicate falsely that the Germans were making soap out of the bodies of their soldiers. This idea spread contagiously throughout the allied world.

In ancient Greece, shortly before the time of Christ, the old religion was falling into decay. The Chaldeans had been studying the stars for centuries and had built up a pseudo-science called astrology for predicting human events from movements of the heavenly bodies. This system was introduced into Greece. Gilbert Murray says that astrology fell upon the Greek mind as a new disease falls upon some remote island people who have never built up immunity to it. Every one was ready to receive the astrology germ.

Rumors are easily started and hard to stop. We pick up most of our ideas uncritically from those around us. Le Bon says:

Affirmation pure and simple, kept from all reasoning and proof, is one of the surest ways of making an idea enter the minds of crowds. The conciser the affirmation is, the more destitute of every appearance of proof, the more weight it carries.... Affirmation, however, has no significance unless it is constantly repeated and so far as possible in the same terms.

CONTAGIOUS EMOTION

While emotions cannot be separated from actions and ideas, activities which are especially emotional are also especially contagious. Watson tells of a boy less than two years old who showed no fear of a rabbit, laughing and reaching for it even when it was put against his face. The same day he was taken into a pen with a little girl who cried at the sight of the rabbit. The boy immediately developed a fear response, and continued for two weeks to be afraid of rabbits.

A crowd was gathered in a theater. Some one back of the stage dropped a match where it caught in a pile of waste. A voice called "fire!" Instantly the audience turned into a raging mob, fighting toward the exits. Scores of people were hurt by being crushed or trampled; many were killed. All might have escaped safely if every one had been self-controlled. But fear is contagious.

A group of pioneers were journeying westward in the early days. A scout met them and warned them that Indians were in ambush a mile away. One of the reckless young men said, "Come on - let's charge them!" Without waiting to plan their attack, the entire party charged. When the Indians opened fire the leaders of the whites waved and turned back. The others followed their example and the epidemic of bravery turned into an epidemic of cowardice. Emotions are contagious.

Children seeing others eating or drinking are likely to discover that they, too, are thirsty or hungry, but without thereby necessarily sympathizing with the other children; want may thus, in a sense, be said to be contagious. A certain nine-year-old girl often complains of having nothing in the house to read. If, shortly after making such a complaint, she hears her father reading to the younger children a perfectly familiar book, which has been lying about all the time, she is likely to pick it up when he stops reading and finish it for herself with great interest.

Sometimes this infection with the interests, action patterns, and purposes which one finds in others may prove disastrous. O. O. McIntyre suggests this possibility in the contagiousness of Marion Talley's aspiration:

Marion Talley is a little nineteen-year-old girl with the world at her feet. The most brilliant audience the Metropolitan Opera House ever held hung on the golden notes of this plump corn-fed child so vibrant with health and girlish freshness.

Tickets sold for as high as $300 each. The famed Horseshoe Circle sparkled with customary jewels. The Social Register was there *en masse*. It was the night of nights for the girl from Kansas City who had achieved where a hundred thousand failed....

The real tragedy of Marion Talley's dıbut is to come. Thousands of obsoure homes bloom with a new hope. Thousands of potential Marion Talleys are girding themselves for the futile fray. Homes will be mortgaged, bent mothers and work-worn fathers will renew the unending sacrifices to send their daughters to New York and abroad to duplicate Marion Talley's success. This is a mere prediction. To find the realities one has only to consult the social workers who deal with the problems of the young people who "go broke" in Hollywood, seeking a career in the movies.

PUTTING THE SELF IN THE PLACE OF THE OTHER

All of the instances thus far given in this chapter relate simply, or primarily, to the taking over of action-patterns without a merging of purposes. In the following instances, however, the similarity of behaviour is clearly due to the fact that one individual puts himself in the place of the other. We have been talking of the copying of purpose; what we are now to consider is a sharing or merging of purpose. In one of Kφhler's photographs of his chimpanzees, the ape on top of a pile of boxes was reaching up for the coveted banana, and the ape on the ground, which had been prohibited from engaging in the activity, had his own arm raised in the same position, as though he too were reaching for the fruit.

The writer has observed a similar incident among children. A six-year-old girl had a loose tooth and stood beside her mother with open mouth to have it extracted. Close beside her, quite spontaneously and with serious face, stood the five-year-old daughter, with her mouth open as though she too had a tooth to be taken out. Apparently the imitation was entirely unconscious until the mother laughed about it. Similarly a hunter told the writer that while watching another hunter try to pull a rusty trigger he himself by unconscious contagion pulled the trigger of a gun which happened to be in his hand, and wounded the man who held the rusty piece. Experienced automobile drivers, when sitting beside other persons who are driving, will, when the speed needs slackening push their feet against the floor as if applying brakes. In each of these instances, note that the individual unconsciously puts himself in the place of the other person.

SYMPATHY MEANS PUTTING THE SELF IN THE EMOTIONAL SITUATION OF THE OTHER

This tendency to put oneself in the place of another is vividly illustrated by the contagious sense of guilt. One of the apes showed clearly that she felt guilty in behalf of another:

Their habit of eating their excrements was often, and finally very sharply, punished, but all to no purpose.... Chica once began to hop agitatedly from one foot to the other, when I happened to come up unexpectedly; I had noticed nothing unusual. As I got nearer, her agitation increased, and all at once she let a mess of rubbish fall out of her mouth. More striking was it when one day Chica received me with the same disquieting hopping and would not stop, although I could not discover guilt in her. Thus made attentive, I became aware that her friend Tercera was missing, or rather that a piece of her black fur kept on disappearing behind a box each time I came round the other side of it. Nearer investigation showed clearly that this time *she* was the sinner.

Putting oneself in the place of another who is suffering is characteristic of the apes, according to instances cited by Köhler:

Considerable - though transitory - interest is shown when an isolated creature's wailings can be heard or seen.... I noticed the strong effect on the others, when they once saw with their own eyes the signs of weakness and illness of one of the little chimpanzees. At the beginning of his fatal illness Konsul was once lying helpless on the floor, with his eyes closed. Rana, who happened to be passing by, placed Konsul's hands on her own shoulders as an invitation to accompany her. As he hardly moved, and immediately sank back again, she grew attentive, first lifted his head, and then, putting her arms around the little fellow, carefully lifted his weak body, and seemed by her bearing and her look so deeply concerned that there could be, at this moment, no doubt whatsoever as to the state of her feelings.

When some days later, during which he had been kept away, she again saw the poor creature, in a very wretched state, she seemed only to shy away. But again, one day when he seemed a little better, the little fellow was once more let out into the open, where the others were gayly eating green stuff. He dragged himself painfully to them, but after taking a few steps he suddenly fell to the ground with a piercing cry of fear. Tercera was sitting some distance away, chewing. She sprang up, her hair standing on end all over her body with excitement. She reached him in a few strides, on two legs, her face filled with the utmost concern, her lips protruding with sorrow, and uttering cries of distress; she caught hold of him under the arms, and did her best to raise him. One could not imagine anything more maternal than this female chimpanzee's behaviour....

It is an indispensable condition that the weakness and helplessness has to be seen or heard first; it must be a concrete fact. More than once I established that the... disappearance of a sick or dying animal has little effect on the rest, so long as he is taken out of sight and does not show his distress in loud groans of pain.

As Köhler points out, the sympathy shown by Rana for Konsul was closely like that of a mother for a child. This relation between sympathy and mother-feeling is reinforced by his observation that although the chimpanzees were violently unfriendly toward a new grown-up chimpanzee that was brought into the group, when little human children and babies were brought near there was no need for the apes to know them at all in order to be very friendly.

Children quite often put themselves into the emotional situations of each other. Among three small children whom the writer has observed, when one of them has started to cry because of being frightened or reproved, the other two sometimes start crying out of sympathy, shedding real tears although not themselves direct victims of the cause of the grief in the child who first cried. Sometimes this sharing of emotions leads to the defense of the reproved child by one of the others. Beatrice says through her tears: "You shouldn't scold Barbara!" Sometimes she takes Barbara away and gives her a present to make up for some richly deserved punishment.

The pre-school children studied by Miss Verry also showed sympathy for the grief of their little associates:

Dorothy, who cried very pathetically, was the object of some solicitation. Belle went up to her, patting her arm and saying, "Poor Dorothy." Gertrude asked the teacher, "Why does Dorothy cry?" And Genevieve went up to her several times and patted her; but none of the children received any response.... Next day Dorothy sat upon her chair, crying dismally. Belle went up to her, touching her arm and saying, "Poor Dorothy," before she went to the slide.

SYMPATHY FOR THE HUNGRY

Putting oneself in the place of a hungry associate occurs among chimpanzees:

There is nothing that looks more undisturbed, more indifferent, more uninterested than, in the ordinary way, a chimpanzee who is eating, and of whom another, with outstretched hands and pleading voice, is begging for some of his superfluity.... But this scene may have a different ending, when the pleader is a good friend of the ape in possession, and the latter happens to be in a good mood.... There are yet enough cases where the whole attitude of the giver is a picture of pleasant friendliness. He will suddenly gather some fruit together and hold it out to the other - as I have seen dozens of times - or will take the banana which he was just going to put in his mouth, break it in half and hand one piece to the other ape, eating the rest himself.

Köhler tells how Sultan, when isolated and starved a little for experimental purposes, persuaded Tschego to feed him:

The isolated ape vigorously began his lamentation the next day as soon as Tschego began to eat, and actually succeeded in making Tschego feed him in this way for five days. But on the sixth day the big female took no notice of the little male's loudest cries; she had probably lost interest in him, for on the sixth day the cold phase of Tschego's sexual period (which was recognizable in other ways) began, and it was not until this was over that her former behaviour recurred.

Thus, while the sympathy of Rana for the sufferings of little Konsul was of the mothering type, the response of Tschego to the hungry pleadings of Sultan were related to another fundamental emotion. Kφhler gives other evidence of the importance of sex feeling in the social functioning of the apes.

Among human beings sympathy for hungry people is very prevalent. For instance, Jane Addams says:

The woman who lives upstairs will willingly share her breakfast with the family below because she knows they "are hard up"; the man who boarded with them last winter will give a month's rent because he knows the father of the family is out of work; the baker across the street, who is fast being pushed to the wall by his competitors, will send across three loaves of bread because he has seen the children looking longingly into his window and suspects they are hungry.

Similarly Lillian Wald tells the story of a man living in a tenement in New York who happened to have work during a period of unemployment, and who had taken into his home and was feeding, in addition to his own family, four friends and three strangers who were less fortunate than himself.

CONTAGION OF PURPOSE

The sharing of action-patterns and of emotions, illustrated by the preceding instances, grew out of a merging of purpose through feeling as though one were in the place of the other individual. This merging of purpose is admirably illustrated by the following instance, relating to the tests which Köhler carried out, in which a banana was hung up out of reach of the chimpanzees. The banana could be gotten in no other way than by piling boxes under the fruit and climbing up:

It is only rarely that one animal helps another, and when this happens, we must carefully consider the meaning of such action. As Sultan was much more expert than the others, in the beginning, he was often obliged to be present without helping, as I wished to ascertain of what the others were capable....

If one's vigilance is at all relaxed, and the veto on building not continuously renewed, he does not venture to enter fully into the work, but he cannot keep from "lending a hand" here and there, supporting a box that threatens to fall under some adventurous and decisive effort of another animal, or otherwise taking a less important part in the work. On one occasion when we had forbidden him to participate in the building, he could not keep to the role of passive spectator, when Grande had piled one box on the other and was still unable to reach the prize.

He fetched a third box from a distance of about 12 meters and quickly left it close to the pile; then he squatted down again and watched, although he had not been reminded of my prohibition by either word or gesture. But we must guard against misconceptions; Sultan's motive is not the wish to help his fellow, at least not predominantly. When we watch him, squatting beside the other animal, following all Grande's movements with his eyes and often with slight sketchy movements of arm and hand, there can be no doubt that these proceedings interest him in themselves and to a very high degree; that he follows and "feels" them himself, and all the more keenly as they grow more difficult and crucial.

The "help" he offers at the critical moment is simply a heightening of his already indicated participation in the process; and interest in the other animal can only play a very secondary part, for Sultan is a pronounced egoist.... We are all acquainted with similar states of mind. It is difficult for any one who understands any form of work as a result of long practice, to stand aside, while another bungles it; his fingers itch to intervene and "do the job." And we humans, too, are far from wishing to help such a bungler from motives of pure altruism our feelings towards him at the moment are not particularly cordial). Neither do we seek some external advantage for ourselves; the work attracts and dominates us.

Miss Verry's pre-school group furnished instances in which one child put itself in another's place and functioned in behalf of the other, as Sultan did for Grande. For instance, when Dorothy and Fred persistently refused to answer "Present" at roll call, Belle looked tearfully at the teacher, saying, "Dorothy can't." Genevieve looked up appealingly as though to plead for Dorothy and Fred, and answered "Present" for each of them. Sylvia and Charles also sometimes chimed in. Genevieve kept up this service delightedly until the children learned to answer for themselves. A similar sharing of another child's purpose occurred when Henry caught his foot in the slide. Paul sat down at once to help him get it out.

Chimpanzees at times may even take satisfaction in rendering service to human beings:

Chimpanzees like very much to remove splinters from each other's hands or feet, by the method in use among the ordinary human laity. Two fingernails are pressed down on either side or the splinter levered upwards, to be caught and removed by the teeth. At the risk of infection, I went up to a chimpanzee on one occasion when I had run a splinter into one of my fingers and pointed it out to him. His mien and expression assumed the eager intensity proper to "skin treatment," he examined the wound, seized my hand, and forced out the splinter by two very skillful but somewhat painful squeezes with his finger-nails; he then examined my hand again, very closely, and let it fall, satisfied with his work.

That this sort of behaviour is characteristic very often of adult human beings needs scarcely to be pointed out. A striking instance given by Miss Wald has to do with a mother whose dead baby was buried in the potter's field because of her poverty.

Three times that year did Mrs. G. painfully gather together enough money to have the baby disinterred and fittingly buried in consecrated ground, and each time she gave up her heart's desire in order to relieve the sufferings of the living children of her neighbors.

Two other instances which she gives are as follows:

An errand took me to Michael the Scotch-Irish cobbler as the family was sitting down to the noonday meal. There was a stranger with them, whom Michael introduced, explaining when we were out of hearing that he thought I would be interested to meet a man just out of Sing Sing prison. I expressed some fear of the danger to his boys in this association. "We must just chance it," said Michael. "It's no weather for a man like that to be on the streets, when honest fellows can't get work."

A Jewish woman, exhausted by her long day's scrubbing of office floors, walked many extra blocks to beg us to get a priest for her Roman Catholic neighbor whose child was dying.

In other places she speaks of the readiness of physicians and surgeons to set aside paying patients for more urgent non-paying ones, the way in which the janitress (of the building where she and the other visiting nurse first lived) dedicated herself and her entire family to their service, and the ease with which sympathy was excited in the neighbourhood of the settlement for people deprived of books and learning. These are further instances of the contagion of purpose.

A practical application of this principle is given by a prominent settlement worker in a large eastern city. She has said that she never has difficulty in raising necessary money for her work, because she takes pains to have wealthy people visit the settlement and get familiar with its activities. Natural contagion of purpose stimulates them to provide the resources needed for the activities in which they have thus become interested.

The word "sympathy" usually covers this tendency to share the purposes of others who are in need - to feed the hungry, comfort the sorrowing, help the struggling. The term "contagiousness of purpose," however, includes also the process in which a group of people develop a common goal. For instance, the members of the clubs of the University Settlement of Milwaukee have built cooperatively a summer camp which all of them use. The growth of the undertaking has involved continually the spread of purposes from person to person and from group to group.

Infection with each other's purposes seems to occur right often at settlements. On one occasion an outside orchestra, hired to play at a dance at the East Side House Settlement in New York, failed to appear. One of the settlement clubs had a little orchestra of its own, whose members had hoped to take part in the dance as guests, not as performers, and had each brought a young woman friend as partner. When these boys saw the fix in which the settlement was placed they hurried home after their instruments, and gayly took the place of the missing musicians, arranging as best they could for the entertainment of their girl partners.

When the dance had come to a triumphant dose, Miss Helen Hart, the head resident, took aside the leader of the impromptu orchestra, and suggested quietly that the club was entitled to the money which otherwise would have been paid to the players hired for the occasion. "Oh, no, Miss Hart; we couldn't take a cent!" was his instant response. She urged him to consult his associates, and suggested that the club had long been wishing to raise a fund for baseball uniforms, which might very properly be purchased with this dance money. He consulted with the other boys, but at once returned with the news that these lads, who were all working to earn their livings, thought of themselves as part of the settlement, and had done their bit at the dance simply to help make the common cause successful.

An orthodox Jew had come into contact with Miss Wald's work for distressed families:

This man, when I called on a Sabbath evening, took one of the lights from the table to show the way down the five flights of dark tenement stairs, and to my protest, - knowing, as I did, that he considered it a sin to handle fire on the Sabbath - he said, "It is no sin for me to handle a light on the Sabbath to show respect to a friend who has helped to keep a family together."

VICARIOUS FUNCTIONING

The tendency to share in the purposes of others may explain the popularity of functioning through other people (vicarious functioning), as, for example, when crowds watch a piece of construction work or when spectators "go wild" over a ball game or a prize fight. When you go to the ball game you get infected with the purposes of the players. When you go to the movies you get infected with the purposes of the hero and heroine - so much so that you are frightened when they are in danger and you are joyful when they have good fortune.

Commander Byrd, who was the first to fly over the North Pole in an airplane, received many letters, of which the following, from a lady, was typical:

"Little do you realize," she wrote, "that thousands of people who have no chance of adventure live your adventure with you. Probably you have no idea what pleasure you give us."

PUTTING THE SELF IN THE PLACE OF THE OTHER IS AS NATURAL AS EATING -OR FIGHTING

A vital point to remember is that contagious behaviour is as natural and normal as are hunger, fear, rage, and the other "instinctive" springs of action. The word "unselfish" has been used to mean acts involving contagious purposes or sympathy. But it is as truly an expression of the self to absorb the emotions and the purposes of others as it is to function in other ways. We may take it for granted that, if conditions are favorable, people will take up the purposes of people near them. Only by recognizing this fundamental tendency can human behaviour be understood and directed.

Like other human motives, the tendency to put the self into the place of the other may be used for constructive social purposes or may be made a means of exploiting others. Efforts to raise money for philanthropic purposes make use of the sympathy motive. For example, in the course of a campaign for more adequate mother's pensions the following appeared in an editorial in the Philadelphia *Evening Public Ledger* for November 19, 1926:

There are by actual count 450 mothers and 1,600 children in this city to-day who will in all probability go to bed hungry to-night. With chill fall winds gnawing through every crevice of door and window, they will, more than likely, have to huddle together to keep warm under inadequate bed coverings.

If the children are old enough, they may have scavengered enough wood in the neighbourhood to boil some cocoa to drink with their portions of butter less bread for supper.

On the other hand, beggars often make use of this motive to get money on false pretenses. Conditions in Russia have been described recently as follows:

Begging is a lucrative profession in Moscow.... One day I asked a familiar member of the profession, daughter of a former Russian nobleman ambassador, why she did not take a few language pupils, especially in English which now is the popular accomplishment. She replied that she liked the outdoor work and that begging was much easier and also profitable, averaging $4 to $5 a day more than a commissar's salary.

We shall find that out of the contagiousness of behaviour arise cultural functioning, the sense of justice, the willingness to follow leadership, and integration of purpose-phenomena which are basic in the development of social relations.

A.Action patterns are much more likely to be borrowed than invented:

1. The hunger for interesting ways of functioning leads to the exploration of the ways of behaving suggested by one's associates.

2. Even when behaviour patterns involve acute suffering, they may be so contagious as to become epidemic.
3. Ideas and emotions, as well as forms of muscular behaviour, are catching.

B. Putting the self in the place of an associate is a fundamental cause of the sharing of functioning and of purposes.

4. Simple muscular imitation is often due to involuntarily imagining that one is in the place of some one whom one is observing.
5. Sympathy means putting the self in the emotional situation of the other.
6. Putting the self in the place of the other is likely to result in taking over in part his purposes as one's own.
7. The contagiousness of a plan for meeting some common problem may lead to a coφperative sharing of effort to reach a joint goal.
8. Putting the self imaginatively in the place of the other is the basis of vicarious functioning, in which one functions through some one else.

9

Ethical Principles with Reference to Migration

It was suggested that an impartial observer might look upon migration not only as productive of serious social problems, but also as a source of stimulating contacts for the individual and of culture progress for the group, as well as a means to the more even distribution of economic opportunity. It was implied that only the unprejudiced student could thus visualize migration as a world phenomenon. Actually, migration is viewed by many different groups from many angles and therefore not without considerable prejudice.

Specific attitudes toward migrants themselves are dependent upon many types of experiences, and these we shall consider. Here more general viewpoints may well be related to varying interests.

People interested in migration may be conveniently divided into four major groups: migrants themselves; the people left behind in the old country; the people receiving migrants in the country of immigration; and supposedly impartial scientific students of migration. Let us consider the viewpoints of these groups and ask ourselves whether and how far a scientific point of view is possible. These viewpoints concern migration itself and its control.

THE VIEWPOINT OF MIGRANTS

Through change of residence migrants normally seek an economic advantage. They expect a larger income, more and better food, more attractive clothing, a more spacious dwelling, more varied and satisfying recreation - in short, a higher plane of living. To this end they are interested in a wider free labor market. Some have also been actuated by less material motives. They have wished release from political or religious handicaps at home. They have sought a larger freedom and, often unconsciously, a fuller development of personality.

Such aims have implied the wish for a minimum of control over their movements. They may recognize the need for guidance and information, but for the most part they wish to make their own choices as to whether to stay or leave; retain their own culture or become assimilated; remain permanently as citizens abroad, or return to their homeland. Migrants, of course, are not all alike. Some may wish restriction upon other types of migrants. Certain white èmigrants wish Orientals shut out of the lands to which they go. Yet migrants themselves are naturally liberals in the matter of migration policy.

But migrants are always a minority group. As a rule they are politically uninfluential in their homeland, and, as individuals, quite without political power in the land to which they go. It is true that national blocs are sometimes formed in the country of immigration after a considerable number of immigrants have become naturalized. As a balance of power these sometimes attain strength. But their influence has been grossly exaggerated. Moreover, they do not represent strictly the viewpoint of the new immigrant. On economic grounds some may even desire restriction upon the further immigration of their fellow countrymen. As we shall show later, there is no "foreign vote" in the United States, and the nationalities are divided in their political affiliations. As a class, migrants are politically uninfluential.

For this reason the viewpoint of migrants has often been neglected in the development of migration policy. Nationalities can count on some interest and protection from their home governments. But this interest has often been found to have the welfare of the homeland at heart rather than that of the migrant as such. Yet the migrant does face problems and these are an important part of the total picture of the "problem of migration." If all migrants could be organized, these problems would receive more consideration than they do. Being unorganized, migrants are a neglected group relying on the interest of philanthropic organisations, to some exten t upon that of their several consular offices, and upon occasional gestures of friendly interest from legislatures or from other sources.

Yet a rational migration policy would consider the effect of international change of residence upon migrants themselves. It would appreciate the economic and cultural gains through escape from a difficult situation in the homeland, and it would appreciate as well the personal losses involved in separated families, exploitation, bitter economic struggle and disappointment, the resentment at race and nationality prejudices directed toward them, and a thousand other benefits and ills which migrant flesh is heir to. If migrants could be organized and made both vocal and influential, they might quarrel over some items in a migration code, but they would develop one vastly different from that which obtains today.

THE VIEWPOINT OF PEOPLE LEFT BEHIND

The folks at home also have their attitude toward migration. To the government and the nation as a whole emigration may spell loss of manpower for field and army, or relief from a too bitter competition for bread and jobs. If intensely nationalistic, the homeland may weep over the loss of patriots who are thought of as generous gifts bestowed upon ungrateful foreign lands. Or it may look hopefully to anticipated extension of the influence of home trade and home culture through emigration of nationals who are conceived of as remaining ever loyal to their nation, however great the attractiveness of the new country may be.

Similarly, the point of view of the homeland includes the attitudes of the members of the immediate family left behind. Sometimes the chief breadwinner has gone abroad to seek sustenance for his family in Europe. Sometimes emigration has meant desertion and easy avoidance of undesired responsibilities. Sometimes it connotes a good riddance and sometimes it means an unbelievably hard pull upon the heartstrings of the two divisions of the family.

In formulating a comprehensive migration policy surely these good and bad effects upon the folks left behind must be weighed in the balance. If migration really relieves overpopulation, broadens the viewpoint, increases the income and happiness of millions of people in the homeland, these influences are part of the total picture, as much as the corresponding effects abroad.

THE VIEWPOINT OF THE RECEIVING COUNTRY

The neighbor who objects to the coming of darker-skinned, strange-speaking, gesticulating, garlic-scented Italians has a viewpoint on immigration from first-hand experience. Furthermore, to him the immigration problem is the problem of one type of Italian. The member of a labor union who has been told that these "wops" and "hunkies" are taking the bread out of his mouth because they eat cheap food, live in squalor, breed prolifically, and especially because they undercut him unfairly in the wage bargain or even throw him out of a job - such a man has a very decided viewpoint on immigration.

The employer who has made what he considers a good bargain hiring foreign, hands - whether he has purchased much in the way of heads and hearts or not -has a different attitude toward migrants. If indeed he happens to have succeeded in playing one nationality against another and thus breaking the backbone of a troublesome and presumptuous trade union, he will think of the immigrant as essential to the maintenance of "American individualism." But if, by chance, aliens have been involved in a strike in his factory or in agitations savoring ever so slightly of a socialistic trend, he will look upon immigration as the source of "bolshevistic" propaganda, and decide that the "iron man" who does not talk back is after all preferable to "imported" critics of the status quo.

Social workers, though few in number, also contact the immigrant and to some extent interpret him to a larger group of people. If these contacts are chiefly indirect and impersonal, the immigrant may loom as a costly and complicating aspect of the problems of dependency, deficiency, or crime. If, however, the social worker makes first-hand contacts, he knows more intimately the virtues and vices of an immigrant population. If these personal contacts are relatively superficial, the result may be sentimental interest or perhaps a strengthening of prejudices. If, however, the contacts are sufficiently thorough to make possible a real understanding of the migrant - of his experiences and handicaps and especially of the culture which he brings with him - the social worker obtains a more balanced view. He becomes an important, but hardly determining, element in the general American viewpoint.

Finally, government representatives have the "official" viewpoint on migration. Among them will be a few who through direct personal contact develop a humane interest in the problem and often a very intense interest in certain individuals. But for the most part officials of necessity have more mechanical impersonal relations with immigrants. They must "do their duty" in enforcing the law. They have their instructions from higher up, and their success will be judged in proportion to their efficiency in carrying out those instructions. Some of them become "hard-boiled" and "officious" as well as official.

Perhaps as nearly as any group these government men reflect the true "American" attitude, although in the past some of them have sometimes appeared to be even more anti-alien than the typical American. At least until recently, they have felt more keenly the pressure of groups interested in protecting America against real or imaginary dangers through immigration, than they have felt the modifying attitudes of other interest groups. They have expressed majority opinion, hardly at all modified by the more liberal minority.

The above by no means is a complete catalog of the different elements in the American viewpoint on migration. We shall return to this question later in considering the development of immigration policy. But enough has been said to show that the American viewpoint is not homogeneous. It is the combination of many viewpoints of individuals and interest groups.

THE SO-CALLED VIEWPOINT OF HUMANITY

In each country the processes of developing policy combine to some extent these varying viewpoints. But there is little if any opportunity for the three fundamental types of attitudes to influence each other. The viewpoints of immigrants, of the country of emigration, and of the country of immigration, remain somewhat distinct and respectively incomprehensible to the other two groups. International conferences and especially the organized work of the International Labor Office have barely begun to bring the countries of emigration and of immigration together for discussion. Through the activities of a few international service organisations, the interests of migrants themselves have achieved some slight recognition.

Is it possible to see the problem of human migration as a whole? Is there a viewpoint of humanity? Can any one at the same time appreciate with equal force the needs and desires of the migrant, the hopes and fears of his homeland, and the needs and ambitions of the land into which migrants seek to move? Clearly no one individual can achieve such a world view completely, because he cannot have the experiences of all the individuals and groups involved. But it is equally clear that the student cannot claim to understand the problem of migration except in proportion as he is able to do this.

And only in this way can he formulate a program for the control of migration which will protect the interests of all concerned. It may be that such a program is impossible even after such an understanding. It may be that conflicting interests are too real and permanent. But clearly without such a many-sided view and complete understanding, a generally satisfying world migration policy is impossible. There seem to be two groups of people who most nearly approximate this viewpoint of humanity. These are, first, research students who having consecrated themselves to the ideal of objectivity and having come to some understanding of how prejudices are acquired, strive by study and experience to see the problem from all angles.

Unfortunately, such impartial research is yet rare and is too often most nearly approximated by impractical dreamers rather than by leaders of men. Secondly, this viewpoint is less perfectly achieved by members of international organisations who meet and discuss with representatives of the different national and interest groups. Their success is more limited because each often has to act and speak as the mouthpiece of a group with great interests at stake. And just as a debate is rarely the best source of information on a controversial question, so an international gathering of representatives of governments or interest groups may arrive at a compromise, without arriving at an understanding of the problem discussed. We shall later consider the achievements to date of a few such international organisations, and perhaps the possibility of greater success in the future.

Pure science seeks to understand. It does not seek to act. In that sense it has no program - no viewpoint. Ideally, the scientist stands coolly and indifferently by and records the most dramatic events in human experience without "turning an eyelash." But equally science cannot understand unless it knows all the facts. There is no such thing as one-sided science. A man does not understand human migration "scientifically" unless he understands the emotions of all the human beings involved. He cannot understand these emotions unless he is able to put himself actually or vicariously in the position of each of the individuals and groups involved.

As a scientist such a man, strictly speaking, develops no program of migration. But he is at the same time a human being with human emotions. As a man he cannot avoid having a viewpoint. But if he has been successful as a scientist - if he has achieved an understanding of the interests and ambitions of each of the groups mentioned above - his attitude toward migration will be the fusion of these often conflicting forces. His attitude will then represent the viewpoint of humanity. This is a difficult, but enviable achievement. It is the contention of this book that the international or world viewpoint is the only one which can rightly be called "scientific."

THE ETHICS OF MIGRATION

DEPENDENCE OF ETHICAL PRINCIPLES ON VIEWPOINTS AND INTERESTS

At first sight the connection between the viewpoints discussed above, and notions of "rights" involved in migration, may not be evident. If some one asks whether there is a "right" to migrate, or whether a country is "right" in restricting migration, or what "rights" the alien has abroad, or whether the migration policy of any country is "justified," we turn to some legal authority, or to some moral treatise, or we base our judgment upon long-established practice. We are apt to think of such ethical principles as existing in their own right, as absolute, as final, rather than as dependent upon group experience and evaluations of group interests.

Yet if we analyze the source of such definitions of right and wrong we discover their subjective origin - their close dependence upon the relationship of the group to migrants and migration. Most Americans think it is "right" to restrict immigration, or deport undesired foreigners, or give citizens preference over alien, say in employment. They may not stop to think that other groups talk of the "right of free migration," the "injustice" of deportation, or the "inhumanity" of discriminating against a man merely because he is an alien. If the advocate of either of these conceptions of "rights" is challenged, he may attempt to justify his position by appeal to authorities, to international law, or to so-called "Christian principles." Today the restriction of migration is easily defended in terms of the time-worn principle that "everybody's doing it."

Analysis reveals, however, that ideas of the ethics of migration vary considerably between groups, and that this variation is correlated with different real or supposed interests which groups have in migration. Countries of emigration and countries of immigration differ somewhat on the right to migrate or to restrict migration. It is this dependence of ethics upon experience and group interests which leads us to discuss the ethics of migration in connection with the discussion of varying viewpoints.

THE RIGHT TO CHANGE RESIDENCE WITHIN THE NATION

Before illustrating concretely the dependence of the ethics of migration upon group interests, let us consider the relative freedom of movement within national boundaries. Speaking generally, a free man may move at will within the limits of his own property, and on the public domain of the group to which he belongs, provided that he does not interfere thereby with the rights of other members of the community or state. In the United States, for example, every citizen and every alien lawfully in the country may in normal times travel unmolested in search of work from one end of the nation to the other.

He not only has this theoretical right, but he will ordinarily not be hindered in his movements, although this does not mean that the wage bargain itself is unrestricted. The United States is not only one of the world's largest free trade areas, but one of the largest free labor markets. Employers may control the wage, labor unions may arbitrarily create a partial monopoly of certain trades, and governments may exclude aliens from certain types of work, but these groups do not put up immigration barriers between communities or states. Free movement within a nation is rarely subject to criticism.

Even when in the United States the migration of large numbers of Negroes from south to north created considerable problems of adjustment, few would have advocated restricting the movement itself. It is an interesting question to determine just what the inherent differences between migrations across state lines are on the one hand and migration across national boundaries on the other. Why, one might query, is it considered right to permit free movement in the one case, and wrong to do so in the other? Why are state boundaries essentially unguarded, while national boundaries are often locked against newcomers? Clearly there are many points of similarity and points of difference between intra-national and international migration and social benefits and problems resulting. At this point we do not analyze these. We only note that intra-national change of residence is almost entirely free.

MIGRATION ACROSS NATIONAL BOUNDARIES

The wide prevalence of restriction upon international migration today makes any discussion of a theoretical right to migrate seem exceedingly academic. Indeed, some would not waste time discussing the ethics of migration. They would treat it as a matter of social forces rather than of social ethics. They would simply ask what forces aid and what forces hinder or forbid international migration. These forces may be unplanned by mail, or they may be deliberate policies and laws. Thus geographical distance, cost of travel, ignorance of language and relative economic well-being at home may hinder migration; while desire for adventure, economic distress or ambition, improved means of travel, may stimulate it.

Similarly, the forces may be conscious plans to assist, or laws and rules to hinder population movement. It is possible to discuss the question whether a man may migrate in terms of these forces past and present; and even to attempt to predict whether future conditions will favor or check human migration. In all this there need not be any question of good or bad, praise or blame, right or wrong. Yet many people like to moralize.

To them problems like migration are not merely problems in social mechanics, so to speak; they are also problems of social ethics. People who are so minded ask: "Is there a right to migrate?" Is free migration "justified" under international law or by some other legal or moral standard? Similarly, they will ask: "Is there a right to defend one's homeland against unwanted intruders even though unarmed?" "Does international law, or the weight of authority justify modern legislation restricting emigration or immigration?" Considered from this angle there is an ethics of migration. The student decides in terms of ethical or legal principles what degree of freedom to migrate is "right." He may then, if he wishes, criticize existing policies and laws in the light of these principles.

ETHICAL PRINCIPLES AS PRODUCTS OF SOCIAL FORCES OR PROCESSES

It is perhaps possible to reconcile these two approaches- the one which talks solely in terms of social forces and processes; the other which insists on raising ethical questions.

The reconciliation comes from recognizing the evaluation of behaviour as right or wrongs as itself a product of a general social process. From this intermediate viewpoint the ethics of migration grows out of the process of development of the mores of nations. These mores are patterns of behaviour approved by the group. Originating probably in the trial and error experiences of the individual, certain patterns of behaviour are discussed by the group.

If approved and if thought peculiarly essential to group welfare, and especially if thought to have religious significance, these patterns of behaviour are labeled "right" or "wrong" - they become sacred mores. Such mores thus come to define for the members of the group the "right" way to kill game, the "right" way to marry a wife, the "right" way to behave toward strangers. Most such ethical ideas have arisen unconsciously. But other later ethical values may be the product of long experience and even of some critical examination of the results of behaviour.

Whatever their origin, they come to be passed on to the individual as patterns rarely questioned, and often even conceived as sacred. The family, the community, and religious and play groups are agencies for the handing on of the group's ethical notions; and to these agencies are often added more formal education. We shall later trace some of the processes by which attitudes toward aliens were thus handed on. Now we are interested in these processes as the source of the ethics of migration. They have determined the group's ideas of the "right to migrate," "the right to restrict migration," the "right of aliens to maintain their culture after migration," and the "right and duty of the receiving group to promote and even compel the assimilation of the alien immigrant."

DEVELOPMENT OF CONFLICTING RIGHTS INVOLVED IN MIGRATION

Migration itself and the resulting conflicts have, of course, largely determined the nature of these established rights. The wanderings of peoples have brought them into contact with other peoples. New biological and social relationships have developed between natives and migrants. The wishes of the two groups have often clashed. They have therefore developed on the basis of these experiences not only attitudes toward one another but toward future migrants and toward the desirability or undesirability of migration in general.

These attitudes of individuals have in turn been integrated into group policies -policies of emigration and policies of immigration. The experiences have been further discussed and ethical concepts -notions of rights and duties of migrants and of others - have resulted. Being developed in different national groups and being often the outcome of conflict, these ethical ideas have differed from group to group. Rightly or wrongly, countries of emigration and countries of immigration have often conceived of their interests in migration as opposed.

We shall later try to test the validity of this conception. At any rate, the two sets of countries were isolated. Hence there was a minimum of discussion. Hence they tended to develop different policies and opposing notions of the rights and duties involved in migration. To one group migration came to be considered a "right"; to another restriction became a "right" and movement across national boundaries was felt to be "unethical." These fundamentally different conceptions of interests and also of rights even today hinder discussion and the development of common migration policy.

FOUR SOLUTIONS OF THIS CONFLICT

One may attempt to resolve this conflict of "rights" in any of four ways: (1) one may appeal to international law, and ask whether the right to migrate has an established legal basis; (2) one may review the arguments of authorities on migration; (3) one may attempt the more difficult task of examining the effects of migration and of evaluating them in terms of some general principle such as "the greatest good to the greatest number," the importance of preserving national cultures, the imperative need to preserve world peace, or the dependence of civilisation upon the freest contact of national cultures; or (4) one may abandon the ethical problem altogether as a counsel of perfection. One may decide that in the last analysis there are no ethical principles in these relations between nations, but only a conflict of forces now favoring and now hindering human migration.

APPEAL TO INTERNATIONAL LAW

Professor Paul Fauchille, a well-known international lawyer, has discussed the "rights of emigration and immigration" from the point of view of international law. He has pointed out that authorities are not agreed on this question, being divided into two opposing schools - more opposed in theory, however, than in practice. One school insists that the absolute sovereignty of the state implies an absolute right to prohibit ingress to or egress from its territories and that this leaves the individual with no rights under international law. The second school insists that the individual has an inalienable natural right to emigrate or immigrate, which may not be arbitrarily infringed by the state. But this right of the individual is limited by the state's right of self-preservation. Professor Fauchille favors the latter theory.

INTERNATIONAL LAW ON THE RIGHT TO EMIGRATE

One of these rights is the right to trade and this right to trade implies the right of nationals to cross boundaries. Hence the state cannot arbitrarily forbid its nationals to leave. The right to emigrate is a consequence of the right to life and the pursuit of happiness. But the state has the right of self-preservation, and this in turn implies the right of maintaining the unity and integrity of its population. Hence the right to emigrate may be regulated to the extent demanded by the security of the state.

This right of the individual to emigrate is, however, denied by most Anglo-Saxon jurists. Others declare that free exit can only be limited under abnormal circumstances such as war or revolution. Most authorities and the Institute of International Law are said to support the right of emigration. The latter declared in 1917 that this right may be restricted by decisions of governments "within the strict limits of social and political necessity." Professor Fauchille then attempts to describe specific rules based upon these principles:

1. There may be no general prohibition of emigration.
2. Emigration may be forbidden specifically when men are needed for military service; when minors or wives attempt to emigrate without the consent of their parents or husbands [sic]....
3. When it is necessary to protect the nation.
4. Wholesale emigration is justified, but may be prohibited if it endangers the state.
5. The state may require a statement of the reasons for emigration.
6. Some regulation of organisations dealing with emigrants is needed to protect them against exploitation; and the home state should protect them during their journey while they travel under its own flag.

INTERNATIONAL LAW ON THE RIGHT TO IMMIGRATE

With respect to immigration, Fauchille finds the same two theories. Here too the right of free movement is implied in the right of international trade. He admits that many authorities take the opposite view and that both principles are subject to exception. Here the Institute of International Law has made conflicting declarations. At its meeting in 1897 it concluded: "The contracting parties recognize freedom of immigration whether by individuals or groups, without distinction of nationality. This freedom may only be restricted to the minimum extent required by social or political considerations." But Fauchille points out that the right is really limited by the state's right of self-preservation.

Yet "It is no longer admitted in modern law that every man is indissolubly bound to his native land. He has the right to come and go as seems good to him, in order to seek, in a community which he considers more favorable, greater facilities for achieving material and moral perfection." Moreover, if, as stated above, there is a right to emigrate, there of necessity would seem to be a right to immigrate, for of what avail is the former without a place to go to! Sovereignty to Fauchille and his school is not absolute but relative. Hence, Fauchille concludes, a state may not close its doors arbitrarily, but only to a limited extent in the interests of the community as a whole. Hence:

1. There may be no general prohibition against the entry of foreigners of all nationalities, but the state may select and exclude diseased paupers, vagrants, those too old to make living, immoral convicts, and those who might disseminate subversive or anarchistic doctrines.
2. Restriction may only be in the interest of the preservation of the state. Nor may all the nationals of a given state be excluded for this would infringe upon the principle of the "equality of states." Some nationals may, however, be supervised more strictly than others.
3. A race may be excluded, but only if it has an absolutely different civilisation and when its nationals apply for admission in large numbers.

To the present writer the appeal to international law, though of practical significance as showing roughly what treatment may be expected, by no means solves our problem. At best the principles enunciated are so vague as to permit almost every type of exclusion now practiced, under some fairly reasonable interpretation. Moreover, as has been pointed out, a large number of authorities adopt the theory of absolute sovereignty of the state. Illiberal as that theory is, it is probably pretty nearly in accord with actual practice. Governments today feel so keenly the importance of the control of population that most of them would pay scant attention to a vague "right to migrate" recognized by only part of the authorities and permitting under favorable interpretation almost every form of restriction.

Professor Fauchille's own interpretation is interesting chiefly as an example of what radical exceptions to announced principles even a liberal feels compelled to make. From the point of view of human welfare some "liberals" would feel that military service is precisely the reason least justified for forbidding emigration. Yet no government would hesitate to forbid emigration of soldiers in time of danger. One might inquire also whether the practical exclusion of all Japanese from the United States today is any less an infringement upon the "equality of states" than complete exclusion would be. And if race may justly be a ground for exclusion, are there not cultural grounds equally important?

THE RIGHTS OF MIGRATION AS SET FORTH BY STUDENTS OF MIGRATION

Instead of turning to international law, we may turn to the writings and utterances of specialists in the field of human migration. American writers on immigration have usually wasted little space in discussion of the ethics of migration. Except for an occasional sentimentalist or a still more occasional liberal, they have lately derived their ethics of migration chiefly from a consideration of the supposed rights of natives and residents in America. Professor H. P. Fairchild's brief statement is worthy of quotation:

Many of the favorite arguments against restriction may be boiled down to the assumption that every human individual has a natural and inalienable right to move from one country to another at his will. This idea is forcefully developed by Mary Antin in the early portion of her book, "They Who Knock at Our Gates." Her point of view is typified by the following quotations. After speaking of the numerous analytical and statistical studies of the immigration problem which have been made, she asks, "But what is there in all this that bears on the right of free men to choose their place of residence? Granted that Sicilians are not Scotchmen, how does that affect the right of the Sicilian to travel in pursuit of happiness?

The fundamental fact of his humanity established, we need only rehearse the articles of our political faith to know what to do with the immigrant.... There is nothing left for us to but to open wide our gates and set him on his way to happiness". In spite of the prevalence of this type of argument, little space need be devoted to it in a scientific analysis. In the first place, the whole question of natural rights lies outside the field of argument. The very use of the terms "natural" or "inalienable" puts them in the realm of the intuitive. If a given individual believes that there are natural rights, and that one of them is the right to migrate, there is no possible way of disproving his contention. But the opposite position is equally unassailable. In the second place, modern thinkers have come to agree that for practical purposes, at least, the whole idea of natural rights should be thrown overboard in *toto*.

Every right which has any real bearing on human problems is a socially conferred right. On this basis, there is no evidence whatever that the right to migrate has ever been universally or even generally conceded. Whatever may be said of the right to emigrate, the right to immigrate is of very recent origin, and is in itself indicative of a very liberal attitude on the part of the receiving state. It has never been conceded unconditionally. It is well recognized in international law that inherent in the very idea of national sovereignty are the right to decide who shall make up the body politic and the right to decide who shall compose the electorate - that is, the rights of immigration and naturalisation. And without a correlative right to immigrate the right to emigrate is quite sterile.

It may be noted that Fairchild here argues against a right to immigrate on the ground that national sovereignty implies the right to decide who shall make up the body politic. He earlier quite properly derives "rights" from social conditioning. But by the same token the implications of sovereignty itself are socially derived and might conceivably change with changing conditions. The concept of national sovereignty itself is now under critical discussion, though in fact it is still a very virile force. Recently, however, some foreign writers on migration and especially men connected with the League of Nations and the International Labor Office have discussed the right to migrate from at least a semi-international or world viewpoint.

The American representative of the I. L. O., Leifur Magnussen, speaking at the National Conference of Social Work a few years ago said, however: "It goes without saying, it seems to me, that every country is entitled to decide which of its citizens may depart from its borders and who may enter and upon what conditions. Each country will make its decisions on the basis of its own interest or policy, that is, for political reasons." Mr. Magnussen seems more influenced by his American environment than by his connection with a great international organisation.

On the other hand, D. Christie Tait of the I. L. O. has said: "Migration is one of the questions whose status has gradually developed from its early stages, when it was considered purely a matter of the individual concerned, through an intermediate period when the governments of the countries both of emigration and of immigration intervened - down to the present day, when it is being more and more closely recognized that it is essentially an international question and can be satisfactorily dealt with only on the lines of international collaboration." This implies the end of the right to free migration, but also the substitution of international for national interference. Such interference would seem to be more likely to take the needs of the individual into consideration than national control.

M. Varlez, former head of the migration section of the I. L. O., goes further, for he raises the question: "Has a country the right to retain fertile areas that it cannot at present populate, as an empty reserve ?... Has an over numerous population the right to emigrate, and if so, where to go?" There is here a distinction between the question of the individual's right to migrate without his country's consent, and the country's right to demand territory for him to go to. This question is closely related to that of economic imperialism (colonies), and both to the question of the monopoly of natural resources.

The late Albert Thomas, former director of the I. L. O., has raised directly the question of the conflict between the sovereign right of a nation to determine who should enter, and the idea of the right of overpopulated countries to exist, to send people abroad, and in a way that they shall not lose their nationality too easily. He would solve the problem by controlling migration, but with the right for some international agency to intervene under certain fixed conditions (thus limiting sovereign rights of nations); allowing some right of selection to the receiving country so that it would not be swamped; and providing international rules of naturalisation and assimilation "failing a policy of compulsory birth control."

He points out also that the individual's right to migrate has been limited not in the interest of the migrant himself, but of the state. The clash of rights threatens war. "The right of over-populated nations to occupy certain territories! Granted, but on the condition that these nations before passing their national boundaries and causing international trouble have first tried to solve for themselves the problem of their population."

Yet even Japanese authorities have declared that no nation should send emigrants where they are not wanted; but also that invitations to settle should be issued to all peoples alike, save for temporary conditions due to assimilability.

George H. Knibbs, the Australian population authority, writes of the need for a better distribution of the human race. He further states that the idea is developing that national rights are subordinate to rights inherent in the nature of things. Perhaps J. W. Gregory, an Englishman, has most fully discussed the implications of ethical considerations for definite migration policy. Starting with the very liberal statement that no nation has made the land it occupies or has the right to prevent its adequate use, he adds that the right of an overpopulated land to discharge its surplus into an under populated area is limited by the right of every country to control immigration on several grounds:

1. The occupants must prepare it for a denser population.
2. A country can only absorb immigrants at a certain rate.
3. The pioneers who have done the rough work in subduing a wasteland have a just claim to fair reward.
4. There is a right to prevent the lowering of the standard of living.
5. As there are still sparsely populated areas, overpopulated countries should do their share of breaking up new land and not expect admission free to an area that one people has subdued for the benefit of its own children.

Every nation has the right to protect itself from deterioration by racial intermixture - but not from intermixture with branches of the same (white) race, for there is no biological support for objection to this. It is ethical to prevent the "dumping" of immigrants. It is ethical to exclude the defective classes. Some restriction is justified to protect national institutions. The exclusion of anarchists is justified. A nation must protect itself against crime. A nation must protect the right of a class to organize for its own protection. The need to promote assimilation is debatable.

A nation is justified in protecting its constitution against a minority, though "its impoverished and starving neighbor might denounce the restriction as merciless and inhuman." The reader should not assume from the numerous liberal statements quoted above that liberal notions are widespread or influential. As Fairchild implies, modern nationalism is so firmly entrenched that the right to immigrate receives but scant official recognition. Even representatives of countries with a large emigration often admit the sovereign right to determine the composition of the national population.

Japan, for example, has frequently made such an admission. She does not want to admit Chinese coolies to her own domain without restriction. It is chiefly from the representatives of the International Labor Office that one hears something approximating a recognition of a limited right to immigrate. The significance of the above quotations lies, rather, in their indication of the sources of these varying views with reference to the right to migrate. Knowing the personal interest, and the cultural or interest group to which an "authority" belongs, one can usually predict what will be his notion of an ethic of migration. In other words, ethical ideas, like other attitudes, are the products of the social milieu. Under stress of trying circumstances "expediency" is rechristened "right." Yet when conditions are favorable, humanitarian ethical principles emerge.

Professor Gregory has written a fairly liberal treatise on human migration. Yet note how, in the above summary, he is led to qualify his liberal general principles when he tries to apply them to actual details of migration policy. There is scarcely a limitation upon immigration in force today which might not be partially justified in terms of the long list of exceptions which he makes. Representatives of the International Labor Office tend to recognize the validity of some degree of right to migrate, but they would not leave migration unrestricted. They would increase its control by international rather than national machinery.

ETHICAL PRINCIPLES DERIVED FROM AN ANALYSIS OF THE EFFECTS OF MIGRATION

The resort to "authorities," therefore, does not seem to solve the ethical problem. A third method is for the student to derive ethical principles from the study of all relevant facts. If in studying the effects of migration he can be equally cognizant of the needs of all concerned, the specialist might theoretically divest himself of previous prejudices and arrive at a rational and liberal and just migration policy. Such a policy would be the basis for possible general principles which would constitute an ethics of migration. This is a gigantic task. It will not be attempted at this point, nor can we ever come to any dogmatic conclusion on so complicated a question. But every objective, impartial study of human migration contributes to such an end.

We have seen that varying views of the ethics of migration result from varying relations to migration and its effects. Man's emotions cause him to evaluate his experiences as "good" and "bad." These evaluations result from the social process. They have no existence apart from it. As soon as one understands this fact he ceases to worry about the justice of one products of the social milieu. Under stress of trying circumstances "expediency" is rechristened "right." Yet when conditions are favorable, humanitarian ethical principles emerge.

Professor Gregory has written a fairly liberal treatise on human migration. Yet note how, in the above summary, he is led to qualify his liberal general principles when he tries to apply them to actual details of migration policy. There is scarcely a limitation upon immigration in force today which might not be partially justified in terms of the long list of exceptions which he makes. Representatives of the International Labor Office tend to recognize the validity of some degree of right to migrate, but they would not leave migration unrestricted. They would increase its control by international rather than national machinery.

ETHICAL PRINCIPLES DERIVED FROM AN ANALYSIS OF THE EFFECTS OF MIGRATION

The resort to "authorities," therefore, does not seem to solve the ethical problem. A third method is for the student to derive ethical principles from the study of all relevant facts. If in studying the effects of migration he can be equally cognizant of the needs of all concerned, the specialist might theoretically divest himself of previous prejudices and arrive at a rational and liberal and just migration policy. Such a policy would be the basis for possible general principles which would constitute an ethics of migration. This is a gigantic task. It will not be attempted at this point, nor can we ever come to any dogmatic conclusion on so complicated a question. But every objective, impartial study of human migration contributes to such an end.

THE CONCEPTION OF RIGHTS AS EXPRESSIONS OF POINTS OF VIEW DEVELOPED BY DIFFERENTIAL EXPOSURE TO THE PROCESSES OF MIGRATION

We have seen that varying views of the ethics of migration result from varying relations to migration and its effects. Man's emotions cause him to evaluate his experiences as "good" and "bad." These evaluations result from the social process. They have no existence apart from it.

As soon as one understands this fact he ceases to worry about the justice of one or another attitude or policy. He rates these attitudes and policies rather as the result of partial and one-sided, or complete and many-sided exposure to the phenomenon of migration. He sees how varied interests lead to varied viewpoints and these in turn tend toward similarly varied conceptions of the ethics of migration.

A scientific viewpoint toward migration is possible to the extent that all its effects are impartially studied. Any policy resulting from such study will be humanitarian. Beyond this, considerations of ethics can be disregarded.

Bibliography

Allen, John C. and Donald Dillman. 1994. Against all odds: rural community in the information age. Boulder, Colo.: Westview.

Allen, Patricia, ed. 1993. Food for the future: conditions and contradictions of sustainability. NY: John Wiley & Sons.

Ann M. Miles. 2004. From Cuenca to Queens: An Anthropological Story of Transnational Migration. Austin, TX: University of Texas Press.

Arthur Wesley Helweg. 2004. Strangers in a Not-So-Strange Land: Indian American Immigrants in the Global Age. Belmont, CA: Wadsworth/Thomson Learning.

Bryant, Bunyan, ed. 1995. Environmental justice: issues, policies and solutions. Washington, DC: Island Press.

Buttel, Fred and Howard Newby, eds. 1980. The rural sociology of advanced societies. Montclair, NJ: Allanheld, Osmun.

Caroline Brettell. 2003. Anthropology and Migration: Essays on Transnationalism, Ethnicity, and Identity. Walnut Creek, CA: Altamira Press.

Elliott R. Barkan, Hasia Diner, and Alan M. Kraut. 2008. From Arrival to Incorporation: Migrants to the U.S. in a Global Era. New York, NY: New York University Press.

Felix Roberto Masud-Piloto. 1996. From Welcomed Exiles to Illegal Immigrants: Cuban Migration to the U.S., 1959-1995. Lanham, MD: Rowman & Littlefield.

Friedland, William F. and et al., eds. 1991. Towards a new political economy of agriculture. Boulder, Colo.: Westview Press.

Jacqueline Knörr, Barbara Meier 2000.Women and Migration: Anthropological Perspectives. Franfurt, NY: Campus Verlag New York: St Martin's Press.

Josiah McConnell Heyman. 1988. Finding a Moral Heart for U.S. Immigration Policy: An Anthropological Perspective. Arlington, VA: American Anthropological Association.

Kloppenberg, Jack R. 1988. First the seed: the political economy of plant biotechnology. NY: Cambridge University Press.

Krimsky, Sheldon. 1991. Biotechnics and society: the rise of industrial genetics. New York: Praeger.

Lasley, Paul and et al. 1995. Beyond amber waves of grain: an examination of social and economic restructuring in the heartland. Boulder: Westview.

LeHeron, Richard B. 1993. Globalized agriculture: political choice. NY: Pergamon Press.

Madhulika Shankar Khandelwal. 2002. Becoming American, being Indian: An Immigrant Community in New York City. Ithaca, NY: Cornell University Press.

McMichael, Philip, ed. 1994. The global restructuring of agro-food systems. Ithaca, NY: Cornell University Press.

Robert C. Kiste. 1974. The Bikinians: A Study in Forced Migration. Menlo Park, CA: Cummings Pub. Co.

Sachs, Carolyn. 1996. Gendered fields: rural women, agriculture, and environment. Boulder, Colo.: Westview.

Solbrig, Otto T. 1994. So shall you reap: farming and crops in human affairs. Washington, DC: Island Press.

White, Richard. 1992. Land use, environment, and social change. Seattle: Univ. Washington press.

Wright, Angus. 1990. The death of Ramon Gonzalez: the modern agricultural dilemma. Austin: Univ. Texas Press.

INDEX

R

S

T

V

W